Taiwanese Firms in Southeast Asia

NEW HORIZONS IN INTERNATIONAL BUSINESS

General Editor: Peter J. Buckley
Centre for International Business,
University of Leeds (CIBUL), UK

This series is aimed at the frontiers of international business research. The study of international business is important not least because it gives researchers the opportunity to innovate in theory, technique, empirical investigation and interpretation. The area is fruitful for interdisciplinary and comparative research. This series is established as a central forum for the presentation of new ideas in international business.

Titles in the series include:

The State and Transnational Corporations
A Network Approach to Industrial Policy in India
Hans Jansson, M. Saqib and D. Deo Sharma

Competitive and Cooperative Macromanagement
The Challenges of Structural Interdependence
Edited by Gavin Boyd

Foreign Direct Investment in Japan
Edited by Masaru Yoshitomi and Edward M. Graham

Structural Competitiveness in the Pacific
Corporate and State Rivalries
Edited by Gavin Boyd

Euro-Pacific Investment and Trade
Strategies and Structural Interdependencies
Edited by Gavin Boyd and Alan M. Rugman

Multinational Firms and International Relocation
Edited by Peter J. Buckley and Jean-Louis Mucchielli

Current Issues in International Business
Edited by Iyanatul Islam and William Shepherd

The Struggle for World Markets
Edited by Gavin Boyd

Japanese Multinationals in the Global Economy
Paul W. Beamish, Andrew Delios and Donald J. Lecraw

Global Competitive Strategies in the New World Economy
Multilateralism, Regionalisation and the Transnational Firm
Edited by Hafiz Mirza

Taiwanese Firms in Southeast Asia
Networking Across Borders
Edited by Tain-Jy Chen

Direct Investment in Economies in Transition
Klaus Meyer

Structural Change and Cooperation in the Global Economy
Edited by Gavin Boyd and John H. Dunning

Taiwanese Firms in Southeast Asia

Networking Across Borders

Edited by

Tain-Jy Chen

Professor of Economics, National Taiwan University and Consultant, Chung-Hua Institution for Economic Research, Taiwan

NEW HORIZONS IN INTERNATIONAL BUSINESS

Edward Elgar

Cheltenham, UK • Northampton, MA, USA

Published by
Edward Elgar Publishing Limited
8 Lansdown Place
Cheltenham
Glos GL50 2HU
UK

Edward Elgar Publishing, Inc.
6 Market Street
Northampton
Massachusetts 01060
USA

A catalogue record for this book
is available from the British Library

Library of Congress Cataloguing in Publication Data

Taiwanese firms in Southeast Asia: networking across borders / edited by Tain-Jy Chen; [contributors, Thomas F. Aquino . . . et al.].
(New horizons in international business)
Includes bibliographical references and index.
1. Investments, Taiwan—Asia, Southeastern. 2. International business enterprises—Asia, Southeastern. 3. Business networks—Taiwan. 4. Business networks—Asia, Southeastern. 5. Corporations, Taiwan—Asia, Southeastern. 6. Taiwan—Foreign economic relations—Asia, Southeastern. 7. Asia, Southeastern—Foreign economic relations—China. I. Chen, Tain-Jy. II. Aquino, Thomas F. III. Series.
HG5798.T34 1998
332.67'351249059—dc21 98–13904
CIP

ISBN 1 85898 746 6
Printed and bound in Great Britain by Bookcraft (Bath) Limited.

Contents

Tables

Contributors

Thomas G. Aquino. Currently Governor, Board of Investments, Manila, the Philippines; formerly Professor, School of Management, University of Asia and the Pacific.

Mohamed Ariff. Currently Executive Director, Malaysian Institute of Economic Research, Kuala Lumpur, Malaysia; formerly Professor, Faculty of Economics and Administration, University of Malaya.

Homin Chen. Currently Associate Professor, Department of International Business, Chi-Nan University, Puli, Taiwan; formerly Associate Research Fellow, Chung-Hua Institution for Economic Research.

Tain-Jy Chen. Currently Professor, Department of Economics, National Taiwan University, Taipei, Taiwan; formerly Research Fellow, Chung-Hua Institution for Economic Research.

Ying-Hua Ku. Associate Research Fellow, Chung-Hua Institution for Economic Research, Taipei, Taiwan.

Da-Nien Liu. Research Fellow and Director of International Division, Chung-Hua Institution for Economic Research, Taipei, Taiwan.

Meng-chun Liu. Associate Research Fellow, Chung-Hua Institution for Economic Research, Taipei, Taiwan.

Sor Tho Ng. Lecturer, Department of Applied Statistics, Faculty of Economics and Administration, University of Malaya.

Mari Pangestu. Director, Center for Strategic and International Studies (CSIS), Jakarta, Indonesia.

Bunluasak Pussarungsri. Currently Executive Vice President, Mutual Fund Public Company, Bangkok, Thailand; formerly Professor, National Institute of Development Administration (NIDA).

James Riedel. Professor, Paul H. Nitz School of Advanced International Studies (SAIS), Johns Hopkins University, Washington DC, United States.

Preface

We were visiting Taiwanese factories in the suburbs of Jakarta in Indonesia. Wherever we went, there was a portrait of Indonesian President Suharto hanging on the wall behind the reception desk or in the middle of the waiting room. The practice was to show respect to the local authority. This routine encounter was repeated until one day we walked into a shoe factory and were met by a gigantic and vivid picture of American basketball star Michael Jordon in Nike shoes instead of the usual solemn portrait of the President. We immediately realized that this place was ruled by multinationals rather than President Suharto. The Taiwanese factory that we visited was an exclusive subcontractor of Nike. When we asked the factory manager about the reason for investing in Indonesia, the manager replied plainly, 'Nike told us to'.

Networking is an essential mechanism through which small- and medium-sized enterprises (SMEs) in Taiwan gain access to international markets. Network linkage provides the impetus to drive an export-oriented economy like Taiwan's in which SMEs play a dominant role. Since the middle of the 1980s, Taiwan's SMEs have become a major force in foreign direct investment (FDI) in Southeast Asia, presumably because their position in the international networks has significantly changed. The predominance of SMEs in foreign direct investment is an unprecedented experience worthy of close examination.

The conventional image of transnational firms is that they are big, resourceful, prestigious and hierarchical. The small Taiwanese transnationals stand in sharp contrast to this image: they are small, short of managerial and technological resources, lack prestige, and are quite independent from the parent company control. When we visited Taiwanese subsidiaries in Southeast Asia, we often found the local factories to be bigger and more splendid in appearance than those owned by parent firms in Taiwan. When local workers of Taiwanese subsidiaries in Southeast Asia were sent to Taiwan for training, they could not believe that they belonged to such small and meager Taiwanese firms. During the interviews, Taiwanese owners or expatriate managers in Southeast Asian subsidiaries often presented us with business cards printed with local names. Many of them also spoke fluent local languages.

When examining the sources of the strength of SMEs in Taiwan, researchers often point out the importance of small-firm networks which provide flexibility and nimbleness. Conventional theory on foreign direct investment has emphasized the firm-specific strength, such as organizational or technological capabilities. Foreign direct investment is perceived as a risky venture; only the large and strong are qualify to enter. Only in recent years has the network approach to international business activities been proposed and discussed. The approach provides a new angle to view FDI and Taiwan seems to be a perfect case to test its explanatory power. Although network is a broad and sometimes obscure concept encompassing business, personal, cultural, social, religious and political relations, among others, our study is restricted to the discussion of business and personal relations.

Southeast Asia is also a perfect choice for case study because it maintains strong business and personal ties with Taiwan, in addition to being the primary destination of overseas investment by Taiwan's SMEs. Included in our study are five countries: Indonesia, Malaysia, Thailand, the Philippines, and Vietnam. Singapore is excluded because it presents a very different picture from the rest of Southeast Asia.

This book is a result of joint research efforts by Taiwanese, American, and Southeast Asian scholars. Major research was conducted between April 1994 and April 1995 with a core team in Taiwan and five country teams in Southeast Asia. The Taiwanese team was composed of Tain-Jy Chen, Ying-Hua Ku, Homin Chen, Da-Nien Liu, and Meng-chun Liu at Chung-Hua Institution for Economic Research, with assistance from James Riedel of the Paul H. Nitz School of Advanced International Studies (SAIS) at the Johns Hopkins University in the United States. The team was responsible for the surveys of and interviews with the parent firms in Taiwan. It also coordinated the works of country teams. To get a full picture of the cross-country operations of Taiwanese transnationals, two of the Taiwanese team members, Tain-Jy Chen and Ying-Hua Ku, also travelled to Southeast Asia to conduct interviews with Taiwanese subsidiaries.

The host country teams were formed by the following researchers: Mari Pangestu of the Center for Strategic and International Studies (CSIS) for Indonesia, Mohamed Ariff and Sor Tho Ng of the University of Malaya for Malaysia, Bunluasak Pussarungsri of the National Institute of Development Administration (NIDA) for Thailand, Thomas G. Aquino of the Board of Investments for the Philippines, and Da-Nien Liu and James Riedel for Vietnam with assistance from Le Van Be and Nguyen Van Vien of the Institute for Economic Research (IER) of Ho Chi Minh City. The host country teams were responsible for the survey and interviews with local Taiwanese subsidiaries, government, and business communities to understand the activities and impacts of Taiwanese FDI.

The successful completion of the project has been aided by many people. First and foremost, this research would not have been possible without funding from Taiwan's International Economic Cooperation Development Fund (IECDF) and the support of its charismatic director, Yan Chou. The Taiwan Investors' Association in each host country also provided valuable assistance. Without them, we would never have been able to locate Taiwanese affiliates, many of which did not appear in the official statistics. Special thanks go to Mr Chung Chin Fu, Chairman of the Taipei Investors' Association in Malaysia, whose hospitality and helping hands extended to unknown visitors like us reminded us of the old Chinese virtue of universal friendship which seemed to exist only in history.

We are also grateful to our research assistants, Miss Chi-Chen Chien at Chung-Hua Institution for Economic Research and Miss Chin-Feng Liu of National Taiwan University. They provided efficient assistance and tirelessly typed our manuscript which has been modified repetitively before publication.

Tain-Jy Chen

1. Introduction

Tain-Jy Chen

1.1 Foreign Direct Investment of Small- and Medium-Sized Firms

Conventional theory states that foreign direct investment (FDI) is undertaken only by firms that possess some intangible asset (Hymer 1960; Caves 1971). These firms invest in a foreign country in order to exploit their firm-specific advantage embodied in their intangible asset. Examining Taiwan's FDI in recent years reveals that most FDI has been undertaken by firms that are export-oriented (Chen 1992a). These firms venture into a foreign country because their competitiveness has been undermined by rising wages coupled with an appreciating currency at home (van Hoesel 1996). If they possess any intangible asset, this asset must be associated with the ability to export, such as a production technology that delivers products in a timely and flexible manner at a reasonable cost, good customer relations with international buyers, and so on. The rationale for these firms to engage in FDI is that their intangible assets are not easily marketable. Therefore, direct investment is sought to internalize the transaction of these assets.

Empirical evidence generally shows that FDI is dominated by large firms (Caves 1974). In the case of the United Kingdom, an estimated 1500 enterprises had 9100 foreign affiliates, where 34 enterprises with net assets over £200 million account for 1550 overseas affiliates and 55 percent of the total stock of investment (Buckley, Newbould and Thurwell 1988). A similar pattern is observed for US investors. Studies on American multinational firms, for instance, Horst (1972), Wolf (1977), and Lall (1980), all indicate that the incidence of FDI is positively correlated with firm size.

Taiwan's FDI may be an exception to this pattern in the sense that small- and medium-sized firms play an important and, in some cases, dominant role in Taiwan's overseas ventures. Between 1986 and 1991, the Southeast Asian countries of Thailand, Malaysia, Indonesia, Vietnam and the Philippines approved 2526 investment projects from Taiwan, with a proposed capital investment totaling US$13.8 billion (see Table 1.2). Among these investment projects, no more than 200 cases can be identified as having been proposed by Taiwan's large firms with sales exceeding 500 million new taipi (Taiwanese currency, NT for short) in 1986 (approximately US$14 million at the time). The rest are presumably undertaken by small- and medium-sized firms.[1]

The only country which came close to this pattern in the history of FDI is Japan. Ozawa has estimated that about half the total number of Japanese foreign investments are made by enterprises with under 100 million Japanese yen of capital stock, or with 300 or fewer employees (UNCTAD 1984).

Foreign direct investment by small- and medium-sized firms raises many issues of theoretical interest. Based on the observation that 'a substantial proportion of Japanese FDI in manufacturing is undertaken by small- and medium-sized firms' (Kojima 1973, p. 5), Kojima argues that Japanese small- and medium-sized firms go abroad to search for low-cost labor rather than to exploit their intangible asset. They need low-cost labor to regain their competitive edge in international markets as their home operations are losing competitiveness due to rising costs. Contrary to the orthodox FDI theory of Hymer and Caves (Hymer 1960; Caves 1971), which asserts that FDI only comes from oligopolistic industries, Kojima argues that Japanese FDI emanates from competitive industries. Kojima falls short of explaining why Japanese firms from a competitive industry feel comfortable about going abroad, although he stresses that changes in macroeconomic conditions in Japan have made it impossible for these firms to continue producing at home.

Lee (1984) has argued that Kojima's competitive firms must also possess some industry-specific intangible asset, for otherwise these firms would have chosen to switch to a new industry, which is favored by the new macroeconomic conditions at home, instead of venturing abroad to carry on the old business. In this vein of argument, Kojima's competitive firms are not so competitive after all, for any intangible asset generates an economic rent which is nonexistent in a competitive industry. And economic rent is precisely what an FDI-bound firm seeks to internalize through transnational operations when the existing markets do not allow the firm to extract this rent through other arrangements such as licensing and direct export (Buckley and Casson 1976).

Although the difference in market power may be only a matter of degree, and the difference between large and small firms may not be large enough to upset the conventional FDI theory, as we will see later, different market structure does lead to different behavior in transnational firms in line with the structure–conduct–performance paradigm.

The other feature of FDI by small- and medium-sized firms, as characterized by Kojima, is its labor-seeking orientation. This feature may be an important characteristic of small investors, but it should not be the one that sets small- and medium-sized firms apart from their larger counterparts. As also expounded by Vernon (1966) in his product life-cycle hypothesis, FDI occurring in the standardization stage of the product life cycle is intrinsically labor-seeking. Motivation for this type of investment is not sensitive to firm size. Empirically we have observed many large, labor-intensive operations that were established overseas to cut costs of production (Mason 1980). Labor-seeking orientation, then, is not unique to small investors. Dunning and Narula (1996) consider the resources-seeking, including labor-seeking, FDI to be the norm of overseas investment by countries with relatively small amounts of strategic assets at their disposal. Resource-based FDI is a primitive form of globalization as opposed to higher orders of FDI in which strategic motivations are involved. According to Dunning and Narula, the reason that labor-seeking FDI dominates Taiwan's overseas investment is explained by the development status of Taiwan rather than its industrial structure.

If motive is not what sets small multinationals apart from their larger counterparts, then it may be their operational characteristics. Whenever one studies small multinationals, some shortage in their operations becomes apparent. Shortages in capital, managerial resources, risk-absorbing capacity, and the like are frequently mentioned (for instance, Buckley 1979; van Hoorn 1979). These shortages lead to distinctive FDI behavior. For example, capital shortage may lead to underinvestment, or may force small investors into a joint venture, which brings about negative consequences. Capital shortage is particularly detrimental in overseas operations because small firms' already shallow pool of capital can easily dry up, as they usually encounter difficulties in obtaining local funding. A shortage of managerial resources limits small firms' scope of internationalization. They cannot afford multi-country operations. Two-country transnational operations seem to be the norm for small firms. Their decision making is much more likely to be personalized, involving ad hoc short-term reckoning based on individual perceptions and prejudice (Buckley, Newbould and Thurwell 1988). Lack of risk-absorbing capacity also limits small firms' overseas ventures. They often invest only if there is some assurance for some important aspect of their business operations. In the case of Taiwan's small- and medium-sized firms, for example, this assurance is often found in the form of a guaranteed market for their products, locally or in other countries. Insufficiently developed administrative procedures and techniques (for instance, market analysis, information systems, cost allocation) force small firms to take shortcuts in decision making and information gathering, which can be disastrous (Buckley, Newbould and Thurwell 1988).

Steinmann, Kumar and Wasner (1980) listed several barriers to small- and medium-sized firms' FDI, resulting from the above shortages, including: (1) inability to establish an economically feasible production facility abroad due to lack of the needed minimum fixed investment; (2) inability to spread risk; and (3) lack of managerial resources to cope with highly divergent environments and to run an internationally coordinated operation.

In addition to deficiencies in resources and other factors, the transaction costs of FDI also affect small firms. Substantial transaction costs will be incurred in collecting information, assessing the feasibility of FDI in competing locations, complying with the regulations of the host and source countries, establishing production facilities abroad, adjusting operations at home, and so on. If the potential benefits from FDI are not large enough to offset the transaction costs, foreign investment will not take place. Potential benefits emanating from an intangible asset are normally correlated with the scale of operation. Meager benefits associated with small firms may be too small to surpass the absolute level of transaction costs, suppressing any incentive for internationalization.

To the extent that resource deficiency and transaction costs matter, the countries that offer geographical, cultural, and structural proximity to the host country will be most attractive to small- and medium-sized firms. The closeness in location, culture, and market structure reduces the transaction costs as well as the managerial resources needed to run a viable transnational operation. In fact, even large firms prefer to operate in a nearby and familiar environment; for instance, most American multinational firms establish their first foreign subsidiaries in Canada (Vernon 1979). But smaller firms are more acutely in need of the advantages of these friendly countries, for otherwise FDI will not be feasible.

When Japanese firms embarked on the course of FDI in the late 1960s and early 1970s, their favorite spots were neighboring Asian countries. A study by Yonekura (1988), for instance, shows that over 70 percent of Japanese electronics subsidiaries are located in Asia. A three-way classification of these firms by size further indicates that while large firms diversify their subsidiaries around the world, medium-sized firms cluster their overseas operations in Taiwan, Korea, and Singapore, and small-sized firms concentrate mainly in Taiwan. The explanation for this pattern is obvious. Besides geographical proximity, Taiwan, Korea, and Singapore all offer a pro-trade policy environment. The former two countries are also inhabited by a sizable Japanese-speaking population and certain Japanese-style industrial infrastructures, the roots of which can be traced back to the Japanese colonial era. In addition, Taiwan has a business environment particularly conducive to the development of small- and medium-sized enterprises as exemplified by the predominance of such firms in Taiwan's own industries. Such friendly countries offer an expedient FDI location for Japanese small- and medium-sized firms.

Buckley, Newbould and Thurwell's (1988) study on FDI by small British firms indicates that most British small investors locate their overseas production subsidiaries in former British colonies (South Africa and Australia) and member countries of the European Economic Community. Among the small sample (43) they studied, the group located in former colonies were more successful than others. This suggests that cultural and ethnic proximity is also conducive to success.

In comparison, small investors from the US are less noticeable internationally. The US is surrounded by inward-looking neighboring countries which have opted for the import substitution development strategy since the 1950s. Canada is a congenial environment as far as the US is concerned, but it does not present an alternative to American firms that are in need of low-cost labor. In fact, most US FDI in Latin America is either geared toward resource exploration or toward domestic markets which are protected by high tariffs. When it comes to export-oriented, labor-hunting investment, American firms have to look across the Pacific to find suitable locations. Transactional cost precludes small firms from this activity and, therefore, only large US firms are observed to engage in FDI in this region.

Another factor which may explain why small- and medium-sized firms are more prevalent among Japanese transnationals is the unique *keiretsu* system embedded in the Japanese industrial structure. The *keiretsu* system is characterized by an interwoven network of suppliers centered around a core firm which takes charge of product and technology innovation as well as marketing responsibilities. The satellite supplier firms, which can be very small, often adopt an internationalization strategy in connection with the core firm's overall global plan (Adachi 1991). Due to the intimate relation with the core firm which provides technical, managerial, and financial support, small firms may also overcome the barriers to internationalization mentioned in Steinmann, Kumar and Wasner (1980). With the core firm's support, the market for a subsidiary's products is often guaranteed, reducing the risk of technical failure in overseas production to a minimum. Technical failure seems to be the predominant concern of small- and medium-sized firms in their offshore operations (Chen and Wang 1995).[2]

Existing literature on FDI by small- and medium-sized firms generally focuses on identifying firm-specific assets that enable SMEs to venture abroad. For example, Lecraw (1977) studied multinational firms from developing countries and found them smaller than those from developed countries. He suggested that these small firms' advantages are in low-volume production and in designing and adapting machinery to permit flexible production. These firms emphasize production rather than marketing. Where marketing expertise is required, these firms may link up with large firms in developed countries, or even larger firms in developing countries to compensate for their weakness (Wells 1983, p. 45; Giddy and Young 1982, p. 73). White (1983, p. 274) characterizes the overseas operations of small third-world multinational firms as being highly specialized, covering only one or two product lines, with short production runs, often serving the 'contractual markets' given by other industries. This empirical evidence seems to suggest that small firms make use of external resources in their globalization process. Recognizing their intrinsic weakness in firm-specific (internal) resources, external resources may be the key to their survival or success in cross-country operations. The theory that seems suitable to explain this phenomenon is the network approach to FDI.

1.2 Network Approach

The network approach views foreign direct investment as a process of constructing linkage between a domestic network and a foreign network (Johanson and Mattsson 1987). Linkage via FDI is considered to be a strategic move that enhances, maintains, or restores the investor's competitiveness in a globalized market, rather than a profit-seeking motive aimed at extracting economic rent from a foreign market by exploiting the investor's firm-specific advantage. FDI is, therefore, motivated by the quest for a specific advantage rather than a result of the possession of such advantages (Lall 1996).

According to the network approach, all firms in the markets are embedded in one or more networks via linkages to their designers, suppliers, subcontractors, customers, and the like. Markets can be partitioned into numerous interwoven networks which are mutually nonexclusive and constantly evolving over time. Coordination of market activities is not brought about by a central plan or an organizational hierarchy, nor does it take place through the price mechanism only. Instead, coordination takes place through interactions between firms in the networks, where price is only one of several decision factors (Lindblom 1977). Part of the success of East Asian NICs was attributed to interfirm linkages that indigenous East Asian firms had built with their counterparts in the advanced countries. These linkages provide technology, entrepreneurial and managerial know-how, and market access to aid an export-oriented development strategy (Gilroy 1993, Chapter 5).

Under the purview of the network approach, FDI is nothing but a linkage to a foreign network. The sole purpose of linkage to a foreign network is to access the resources therein. These resources may include market opportunities, natural resources, labor, capital, technology, and other strategic assets that are essential to the investor's long-term survival. Linkage to a foreign network, although initiated by an individual firm, may entail actions of the other members in the network to make the attempt successful. A firm's position in the national network determines its ability to mobilize the resources within the network for such an endeavor and therefore its likelihood of success (Johanson and Mattsson 1987). For example, a core firm in the Japanese *keiretsu* can orchestrate concerted actions of *keiretsu* members to jointly penetrate a foreign market or to establish an overseas production system (Ozawa 1979). In contrast, small firms in Taiwan's loosely structured small-firm networks usually take independent actions when making FDI. They, however, may rely on resources within the national networks to support their cross-border operations, as we will see in this study. In fact, we may say that national networks in Taiwan provide the Taiwanese small firms with the competitive edge in overseas productions.

How difficult it is to establish linkages with foreign networks also depends on the nature of foreign networks. If foreign networks are structurally similar to domestic ones, creating a linkage is relatively easy because there is little need for adaptation on both ends of the bond. Networking is an adaptation process because interdependent production, logistics, development, and administrative activities and resources need to be modified and coordinated to bring about a better match between the firms in the network (Hallen, Johanson and Seyed-Mohamed 1991). In other words, network similarity reduces transaction costs and is therefore conducive to FDI. Since the structure and the functioning of a network is shaped by economic as well as political, social, religious, and cultural factors, the closer two countries are in terms of these factors, the more likely FDI will take place between them. Network similarity is a concept synonymous with the aforementioned psychological distance, which has an important bearing on the small firm's FDI decisions. Due to shortages in managerial resources, small firms are less capable of coordinating their activities with local networks that are intrinsically different from the ones they are used to working with. Hence, small firms do not travel far in terms of psychological distance to make FDI.

The network approach has important implications for Taiwan's small- and medium-sized firms which are known to be weak organizations linked by strong networks (Redding 1991). They may therefore exploit the network strength at home to obtain logistical support, market information, technological assistance, and so on to aid their overseas operations. Unique network ties in the Chinese business community built upon cultural and ethnic bonds (Hamilton 1996) may also play a role in Taiwanese firms' attempt to link to other Chinese business webs. Cultural and ethnic bonding is particularly effective in penetrating a primitive market where institutions facilitating internationalization are still lacking. As argued by Johanson and Mattsson (1987), in a primitive market a firm which has no experience of foreign operations has little chance of establishing a position in a local network. Dunning and Narula (1996) argued in their investment development path framework that in primitive markets only firms possessing some dominating ownership advantages can establish themselves to exploit the resources available in the local economies.

Network resources are less important for entry to a mature market like the US where institutions facilitating internationalization are well in place.

However, since this type of market is well structured and highly specialized, only firms with powerful and abundant internal resources are qualified to enter. Linkages to this type of market are more 'strategic' than those to primitive markets in the sense that such linkages enhance strategic capabilities of investors, which in turn reshapes their courses of future action and broadens their scope of market opportunities, rather than just maintaining their market positions as linkages to primitive markets will do. A study on the pattern of Taiwanese FDI has indicated that only strategically capable and organizationally strong firms are able to make FDI in the US. Less capable and weaker firms can only venture into China and Southeast Asia (Chen and Chen 1998).

Getting established in local networks requires adaptation. In a primitive market, adaptation occurs mostly on the production side as the investors attempt to integrate themselves into the local supplier networks with an ultimate aim of cost reduction. In a mature market, adaptation occurs mostly on the demand side as the investors' main motive is to build closer bonds with local customers. Small firms are generally more adaptive on the production side than large firms which may have difficulty finding a niche in highly internationalized networks (Johanson and Mattsson 1987). Large firms, however, may find it easier to penetrate a primitive and large market because their products can be replicated in the local market and their sheer size reduces the need for adaptation. For a large investor which commands sizable forward and backward linkages in production, local agents and suppliers may modify themselves to accommodate its needs.

According to the conventional theory of FDI, an investor chooses a location where the local resources enable the investor to upgrade or to make best use of its internal capabilities. In terms of the network approach, while complementarity between local resources and internal capabilities remains important, local factors that minimize transaction costs or coordination costs of markets, or factors specific to the functioning of network activities also matter in the location decision of FDI (Dunning 1995).

Empirical studies on location decisions of FDI have uncovered the importance of agglomeration effects emanating from clusters of interfirm linkages (Wheeler and Mody 1992; Harrison 1994; Audretsch and Feldman 1994). One possible explanation of the agglomeration effect is that information flow within local networks and institutional thickness (Amin and Thrift 1994) underlying these networks make it easy for a potential investor to establish itself in the local networks. In other words, agglomeration increases the possibility of mapping national networks with foreign networks and reduces the transaction costs of FDI.

Our study shows that the network approach explains the FDI pattern of Taiwanese small firms fairly well. Indeed, Taiwanese small firms depend on network strength more than their own organizational advantage or technological superiority to invest abroad. They use the relational linkages, particularly those based on ethnic and cultural bonds, to make connections to local networks. When running cross-border operations, they rely on network resources at home to beat off their overseas competitors. They tend to cluster in certain locations through agglomeration although their FDI moves are largely independent actions rather than a concerted effort. All this can be extrapolated from the network approach to FDI.

Moreover, our study shows that Taiwanese small firms adapt themselves not only to get established in local networks after FDI but to move the core business operations to local networks in order to save transaction costs in running cross-border operations, although they retain linkages to Taiwan's networks in order to access some crucial resources such as market intelligence and technologies. In other words, for Taiwanese small firms, FDI is not only a linkage to foreign networks but a relocation to foreign networks. Relocation is forced by competitive pressure which quickly eradicates their shallow firm-specific advantage. By relocation, they increase local sales, procure more local raw materials, components and parts, and may ultimately diversify into new areas of production which they do not even do at home, to take advantage of assets accumulated locally. It is not uncommon that owners of Taiwanese small firms adopt local names in an attempt to integrate with the local society.

Small firms, however, encounter more difficulties in localization than do medium and large firms. One major reason is that small firms lack the capacity to nurture their own subcontractors and suppliers due to the small size of their demand. They have to adapt themselves to locally available subcontractors and suppliers whose major patrons may be local competitors or other multinational firms. They are also less successful in advancing technology transfer because they are less willing and able to invest in training and their technologies may be tacit and not codified. When the difficulties of localization are insurmountable, competitive pressure may force these small transnationals to relocate again, often to a country with even lower wages. These 'footloose' firms pursue a 'one-step-ahead' strategy in FDI by venturing into areas where FDI competitors are still rare. They make a small investment to take advantage of low wages and market opportunities through exploiting their small margin of technological superiority.

Due to a strong inclination toward localization and a lack of the managerial resources necessary to run a sophisticated cross-country operation, Taiwanese transnational firms are usually binational rather than multinational. In a binational operation, it is not uncommon for Taiwanese subsidiaries to overtake their parents in terms of production and revenue in a fairly short span of time because of the reallocation of resources from Taiwan to overseas locations. For small firms that are owner-managed, it is not unusual for the owners to spend most of their time with the growing subsidiaries while the parent firms degenerate into nothing more than information-collecting agencies. Parent firms control neither marketing channels nor technologies. Traditional theory asserts that the parent firm extracts rent from the subsidiary through the internal market by exploiting its intangible asset. In Taiwan's case, the subsidiary may actually extract rent from the parent which gathers market and technology information available in Taiwan and enables the subsidiary to innovate and capitalize on market opportunities overseas.

1.3 Patterns of Taiwan's Foreign Direct Investment

Taiwan's foreign direct investment took off in 1986 when the domestic wage rate and the value of the Taiwanese currency skyrocketed simultaneously. It would, however, be premature to conclude that FDI takes place only when a country's wage rate rises above a certain level. There was FDI, albeit small in amount, undertaken by Taiwanese firms before 1986. According to the Taiwan government statistics, a cumulative amount of US$214.9 million was invested abroad by Taiwanese firms from 1959 to 1985. Among the host countries, the US was the most popular destination, accounting for 54.5 percent of the total investment. Most investment in the US involves the establishment of sales subsidiaries, among which some also install simple assembly lines to accommodate the sales function in terms of adapting to special local market needs. Establishment of full-fledged production facilities is rare.

The wage rate increase, which started in 1986, added extra incentives for FDI. Losing their competitive edge at home, many Taiwanese firms relocated to lower-wage countries, mainly Southeast Asian countries and China. The enlarged wage gap between Taiwan and its neighboring Asian countries also provided incentives for multi-plant operations to benefit from an international division of labor. Additionally, there was a dramatic appreciation of the Taiwanese currency, setting off an explosion in asset values. The wealth increase engendered a portfolio reallocation effect, directing investment towards high-wage as well as low-wage countries. Thus, we have observed a rapid increase in Taiwan's outward investment since 1986, not only in the Southeast Asian countries, but also in the US, Europe, and Japan.

A study by Chen (1992a) shows that the motivational factors for Taiwan's FDI changed significantly after 1986. Before 1986, FDI was mainly motivated by the aspiration for market expansion; after 1986, FDI was mainly a bridge to sources of low-cost labor. The change in FDI motives was manifested in the substantial investments made in Southeast Asia and China, which have overshadowed the US as the major destinations of Taiwan's outbound capital since 1986.

Table 1.1 shows the geographical distribution of Taiwan's outward direct investment based on FDI projects approved by the Taiwanese government. It can be seen that in 1959–85, Taiwan's outward investment was concentrated

Table 1.1 Taiwan's Outward Direct Investment Approved by the Taiwan Government (by number of cases, amount US$ million)

Year	Southeast Asia[a]		North America[b]		Europe		China		Other Area		Total	
	Case	Amount	Case	Amount	Case	Amount	Case	Amount	Case	Amount	Case	Amount
1959–85	72	54.1	60	117.2	5	4.3	–	–	81	39.3	218	214.9
1986	4	7.7	16	46.0	1	0.2	–	–	11	3.0	32	56.9
1987	13	14.8	21	70.1	1	0.2	–	–	10	17.7	45	102.8
1988	30	52.7	42	123.3	15	12.1	–	–	23	30.6	110	218.7
1989	62	276.9	57	532.3	7	2.3	–	–	27	119.5	153	931.0
1990	109	519.8	116	449.4	21	96.2	–	–	69	486.8	315	1552.2
1991	100	707.2	129	312.0	28	60.3	237	174.2	107	576.5	601	1830.2
1992	72	300.3	87	193.5	36	45.9	264	247.0	105	347.6	564	1134.3
1993	82	364.2	87	529.1	27	255.9	9329	3168.4	130	511.7	9655	4829.3
1994	84	297.0	73	144.9	21	22.2	934	962.2	146	1152.7	1258	2579.0
1995	87	294.0	97	248.2	16	59.9	490	1092.7	139	754.8	829	2449.6
1996	79	422.3	175	272.4	10	11.9	383	1229.2	206	1458.8	853	3394.6

Notes: [a] Southeast Asia: includes Indonesia, Thailand, Malaysia, the Philippines, and Vietnam.
[b] North America includes the US, Canada.

Source: Investment Commission, Ministry of Economic Affairs, ROC, *Statistics on Overseas Chinese and Foreign Investment, Technical Cooperation, Outward Investment, Outward Technical Cooperation*, December 1996.

Table 1.2 Taiwanese Investment toward Southeast Asian Countries (in US$ million)

Country	Year	Approved by Local Government		Approved by Taiwanese Government	
		Value	Number of cases	Value	Number of cases
Thailand	1986	37.59	21	5.81	3
	1987	307.58	102	5.36	5
	1988	859.95	308	11.88	15
	1989	892.20	214	51.60	23
	1990	782.69	144	149.39	39
	1991	583.46	69	86.43	33
	1992	289.92	44	83.29	23
	1993	215.00	61	109.17	19
	1994	477.48	88	57.32	12
	1995	1803.91	102	51.21	15
	1996	2688.20*	45*	71.41	9
Malaysia	1986	4.08	15	0.00	0
	1987	91.70	37	5.83	5
	1988	313.06	111	2.70	5
	1989	815.07	191	158.64	25
	1990	2383.00	270	184.88	36
	1991	1314.21	182	422.01	35
	1992	602.00	137	155.73	17
	1993	346.50	86	64.54	18
	1994	1149.60	100	101.13	17
	1995	565.49	123	67.30	13
	1996	310.40	79	93.53	12
Philippines	1986	0.35	8	0.07	1
	1987	9.04	43	2.64	3
	1988	109.87	86	36.20	7
	1989	148.69	190	66.31	13
	1990	140.65	158	123.60	16
	1991	11.61	109	1.31	2
	1992	9.27	27	1.21	3
	1993	5.37	21	6.54	12
	1994	292.37	42	9.60	10
	1995	183.80	86	35.72	17
	1996	52.70	22	74.25	20

Country	Year	Approved by Local Government		Approved by Taiwanese Government	
		Value	Number of cases	Value	Number of cases
Indonesia	1986	18.00	0	1.78	0
	1987	8.00	3	0.95	0
	1988	914.00	18	1.92	3
	1989	157.00	49	0.31	1
	1990	618.20	94	61.87	18
	1991	1056.50	57	160.34	25
	1992	563.30	23	39.93	20
	1993	131.00	21	25.53	11
	1994	2487.50	48	20.57	12
	1995	567.40	89	32.07	8
	1996	534.60	111	82.61	13
Vietnam	1989	1.00	1	0.00	0
	1990	104.43	18	0.00	0
	1991	457.66	28	17.14	5
	1992	531.41	23	20.17	9
	1993	436.54	47	158.40	12
	1994	524.01	76	108.38	33
	1995	1215.10	63	108.15	34
	1996	844.61	61	100.48	25

Note: * January–October data.

Source: Investment Commission, Ministry of Economic Affairs, ROC.

in North America (mainly the US). FDI in North America accounted for 27.5 percent of the total projects and 54.5 percent of the total capital investment. The dominance of North America quickly retreated after 1986. Between 1986 and 1996, according to the table, FDI in North America only accounts for 6.4 percent of the total projects (916 out of 14 415), and 15.3 percent of the total capital commitment (US$2921.2 million out of US$19 078.6 million). The decline of the North American share is attributable to the emergence of small- and medium-sized firms which were virtually nonexistent on the foreign investment scene before 1986, but rushed to join the FDI bandwagon afterwards. In fact, the official statistics understate the decline of the North American share because many small firms, whose FDI was concentrated in Southeast Asia and China, made investment without government approval. The Taiwan government lifted foreign exchange controls in July 1987, and allowed each citizen to remit up to US$5 million abroad per year. Taking advantage of capital account liberalization, small firms made overseas investments with the personal allowance for the foreign exchange quota. In addition, Taiwan's tax laws exempt foreign-sourced individual income from personal income tax, whereas corporate income tax is assessed on consolidated global income. This provision, initially designed to encourage Taiwanese citizens to remit their overseas earnings to Taiwan during an age of foreign exchange shortage, has become a distortive measure encouraging personalized FDI. Smaller firms can take full advantage of this loophole because both their ownership and management are personalized anyway. Larger firms, especially public companies, have more difficulty doing so. Therefore, Taiwan's official statistics on FDI are biased towards the activities of larger firms.

Table 1.2 compares the FDI statistics of the investment projects approved by the Taiwanese and host country investment authorities. It can be seen that the discrepancy between the two sets of statistics is amazingly large. In some years, the Taiwanese government statistics capture only 5 percent of the investment projects approved by the host countries. This discrepancy is mainly caused by smaller investors who failed to report their overseas investments to the Taiwanese government. Even if we take into consideration that some of the small investment projects approved by host countries may not materialize, the discrepancy is still large. For example, between 1986 and 1996, a total of 4151 investment projects from Taiwan were approved in Thailand, Malaysia, the Philippines, Indonesia, and Vietnam altogether. If we assume an average realization rate of 30 percent, then an estimate of 1245 Taiwanese projects were actually implemented in these countries.[3] This figure still exceeds the number of projects approved by the Taiwan government, 712, by a large margin. In fact, according to local Taiwanese Investors' Associations or their equivalents in various countries, the actual number of investors may even exceed the figures reported by the host-country governments, because many Taiwanese investors did not even register with the foreign investment authorities in the host countries – they registered as local investors, using the names of local partners or dummies.[4]

The prevalence of small- and medium-sized firms in Taiwan's direct investment in Southeast Asia is partly explained by smaller firms' pressing need for a new export platform to cut production cost. Generally speaking, when a firm's export market position is threatened, two reactions are possible. One is cost cutting, whereby a competitive edge may be regained. The other is product differentiation, whereby the value of products may be enhanced. The second option may require local production in markets which were originally served by export, leading to direct investment in developed countries such as the US and in Europe. For small- and medium-sized firms, the product differentiation option is less affordable because their limited managerial, financial, and technological capacities constrain their ability to do so. Both the US and Europe also present a high degree of foreignness (long psychological distance) to small Taiwanese firms, in terms of language and culture, making linkage to local networks a daunting task. The cost-cutting approach, therefore, becomes the option chosen by most smaller firms.

1.4 Literature on Taiwanese FDI

Due to its short history, studies on Taiwanese FDI are limited. Chen's (1992a) study on the determinants of Taiwan's FDI found that FDI undertaken before 1986 was primarily aimed at expanding the overseas markets whereas FDI undertaken after 1986 was in search of low-cost labor and market expansion. Wage increase and currency appreciation since 1986 were considered to be the underlying macroeconomic forces that prompted the labor-seeking FDI. The study also found FDI by small and large firms to be driven by distinctive microeconomic factors. Growth performance prior to FDI was found to have a positive and significant impact on small firms' propensity to invest abroad while it is inconsequential to large firms' decision on FDI. In contrast, large firms may invest abroad to secure a steady supply of raw materials while this motivation is not observable among small firms. Export-oriented firms, regardless of their size, are more likely to invest abroad than those oriented toward the domestic market. This result is in conformity with Vernon's product-cycle hypothesis (1966), in which Vernon argues that foreign investment is often preceded by export activities, and foreign investment made by the exporter is seen as a prudent means of forestalling the loss of the export market. The result is also consistent with the cumulative approach to internationalization (see Johanson and Vahlne 1990) whereby internationalization is seen as a cumulative process, starting from a low level of resources commitment such as export, and gradually moving to a higher level of commitment, such as FDI, after the firm has accumulated enough 'internationalization' assets to enable a more risky engagement.

A survey study conducted by Taiwan's Council for Economic Planning and Development (CEPD 1992) detected a significicant difference in motives of FDI between investors making a different location choice. Table 1.3 reproduces the survey results in which Taiwanese investors in the US are compared with their counterparts in Southeast Asia. It can be seen that the primary reason for Taiwanese firms to invest in the US is to expand their local or third-party markets. The secondary and tertiary reasons are to acquire or develop new technologies, and to collect market information in the US. All the other reasons, with the exception of risk diversification concerns (portfolio diversificaion), are minor considerations. This motivational pattern is largely the same as that of the Taiwanese FDI that took place before 1986 when the US was the predominant destination of investments (Chen 1992a), except that the technology acquisition motive became more prominent after 1986. As Taiwan's technology level upgraded and Taiwanese firms were seeking frontier technologies rather than outmoded ones, the conventional way of acquiring technology through the market (licensing) became more difficult, forcing firms to internalize their R&D activities, and the US appeared to be the best location for that function because scientists and technicians needed for R&D were readily available and the US was also the largest market for the products targeted by R&D.

Table 1.3 Rankings of Motivational Factors for Taiwan's FDI toward Different Locations

Reasons given by Taiwanese FDI company	US	Southeast Asia
To expand local or third-party markets	1 (36.1)	2 (23.7)
To acquire or develop new technologies	2 (14.8)	– (0)
To collect market information	3 (13.1)	8 (1.4)
To diversify risks, including exchange rate risks	4 (7.5)	3 (14.2)
To secure raw-material supply	5 (2.9)	6 (3.6)
To utilize local labor	6 (2.3)	1 (35.4)
To circumvent trade restrictions	7 (1.3)	7 (3.1)
To access cheap land	7 (1.3)	4 (8.8)
To capitalize on tax incentives or other trade preference	9 (0.4)	5 (4.2)
Others	(20.3)	(5.6)
Sample size	46	102

Note: Percentages in parentheses indicate the average weights of motivational factors; weights are assigned to each factor in line with its ranking by individual firms: the ith ranked factor weights (n−i+1)/n!. Such information is not available for FDI in mainland China.

Source: CEPD (1992).

In contrast, low-cost labor ranks at the top among the factors which motivate Taiwanese investment towards Southeast Asia. The market expansion motive is a distant second, followed by the risk diversification concern, and the desire to obtain cheaper land in the host country. In both the US and Southeast Asia, securing a supply of raw materials is only a minor consideration for FDI. It is also noteworthy that tax incentives and other trade-preferential policies, such as GSP privileges afforded by the US and European countries, are not a major factor in motivating Taiwanese FDI either.

The results suggest that, under the same external conditions, firms in Taiwan pursue FDI in various locations for various reasons.[5] It is tempting to say that the US and Southeast Asian countries possess distinct location-specific advantages for Taiwanese businesses. We might surmise that the advantage of the US is a large market and that of the Southeast Asian countries is low-cost labor. The problem is that Southeast Asia's advantage did not seem to be effectual before 1986; the scant investment made by Taiwanese firms in Southeast Asian countries prior to 1986 was rarely in pursuit of cheap labor.[6] This seems to suggest that the advantage of low wages in Southeast Asia became exploitable by Taiwanese firms only after Taiwan reached a certain stage of industrialization, or, in John Dunning's words, accumulated a certain amount of 'strategic asset' (Dunning 1995). This strategic asset may have been created out of many years of export experience.

Recognizing the motivational differences between FDI in high-wage countries like the US and FDI in low-wage countries in Southeast Asia, Chen, Ku and Liu (1995) termed FDI in high-wage countries as expansionary investment because it is aimed at market expansion, and FDI in low-wage countries as defensive because it is aimed at protecting the export markets. Examining the profiles of Taiwanese investors, they found that investors in high-wage countries are generally larger in size and superior in technology than those investing in low-wage countries. The latter group, in turn, is larger than and superior to those which did not engage in FDI at all. After FDI, both high-wage, and low-wage country investors gained revenues but the high-wage country investors gained more than their low-wage country counterparts. High-wage country groups also substantially expanded their exports after FDI whereas the low-wage country group saw their exports largely stagnate. This suggests that investors in low-wage countries like Southeast Asia shifted their export platforms to overseas while the parent firms struggled to upgrade product lines at home. In contrast, investors in high-wage countries promoted exports through local production in overseas locations and made other investments that enhanced the product value.

Van Hoesel (1996) also noticed the difference between Taiwan's FDI in developing countries, such as Southeast Asia and China, and 'upward' investment in the US and Europe. He attributed Taiwan's active investment in Southeast Asia to the erosion of Taiwan's comparative advantage in labor-intensive industries and pro-FDI policies adopted by Taiwan and the host-country governments. In comparison, FDI in the US and Europe is to acquire brand names, marketing channels, and technological capabilities. By establishing local operations in industrialized countries, Taiwanese firms can hire local skills to conduct product and marketing research and tap into locally available technological and commercial know-how. The trend of regionalization in North America and Europe also induced FDI from Taiwanese firms which were wary of a market lock-out.

Van Hosel also noticed the small number of technology licensing cases to parallel Taiwan's zealous outward investment. A few technology cooperation cases were arranged with developing countries in Southeast Asia, such as Indonesia, Thailand and the Philippines. This suggests that the technological capability of Taiwanese firms is unparallel to other 'intangible assets' which can only be exchanged through an internalized market. The 'intangible assets' may include their position in Taiwan's networks.

Chen and Chen (1998) used the theory of strategic linkage developed by Nohria and Garcia-Pont (1991), among others, to examine Taiwan's investment pattern. Strategic linkage theory is conceptually analogous to network linkage but it emphasizes the 'strategic' aspect of network linkages that enhances the competitive position of linkage seekers. In particular, they looked at the technology-sourcing and market-enhancing linkages and found that these types of strategic linkages are evident in Taiwan's FDI in the US but lacking in Taiwan's FDI in Southeast Asia and China. Taiwanese investors in the US were also found to be larger in size and stronger in technological capabilities than their counterparts in Southeast Asia and China.

The results suggest that firms possessing more organizational and technological advantages are more capable of seeking linkages to strategic assets overseas. Those which are short of such advantages have little chance of seeking strategic linkages. They do, however, have the option of linking to natural resources and cheap labor in a foreign location to which psychological distance from the home country presents a reasonable risk for investors. Southeast Asia and China are two of these locations. Small Taiwanese firms without technological superiority and organizational strength have hence concentrated their FDI in Southeast Asia and China.

1.5 The Purpose, Scope and Methodology of this Study

Purpose

The purpose of this book is to study the FDI behavior of Taiwanese firms in general, and that of small- and medium-sized firms in particular. As eloquently argued by Lecraw (1979) and Wells (1983), among others, the strength of small firms lies in their ability to conduct small-scale and flexible production.

In Taiwan, small firms are able to do this not so much because they possess specific intangible assets but because they are supported by an efficient production network encompassing a large number of specialized producers. Redding (1991) characterizes Taiwan's SMEs as weak organizations with strong linkages. The fundamental question that we set out to answer is how networks matter in small firms' FDI. Is the advantage of strong linkages sufficient to support overseas operations? Moreover, once these SMEs venture abroad, how can this domestic advantage be extended to overseas production?

In theory, there are two possible arrangements to extend these linkages abroad. In the first arrangement, overseas subsidiaries maintain a close connection with their domestic production network, which enables them to preserve the advantage of being small and flexible. In the second arrangement, overseas subsidiaries follow their parent firms by establishing a similar network in the host country. In the first case, small firms have to overcome distance and artificial barriers to trade when they try to access the local production networks from abroad. Hence, distance constrains SMEs to invest mainly in neighboring countries. For similar reasons, countries with high artificial barriers in the form of tariff and import restrictions may not attract small investors although they may attract large multinational firms to invest for the purpose of circumventing trade barriers.

In the second case, the overseas subsidiary will have to bear large costs in searches and organization of a new network. The two approaches yield completely different results for the host country. The first approach promotes trade between the source and host countries, and the second creates linkage effects in the local economy. In terms of technology, the first approach emphasizes the application of original technology while the second emphasizes the adaptation of the original technology to local conditions. Again, their implications for the local economy are different. The two approaches may also produce different effects in the area of employment, trade, technology transfer, induced local production, and so on.

The actual situation is likely to be a mixture of the two approaches. That is, small firms extend some domestic networks to overseas production and also duplicate some portion of the network abroad. They apply their original technology to local production but also make adaptations to suit the local environment. The relative share of these two elements probably depends on the characteristics of the firm, the nature of the products, and the structure of the market in which small firms operate. Our interest is to connect these factors with small firms' approach to overseas production. From this connection we hope to draw inferences about the effect of their direct investment on the host country economy.

Scope

We will investigate the relationship between firm characteristics, products, and market structure on the one hand, and the FDI behavior of small firms on the other. From this pattern, we will study the effects of small firms' investment on: (1) employment; (2) trade; (3) linkage effect; and (4) technology transfer, in both investing countries and their host countries.

The study will also draw on the FDI experiences of large Western multinationals. We hope to identify distinctive features of Taiwan's small- and medium-sized firms' cross-country operations. For example, in the area of employment, we are interested not only in the number of jobs created, but also in the type of job created and the location of job opportunities. In the area of trade, we are concerned not only with the volume of imports and exports, but also with the kind of commodities and services which are traded and their impact on the trade structure of the host country. In the area of linkage effects, we are concerned about the possibility of linking Taiwan's small transnationals to indigenous small- and medium-sized firms. In the field of technology transfer, we are concerned about the 'appropriateness' of the technology transferred and the speed of transfer. In other words, we are interested in investigating to what extent and how fast the technology is absorbed by the host economies, and how effective the transferred technology is in improving productivity of the host country.

Method

Our study covers Taiwan's direct investment in Southeast Asia, including Indonesia, Malaysia, Thailand, the Philippines, and Vietnam. We focus on the manufacturing sector and emphasize the roles of small- and medium-sized firms, although the behavior of large firms is also analyzed. Singapore is excluded from the study because Taiwan's FDI in Singapore is mainly for the purpose of trade rather than manufacturing. FDI in Singapore is also dominated by large Taiwanese firms which sometimes use Singapore subsidiaries to coordinate sourcing and marketing activities elsewhere in Southeast Asia.

We explored the issues of interest from two fronts. We organized a research team in Taiwan to survey and interview parent firms which hold subsidiaries in Southeast Asia. We also organized a research team in each host country to survey and interview Taiwanese subsidiaries. A common survey questionnaire was used for the five host countries to provide uniformity upon which inter-country comparisons can be made. A separate questionnaire was used to survey the parent firms. The sample of parent firms was drawn from the database containing FDI projects approved by the Taiwan government and corresponding investors. As previously mentioned, these data tend to be biased toward large firms. Our sample, however, includes a substantial number of small- and medium-sized firms that enables us to make meaningful comparisons between large enterprises and SMEs. The population of Southeast Asian subsidiary samples is based on the membership of each country's Taiwan Investors' Associations, or their equivalents (for instance, Taiwan Business Club) in the host countries. These samples include independent individual investors (who do not own a parent firm in Taiwan) as well as normal company investors.

Interviews conducted following the survey explored the issues in depth. Interviewees were selected such that firms of all sizes were covered. In countries where FDI is dispersed, we strove to cover various locations to avoid selection bias. For example, in Malaysia, we interviewed firms in Penang and also in the Klang Valley area. In Indonesia, we interviewed firms in Bandung and Surabaya, in addition to Jakarta. In Thailand and the Philippines, interviews were mainly conducted in suburban areas surrounding the capital cities; in Vietnam, in suburban Ho Chi Minh City.

There is not a universal standard used to define small- and medium-sized firms. Some countries use assets as the criterion; some use number of employees. The cut-off point also varies from country to country, and even differs in different times within a country. In our study, we chose employment as the criterion, and classified firms employing fewer than 300 persons as SMEs.

The rest of the book is arranged as follows: In the next chapter, a review of foreign investment experience of SMEs from developed countries is made. In Chapter 3, the survey and interview results of parent firms in Taiwan are presented and discussed. In Chapter 4, we discuss the economic effects of Taiwanese FDI on host countries with a focus on small Taiwanese affiliates, based on the survey and interviews with the Taiwanese subsidiaries in Southeast Asia. In Chapter 5, we discuss the noneconomic elements of Taiwanese FDI, emphasizing the unique features of Taiwanese SMEs and their relationship with local Chinese communities and indigenous labor in general. The discussions are drawn from surveys and interviews of both parents and subsidiaries. The country studies of the five host countries are presented in Chapters 6 through 10. Chapter 11 summarizes the major research findings and makes some remarks on the implications of the findings.

Notes

1. According to data provided by the Foreign Investment Commission, Ministry of Economic Affairs of Taiwan, among the 674 firms with sales exceeding 500 million NT in 1986, 149 firms have invested abroad between 1986 and 1991.
2. Most Taiwanese investors indicate that their primary comparative advantage in overseas production is technical superiority in production. Therefore, successful transfer of production technology to the subsidiaries is a precondition for success

in overseas operation.

3. Most empirical data show the realization rate of approved FDI projects to be in the order of 30 to 50 percent. Here we take the lower bound.
4. Our estimated Taiwanese investors, as of 1994, are 600 based on membership of Taiwanese Investors' Associations in Thailand, 400 in Malaysia, 300 each in Indonesia and Vietnam, and 200 in the Philippines. The total comes to 1800 firms.
5. To verify statistically the difference in the distribution of motivational factors between the FDI directed toward the US and that toward the Southeast Asian countries, we conducted a Pearson's x^2 test. The test yields a statistic of 51.8, indicating that the two distributions are different at the 1 percent significance level (with nine degrees of freedom).
6. In fact, the motivation for FDI in Southeast Asia before 1986 is also mainly in pursuit of market access and market expansion. See Chen and Su (1987).

2. FDI by Small- and Medium-Sized Enterprises in Developed Countries

James Riedel

The aim of this chapter is to put the foreign direct investment by Taiwan's small- and medium-sized enterprises (SMEs) into perspective by examining the role and key characteristics of FDI by SMEs in other countries, principally the developed countries. While the literature on FDI is immense, there is little in it that refers to the experience of SMEs *per se*. Fortunately, however, the United Nations recently published the results of a survey of transnational corporations, based in developed countries and investing in developing countries, that distinguishes large firms from small- and medium-sized ones (UNCTAD 1993). That survey, together with the *White Paper on Small- and Medium-Sized Enterprises* of the Japanese Ministry of International Trade and Industry and selected secondary sources, provide enough information to begin to form a picture of the nature of FDI by SMEs in other countries, which can usefully serve as a benchmark for evaluating the operations of Taiwan's SMEs in Southeast Asia.

2.1 The Relative Importance of Small- and Medium-Sized Transnational Corporations (TNCs)

The term 'multinational corporation' conjures up the image of a large conglomerate enterprise based in the US, Western Europe or Japan, with operations worldwide. Much of the academic literature on multinational corporations is written with this kind of firm in mind, a company whose 'Global Reach' (Barnet and Muller 1974) puts 'Sovereignty at Bay' (Vernon 1971). Nevertheless, the number of foreign investments made by SMEs in developed countries is not insignificant, although their share of the assets of foreign affiliates of transnational corporations (TNCs) is not great. Small- and medium-sized TNCs are more important in Japan than in other developed countries, and in the mid-1980s accounted for about half of Japanese new equity foreign investments and about one-fifth of the value of Japanese foreign equity assets (UNCTAD 1993, pp. 50–51). By comparison, during the same period in the US, small- and medium-sized TNCs accounted for only 28 percent of foreign investments and only 3 percent of all US TNCs' foreign assets (ibid.)

From 1985 to 1988 the number of Japanese foreign investments by SMEs increased dramatically, and then subsequently declined equally dramatically. The boom in the number of foreign direct investments by Japanese SMEs after 1985 has been attributed to the concurrent real appreciation of the yen. The subsequent decline in the number of investments in the 1990s has been attributed to several factors, including rising interest rates at home, recession in host countries, and finally depressed business conditions in Japan after 1991 (Japanese Ministry of International Trade and Industry 1994). What is unclear, however, is why these factors did not have the same impact on the number of investments of large TNCs in Japan, which increased steadily from mid-1980 until 1991. The widely divergent experience of large and small TNCs would seem to suggest that the two types of firms are subject to different kinds of constraints and hence may be affected differently by changing business conditions at home and abroad, an issue which is explored below.

2.2 Where Small- and Medium-Sized TNCs Invest

The geographic pattern of FDI by SMEs in Japan and the United States is shown in Table 2.1. The geographic pattern of FDI by SMEs is not much different from that of large TNCs, either in Japan or in the United States. However, as between Japan and the United States, a significant difference in geographic pattern is observed, with Japan concentrating far more of its FDI in developing countries, especially Asia. Proximity clearly plays a role in determining the geographic pattern of FDI, especially that which goes to developing countries, with the US firms locating predominantly in Latin America and Japanese firms in Asia, and within Asia primarily in China, the Newly Industrializing Economies (NIEs) and Southeast Asia.

The industrial composition of FDI by SMEs in Japan and the United States is shown in Table 2.2. Naturally, the FDI in the primary sector is more important for the US SMEs than for Japanese ones, though in both countries the majority of investments are in the manufacturing and service sectors, with the latter marginally more important. The industrial composition of FDI by SMEs, both in Japan and the US, is quite different from that of their large-firm counterparts, whose investments are far more concentrated in manufacturing. About two-thirds of the foreign affiliates of large US TNCs are in manufacturing with a comparable figure for Japan.

Table 2.1 The Geographic Pattern of FDI by SMEs in Japan and the United States (%)

	Japan[a]	United States[b]
Developed Countries	55.3	70.0
United States	42.1	–
Europe	8.3	42.5
Japan	–	4.1
Other	4.9	23.4
Developing Countries	44.7	27.6
Asia	43.0	8.4
Latin America	1.4	13.3
Middle East	0.1	3.1
Africa	0.1	2.8

Notes: [a] Distribution of the number of foreign equity investments by Japanese SMEs from 1986 to 1991.
[b] Distribution of the number of foreign affiliates of small and medium US TNCs in 1988.

Source: UNCTAD (1993), pp. 57, 63.

Table 2.2 The Industrial Composition of FDI by SMEs in Japan and the United States (%)

	Japan[a]	United States[b]
Primary	1.8	15.0
Manufacturing	42.4	39.4
Services	55.8	45.6

Notes and source: Same as for Table 2.1.

2.3 Why Small- and Medium-Sized Enterprises Invest Abroad

The alternative to FDI as a way of serving foreign markets is exporting from the home country. When profit-maximizing firms invest abroad they presumably believe that by establishing foreign affiliates they can thereby either market their products more effectively or produce them more cheaply. The importance of having production facilities located in foreign markets for the purposes of marketing would presumably be greater in industries in which many highly differentiated products compete, such as those in which intra-industry trade predominates, a phenomenon that occurs mainly among the developed countries. In such industries, marketing and the ability to adapt products to local tastes are likely to be decisive factors. The informational requirements for taking advantage of these factors may well necessitate the establishment of affiliates in foreign markets, especially when that market happens to be in a developed country.

The motive for FDI in developing countries, on the other hand, is more likely to be based on relative production costs, especially relative real wages (Riedel 1975). Since the early 1980s, protection levels have been falling throughout the developing world, and with the fall in trade barriers it has become easier for foreign firms to serve the markets of developing countries through exporting to those countries rather than by investing in them directly. By the same token, the fall in trade barriers and improved incentives for exporting in developing countries have expanded opportunities for multinational companies to cut production cost, especially in labor-intensive activities, by investing in these countries for the purpose of establishing a base for exporting back to the home country and to third countries.

Some evidence in support of these hypotheses, as they relate to the experience of small- and medium-sized TNCs, is provided in Table 2.3. According to the results of the UN survey, the single most important motive for SMEs' foreign direct investment in North America is to strengthen their 'information-gathering' capabilities. The strongest motive for SMEs' foreign direct investment in Asia and Europe, on the other hand, is 'expected growth in local markets', followed by 'low labor costs', in the case of Asia, and 'establishing an export base', in the case of Europe.

Our hypotheses about the motives for direct investment by SMEs are given even stronger support by data collected by the Japanese Small and Medium Enterprise Agency, which routinely surveys Japanese SMEs and publishes the results. As Table 2.4 indicates, Japanese investment by SMEs in East Asia is primarily motivated by relative labor costs, a motive which has only been reinforced by the real appreciation of the yen in recent years. The motive behind the foreign investment of Japanese SMEs in North America and Europe, on the other hand, is mainly to strengthen information collection in those markets, and secondarily, to 'better respond to customer needs' in those markets. These findings suggest that there is probably no great difference in the motives behind foreign direct investment of large and small enterprises.

Table 2.3 Motivation for FDI by Small and Medium TNCs by Host Region (% of foreign affiliates responding 'yes' in UN survey)

Motivation	Asia*	N. America	Europe
Expect growth in local market	52.7	5.8	44.3
Lower labor costs	31.2	3.9	3.8
Establish export base	29.0	15.4	24.1
Host country incentives	11.8	–	2.5
Information gathering	16.1	28.9	22.8

Note: * Excluding Japan and West Asia.

Source: UNCTAD (1993), p. 41.

Table 2.4 Motivation for FDI by Japanese Small and Medium TNCs by Region (%)

Motivation	E. Asia	N. America and EC
Secure cheap labor	66.0	7.8
Strengthen information collection	12.4	51.0
Respond to customer needs	24.7	27.5
Counter-measure against strong yen	12.4	9.8
Secure natural resources	4.1	2.0

Source: Small and Medium Enterprise Agency, Japan (1992).

2.4 Characteristics of Small- and Medium-Sized TNCs

2.4.1 Ownership

When a firm establishes a foreign affiliate, be that firm large or small, it normally prefers to own the affiliate one hundred percent. In that way it can better protect its market advantage from its competitors. It is, of course, not always possible for foreign investors to retain full ownership because of legal requirements in the host countries which may obligate foreign investors to take local partners. Moreover, in some cases it might make good business sense to take a local partner, especially if the foreign investor faces financial constraints or lacks sufficient information about the host-country market and policy environment. The case for taking a local partner would presumably be even stronger for small- and medium-sized firms than for their larger counterparts, since SMEs are generally perceived to be weaker financially and to have less access to the information that is needed to operate efficiently in a foreign country. As Table 2.5 shows, there is some basis for this premise, though the differences between small–medium and large TNCs in terms of mode of ownership are not great, with roughly equal proportions of wholly owned and jointly owned affiliates for both types of TNCs.

Table 2.5 Form of Ownership and Mode of Entry of Small, Medium and Large TNCs in Developing Countries (%)

	Small–Medium TNCs	Large TNCs
Wholly owned affiliates	47	53
Newly established	47	51
Acquired	0	2
Non-wholly owned affiliates	53	47
Newly established	33	28
Acquired	20	19

Note: Based on a United Nations Survey of 91 affiliates of small-medium-sized TNCs and 141 affiliates of large TNCs in developing countries.

Source: UNCTAD (1993), p. 83.

2.4.2 Research and Development

In the theory of foreign direct investment, research and development (R&D) is a key ingredient. Without the technological advantages that R&D supposedly brings, foreign firms would presumably operate at a disadvantage *vis-à-vis* indigenous firms. A positive relation between research and development intensity and foreign direct investment is, therefore, often hypothesized, and evidence in support of the hypothesis exists, at least for US based firms (Pugel 1981; Bergsten, Horst and Moran 1978; Pearce 1989). In the case of Japan, while FDI and R&D are positively correlated across industries, they are negatively correlated across firms within an industry (Pearce 1989).

Table 2.6 R&D by Small and Medium TNCs (%)

	Proportion of Small–Medium TNCs that:		
	have R&D facilities		have acquired
Country/Industry	at home	abroad	patents
Japan	34	7	68
United States	56	31	79
Europe	52	36	54
Manufacturing	55	18	78
Services	20	10	38

Note: Based on the United Nations Survey cited in Table 2.5.

Source: UNCTAD (1993), pp. 96, 97.

In the case of small- and medium-sized TNCs, the evidence from the UN survey confirms the importance of R&D, especially for firms based in the US and Europe (see Table 2.6). Japanese small- and medium-sized TNCs apparently do less R&D than those based in the US or Europe. While about two-thirds of all Japanese small- and medium-sized TNCs reported doing some kind of R&D, only about one-third maintained specialized R&D departments at home and only 7 percent maintained them in their foreign affiliates. However, in terms of reliance on patents, the differences between firms of different size and nationality is not significant.

2.4.3 Technology Transfer

Foreign direct investment is an important conduit for transferring technology from developed to developing countries. However, since technology is often the source of market advantage for multinational firms, there is sometimes reticence on the part of parent firms to transfer state-of-the-art technology to their foreign affiliates, especially those which are not wholly owned. Of course, conditions in host countries, especially in developing countries, may favor older technologies over state-of-the-art technologies. As the UNCTAD (1993) study indicates, foreign affiliates of small- and medium-sized TNCs in developing countries obtained frontier, state-of-the-art technology in fewer than half the cases surveyed, while about two-thirds of the foreign affiliates of larger TNCs received state-of-the-art technology (p. 118). It is, however, impossible to determine to what extent this observation is due to the unwillingness on the part of parent companies to transfer the best technology to their affiliates, to what extent it is due to the inappropriateness of state-of-the-art technology in particular host countries and to what extent it is due to sectoral and country-specific factors.

2.4.4 Capital Intensity

The single most important motive for foreign investment in developing countries by small- and medium-sized TNCs, as noted above, is to utilize low-cost labor to manufacture for export. This leads naturally to the expectation that the capital intensity of operations by small- and medium-sized TNCs in developing countries would be relatively low. This expectation is confirmed in Table 2.7, which indicates that the capital intensity of affiliates of small- and medium-sized TNCs is indeed low relative to (a) the affiliates of large TNCs, and (b) indigenous firms in developing countries. It is interesting to observe that the capital intensity of foreign affiliates is apparently also lower than that of the parent companies in developed countries, which is to be expected, of course, because of differences in real wages between the home and the host countries.

Table 2.7 Relative Capital Intensity in Manufacturing (US$ '000 per worker)

Affiliates of small and medium TNCs in LDCs	13.8
Affiliates of large TNCs in LDCs	20.4
Indigenous firms in LDCs	47.6
Parent firms of small and medium TNCs	76.9

Note: Based in part on the United Nations Survey cited in Table 2.5.

Source: UNCTAD (1993), pp. 86, 116.

2.4.5 Linkages

There are two sets of linkages that are important in understanding how small- and medium-sized TNCs operate in developing countries. One is the linkage between affiliates in developing countries and parent firms in the home country. The other is between the affiliate and the local economy of the host country. Some indication of the nature of the linkage between affiliate and parent is given in Table 2.8. According to the UN survey, this linkage is similar for small- and medium-sized and for large TNCs. As indicated in the table, the principal linkage is horizontal – that is, an affiliate producing the same products with the same or modified technology as the parent in the home country. Vertical linkages are significantly less prevalent, according to the survey. However, when Japanese SMEs began to invest abroad in the 1960s, they initially developed vertical linkages with foreign affiliates, exporting basic materials and semi-finished goods to their affiliates in developing countries where they were processed and then re-exported back to Japan and to other countries (Ozawa 1985, p. 4). As the dualistic character of Japanese industry diminished in the 1970s, the relationship between parent and affiliate of small- and medium-sized enterprises changed to reflect more closely that of larger TNCs, for which a horizontal relationship was more prevalent.

Table 2.8 Relationship between Foreign Affiliates in Developing Countries and their Parent Firms (%)

	Small–Medium TNCs	Large TNCs
Horizontal Relationship		
Producing the same product as the parent with the same technology	66	64
Producing the same product as the parent with different technology	23	29
Vertical Relationship		
Turning raw materials into semi-manufactured products	15	19
Turning semi-manufactured products into final products	28	23
No Relationship		
Producing different products	10	14

Note: Based on the United Nations Survey of 79 Small and Medium TNCs and 129 Large TNCs, cited in Table 2.5.

Source: UNCTAD (1993), p. 99.

The second linkage, between the affiliate of small- and medium-sized TNCs and the local economy, is of particular significance to this study, since it has an important bearing on the benefits to the host country from this form of foreign direct investment. Foreign-owned affiliates of TNCs are, of course, linked to the local economy in many ways, such as by hiring workers, purchasing inputs and subcontracting production. Small- and medium-sized TNCs are especially well linked to local labor markets in developing countries since, as noted above, the labor intensity of their operations is greater than that of either their larger TNC counterparts or indigenous firms in developing countries. However, as Table 2.9 indicates, small- and medium-sized TNCs are more footloose, depending less on local sources for inputs and for subcontracting production than do larger TNCs or indigenous firms. This feature of small- and medium-sized TNCs' operations in developing countries may well be due to their relatively strong export orientation, which no doubt requires higher quality and more specialized inputs to be competitive in world markets than may be required to compete in local host-country markets.

Table 2.9 Linkages to the Local Economy: Foreign Affiliates and Indigenous Firms in Developing Countries (%)

	Local content[a]	Subcontracting[b]
Affiliates in LDCs of		
Small and medium TNCs	50	48
Large TNCs	58	49
Indigenous firms in LDCs	67	58

Notes: [a] Share of local purchases in total purchases.
[b] Share of affiliates/firms subcontracting with local firms.

Source: UNCTAD (1993), p. 124.

2.5 Conclusions

To sum up, FDI in developing countries by small- and medium-sized enterprises based in developed countries is not an insignificant phenomenon, though it is minor compared to investment by large TNCs. Among developed countries, Japan is the principal source of FDI in developing countries by SMEs. Like Taiwan's SMEs, Japanese SMEs, motivated mainly by the relatively low labor costs, invest mostly in China and Southeast Asia, and mostly for the purpose of producing for export.

Transnational corporations have been the subject of heated debate largely over the appropriateness, or more precisely inappropriateness, of their investments in developing countries. Motivated by barriers to trade and other market interventions, TNCs were often found to be producing goods in developing countries that could be obtained more cheaply by importing them, and using technologies more suited to conditions in developed countries. Many of the issues about TNCs that were debated in that literature would appear, from the foregoing survey of evidence, to be largely irrelevant to the FDI by small- and medium-sized transnational enterprises. Their investments in developing countries are found to be mainly market determined, with relative wage cost being a decisive factor, and therefore are seen to conform reasonably well to conditions in developing countries. Small- and medium-sized TNCs in developing countries are found to employ relatively labor-intensive technologies and to be reasonably well integrated into the local economy of the host countries in which they operate. Furthermore, small- and medium-sized TNCs are somewhat more apt to take local partners in developing countries than are larger TNCs. They are not found to be heavily engaged in R&D in developing countries, but that is probably all to the good since such activities are likely not to be very appropriate in the circumstances of many developing countries. The evidence presented here suggests, therefore, that FDI in developing countries by SMEs is generally a positive force for economic development and as such should be encouraged.

3. FDI by Small- and Medium-Sized Enterprises from Taiwan

Tain-Jy Chen

3.1 Introduction

The idea that the pattern of foreign direct investment (FDI) differs depending on the source of investment was first suggested by Kojima (1973). He argued that FDI originating in Japan was in line with the host country's comparative advantage and results in a trade promotion effect. In contrast, he claimed that FDI originating in the US did not conform to the host country's comparative advantage and resulted in a trade reduction effect. The difference, as he explained it, came from the fact that Japanese FDI emanated from competitive industries while the American FDI came from oligopolistic industries. In other words, the principle he proposed was that differences in domestic market structure lead to differences in overseas operations, which in turn account for the different effects of FDI. The reasoning of this argument falls into the structure–conduct–performance paradigm in an open-economy context.

Kojima's assertion that Japanese transnational firms come from more competitive industries may have stemmed from the observation that 'a substantial proportion of Japanese foreign direct investment in manufacturing is undertaken by small- and medium-sized firms and on a smaller scale than by American firms' (Kojima 1973, p. 5). In fact, Lee's (1980) study of Japanese and American FDI in Korea uses firm size as a criterion for distinguishing oligopolistic firms from competitive ones. By equating American firms listed in the Fortune 500 to oligopolistic firms, Lee found that American subsidiaries in Korea are predominantly in the oligopoly group, confirming the Kojima hypothesis.

If firm size is what sets Japanese transnational firms apart from American ones, then it is useful to study the relationship between firm size and the behavior of transnational firms. We attempt to do just that in this chapter by examining Taiwanese investment in Southeast Asia. We hope to identify the unique features intrinsic to small firms and to see whether the phenomena represent a deviation from traditional FDI theory.

Taiwanese firms started to make substantial direct investment in Southeast Asia in 1987. Since then Taiwan has become one of the major investors in the region, rivaling Japan and the US. Unlike advanced countries, Taiwan's overseas investment is dominated by small- and medium-sized firms. This is, of course, a manifestation of Taiwan's domestic industrial structure.

Traditional theory as mentioned above asserts that foreign direct investment is undertaken only by firms that possess some intangible asset. If there is any 'intangible asset' possessed by Taiwan's small firms, it must be something related to their ability to conduct small-scale, flexible production. In Taiwan, small firms are able to do this because they are supported by an efficient production network encompassing a large number of highly specialized producers, all of which are generally small firms.

These small-firm networks exist mainly in light manufacturing industries, such as clothing, food, metal working, electronics, furniture, auto components, chemical products, and so on. Firms in the networks are generally independent and are constantly competing among themselves, but they share production and market information that enables them to react quickly and fruitfully to change in technology and market (Perrow 1992). In a Chinese society like Taiwan's, interactions between firms in the networks are often driven and sanctioned by personal relations (Hamilton and Waters 1995). The question that we set out to answer is that once these Taiwanese firms venture abroad, how can this advantage based on domestic industry structure and cultural bonds be extended to overseas operations?

As elucidated in Chapter 1, there are two possible answers. First, overseas subsidiaries could maintain a close connection with the domestic production network which enables them to preserve the advantage of being small and flexible. Or second, overseas subsidiaries could follow their parent firms by establishing a similar network in the host country or getting established in a local network through their cultural connections. In the first case, small firms have to overcome distance and artificial barriers to trade when they try to access the domestic Taiwanese production network from abroad. In the second case, they have to bear large costs in locating and cultivating suppliers and subcontractors and organizing them into reliable networks to support their local production. The two approaches yield completely different results for the host country. The first approach promotes trade between the investing and host countries, and the second creates linkage to the local economy. In terms of technology, the first approach emphasizes the application of original technology, while the second emphasizes the adaptation of original technology to local conditions. Their implications for the local economy are therefore very different. The two approaches may also produce different effects in the areas of employment, technology diffusion, and induced local investment.

The purpose of this chapter is to survey Taiwanese parent firms who made investment in Southeast Asia to distill answers to the above question. Our study found that Taiwan's small- and medium-sized firms generally attempt to adopt the first strategy in the beginning, just like multinationals from advanced countries, but soon find the transaction costs of cross-border and cross-network operations too high to bear and hence switch to the second strategy. Under the second strategy, they get established and absorbed into local networks more often than creating new ones. They localize swiftly through this network linkage. They increase local sales, procure more local raw materials, components and parts, and may ultimately diversify into new areas of production, which they do not do at home, to take advantage of local assets that they have accumulated in host countries. It is also common that owners of small firms adopt local names or seek naturalization in an attempt to integrate with the local society.

It is apparent that Taiwan's small firms are under immense pressure to localize since their competitive edge over indigenous firms is so thin that it dissipates quickly over time. Small firms, however, face more challenges in localization than medium and large firms. One major reason is that small firms lack the capacity to nurture their own subcontractors and suppliers, which are essential to cost cutting. They have to adopt locally available subcontractors and suppliers into their own production systems. They are also less successful in advancing technology transfer because their technology is mostly tacit and not codified. However, they are more likely to develop indigenous technologies in the localization process.

When small firms face bottlenecks in localization, market pressure may force them to relocate, often to a country whose wage is even lower. But once they successfully localize, they do not move to other locations easily even if the macroeconomic conditions of the host country change, say wage rate rises. This is because their investment in localization creates location-specific assets which act as an exit barrier. Instead of escaping the country, the localized firm will restructure itself to cope with a changing environment. These otherwise 'footloose' firms pursue a 'one-step-ahead' strategy in FDI, whereby they venture into areas when FDI from competing countries is still rare.

Taiwanese SMEs usually make a small investment to take advantage of low-cost local labor and market opportunities by exploiting their technological superiority. To establish a foothold in these countries, they often rely on personal connections to gather information, to obtain governmental approval, and to access the local market. For those who succeed in localization, personal connections are also crucial in building local networks of suppliers and subcontractors.

Because of immense pressure to localize, Taiwanese firms investing abroad actively encourage their subcontractors in Taiwan to follow in their footsteps and invest abroad so they can reconfigure a network in the new location. An agglomeration effect resulting from Taiwanese FDI is apparent, but, because there usually is not a dominant firm in the Taiwan network, the agglomeration effect does not constitute an enclave. Instead, there is substantial local participation by indigenous firms and multinational firms based in other countries. Unlike Japanese multinationals, where local subcontractors are typically investment ventures made by members of the *keiretsu* system in Japan, Taiwanese networks show little discrimination against local firms.

Due to a strong inclination toward localization and a lack of the managerial resources necessary to run a complicated cross-country operation, Taiwanese transnational firms are usually binational rather than multinational. Their transnational operations follow a simple pattern: For relatively large firms, the parent firm controls the marketing and technology of the subsidiary until local market sales warrant the establishment of an independent marketing arm in the subsidiary. Local sales may also encourage the development of new product lines, which in turn may lead the parent to install R&D capability in the subsidiary. In the process, the subsidiary becomes less and less subordinate to the parent. Since most host countries in Southeast Asia possess a potential market larger than Taiwan's, it is not uncommon for Taiwanese subsidiaries to overtake their parents in terms of production volume and revenue in a fairly short span of time. For small firms that are owner-managed, it is not unusual for the owners to spend most of their time with the growing subsidiaries while the parent firms degenerate into nothing more than information-collecting agencies. Parent firms control neither marketing channels nor technologies. In many cases, Taiwan serves as a nursery from which small firms are transplanted and grown into big firms in foreign soil. Traditional theory asserts that the parent firm extracts rent from the subsidiary by exploiting its intangible asset. In Taiwan's case, the subsidiary may extract rent from the parent which gathers market and technology information available in Taiwan and enables the subsidiary to innovate and capitalize on market opportunities overseas.

The rest of the chapter is arranged as follows. In the next section, we review the role of small- and medium-sized firms in Taiwan's economy to provide a backdrop of their FDI. In Section 3.3, we describe the nature of the sample in our parent-firm survey. Major findings manifesting the 'localization' phenomena are presented in Section 3.4. The issue of technology transfer is discussed in Section 3.5. Final remarks are made in Section 3.6.

3.2 Small- and Medium-Sized Enterprises in Taiwan

The Taiwan economy has been dominated by small- and medium-sized enterprises (SMEs). According to the 1991 Census of Industry and Commerce, small business establishments with employment less than 30 persons accounted for 96.4 percent of all non-agriculture establishments in 1991. These groups of extremely small establishments produced 25.5 percent of total non-agriculture output and provided 46.2 percent of total non-agriculture jobs.

Table 3.1 The Contribution of SMEs to Sales, Employment and Exports in Taiwan's Manufacturing Sector (%)

Year	Sales	Employment	Export
1966	-	42.7	-
1971	26.7	35.6	-
1976	47.1	59.6	56.8
1981	44.8	62.0	74.8
1986	47.3	64.0	66.4
1991	40.0	79.6	56.9
1995	36.1	83.5	50.7

Note: The share of export includes the contributions of manufacturing and trading firms.

Source: *Chung Hsiao Chih Yeh Pai Shu (White Paper on Small and Medium Enterprises)*, various issues, Small and Medium Enterprises Administration, ROC.

If we take the official definition of SMEs in Taiwan, namely enterprises employing fewer than 200 workers, then SMEs accounted for 40.0 percent of manufactured output and provided 79.6 percent of manufacturing jobs in 1991. The figures point to the significant role played by SMEs in Taiwan's economy.

SMEs have been the central force of Taiwan's export drive. Indeed, some scholars (for example, Chou 1988) characterized the Taiwan economy as dichotomized into SMEs-led export sector and large enterprises-dominated domestic sector. Table 3.1 lists the share of SMEs in Taiwan's manufacturing sector in terms of sales, employment, and export for various years. It can be seen that SMEs had a disproportionately larger share in exports than in sales. For instance, in 1991, SMEs accounted for 56.9 percent of manufactured exports while only contributing 40 percent to manufactured output. This suggests that SMEs were more export-oriented than large firms. On the other hand, SMEs also contributed disproportionately more to employment than their share in output. This suggests that SMEs were more labor-intensive in terms of production method than large enterprises. Moreover, the disparity in labor intensity seems to have increased in recent years as SMEs' share in manufacturing employment increased whereas their share in manufactured output decreased.

All manufacturing firms increased their capital intensity since the mid-1980s as a response to rising wages in Taiwan, but SMEs did not adjust as much as their larger counterparts. Their ability to undergo internal restructuring was limited by their managerial and technological capacities. They were inclined to relocate abroad when internal restructuring was difficult. In fact, SMEs were under more pressure than large firms to relocate because their limited scope of business lines did not allow for a switch of products from less advantageous to more advantageous ones under the concurrent macroeconomic conditions. Their ability to upgrade product quality was limited by lack of technological sophistication and their ability to diversify into new business frontiers was limited by shortages of managerial resources. In fact, Taiwanese FDI was spearheaded by SMEs rather than large enterprises. It was only after SMEs had tested the foreign waters and established a foothold overseas that large enterprises followed with larger investment projects. SMEs' strong inclination to make investment abroad was eventually constrained by their technological and organizational weakness, however. Their investments mainly concentrated in Southeast Asia and China which were close to Taiwan geographically and psychologically.

Taiwanese SMEs worked closely with international production and marketing networks. Through this network linkage, they exported to advanced markets, such as the US, Japan, and Europe. They often served as subcontractors under an original equipment manufacturer (OEM) contract to manufacture goods for Western multinational firms. This close relationship with Western multinationals, which were richly endowed with internationalization resources, facilitates but also confines the FDI activities of Taiwanese SMEs. To continue serving a major international client, which sometimes controlled the lifeline of Taiwanese subcontractors, a prior consent from the client had to be obtained before overseas investment was implemented. The client sometimes even urged or coerced the Taiwanese subcontractors to make direct investment in locations of its choice.

When Taiwanese SMEs made FDI under the purview of international production networks, their FDI was often accompanied by a relocation of this network relationship. For example, when a footwear firm serving as a subcontractor for a brand-name merchandiser, such as Nike, made FDI it usually brought with it the trading company which used to represent the merchandiser in Taiwan as an inspector. Trading company was a crucial node in the international subcontracting system, linking subcontractors to merchandisers (Hsing 1997). The 'wholesale' relocation of the working group was to ensure smooth operations of the new system in order to guarantee the quality and punctual delivery of the product. This working relationship was established over long years of interactions and mutual adaptations which resulted in a bond of trust. The trust had to be relocated together with the production activities.

3.3 Nature of the Sample

In this chapter, we report on a survey of Taiwanese parent firms who own a subsidiary in Thailand, Malaysia, Indonesia, the Philippines, or Vietnam. For those who own multiple subsidiaries, we asked them to answer the question based on the largest subsidiary if different subsidiaries yielded conflicting replies. We sampled all FDI projects approved by the Taiwanese government in 1986–92. According to the Foreign Investment Commission of Taiwan, which processes the FDI approval, a total of 390 projects destined for the above five Southeast Asian countries were approved in 1986–92. We contacted all investing firms and obtained 113 respondents. In other words, the valid samples cover 29 percent of the population surveyed.

Note that we do not include Singapore in our study because the characteristics of Singapore as a host country are distinctive from those of the rest of Southeast Asia. The wage rate in Singapore was higher than in Taiwan, making labor-seeking FDI from Taiwan out of the question. Instead, as a gateway to Southeast Asia and an operations hub for many multinational firms present in that region, Singapore attracted some Taiwanese investments in the service sector. FDI in the manufacturing sector was limited except for a few cases in which investors were seeking a strategic production position in the Southeast Asian market.

Table 3.2 lists the host countries in which the respondents locate their subsidiaries. It can be seen that 35 subsidiaries are located in Thailand, 39 in Malaysia, 22 in Indonesia, 9 in the Philippines, and 8 in Vietnam. Table 3.3 lists the industry distribution of the sample firms. It can be seen that the sample spreads over all industries, but the electrical and electronic products industry dominates the sample with 33 firms. This is followed by 13 firms in the textile industry, and 11 firms in the fabricated metal industry.

There are various ways to define small- and medium-sized firms: by employment, by capital, or by turnover. To facilitate international comparison, we choose a definition which is independent of price level and exchange rate, that is, by employment. We define small- and medium-sized firms as those firms whose employment is less than 300, and denote them 'small firms' in short. The rest are called large firms.

Table 3.2 Sample Firms by Host Country of FDI

Host country	Number of firms
Thailand	35
Malaysia	39
Indonesia	22
Philippines	9
Vietnam	8
Total	113

Table 3.3 Sample Firms by Industry

Industry	Number of firms	Small firms	Large firms
Food processing	5	0	5
Beverage	1	0	1
Textile	13	5	8
Clothing and accessories	2	0	2
Wood & bamboo products	4	3	1
Paper & paper products	4	2	2
Chemical materials	9	6	3
Chemical products	2	1	1
Rubber products	2	2	0
Plastic products	3	3	0
Nonmetallic minerals	2	1	1
Basic metal	2	1	1
Fabricated metal products	11	6	5
Machinery	3	3	0
Electrical and electronic products	33	16	17
Transport equipment	8	7	1
Miscellaneous manufacturing	9	6	3
Total	113	62	51

Using the employment criterion, the sample can be cut into two subgroups: 62 small firms and 51 large firms. The industry distributions of the two subgroups are slightly different. For example, all sampled firms in the food processing industry are large firms, and all sampled firms except one in the transport equipment industry are small firms. Within the major industries of FDI, such as electrical and electronic products, textiles, and fabricated metal products, samples are fairly evenly distributed between small- and large-firm subgroups, however. This suggests that the classification adopted here will probably not cause serious bias when it is used as the basis for comparison.

Since our samples were drawn from the government-approved FDI projects, small- and medium-sized firms may be under-represented. The problem of under-representation is apparent in the clothing and accessories industry, chemical products, and plastic products. In Taiwan these industries are dominated by SMEs who are also active in FDI, as shown by the host-country statistics. Our sample, however, only captures a small number of parent firms in these industries. This deficiency will be made up by our survey of the subsidiaries, which will be presented in Chapters 4 and 5. The survey of subsidiaries is based on membership of Taiwan's chambers of commerce, or its surrogate, Taiwan Investors' Association in the host countries. A sizable number of SMEs in the clothing, chemical, and plastics industries are covered by that survey.

The sample only covers private firms; state-owned enterprises are not included in the survey. FDI by state-owned enterprises may not be driven purely by market incentives. It is sometimes politically motivated. Lack of systematic data on state enterprises' FDI also precludes any attempt to incorporate state firms in the survey. Sketchy information indicates that FDI by state enterprises is limited because their productions are mostly oriented toward the domestic market. Lack of exposure to international markets also makes their involvement in FDI difficult as export is often considered as a precedent to FDI (Vernon 1966). Notable exceptions are state-owned China Petroleum Corporation and Taiwan Sugar Corporation which are actively engaged in overseas oil exploration and sugar production projects, respectively.

The other feature of the survey is that it only covers FDI in the manufacturing sector. FDI in agriculture and services is excluded. It is understood, however, that there is substantial Taiwanese investment in shrimp aquaculture in Thailand, forestry and banana plantations in Vietnam, and pineapple plantations in Indonesia. There is also widespread investment in real estate and financial services in Southeast Asia. Focus on manufacturing FDI sharpens the picture and simplifies the analysis. In fact, FDI projects covered in this survey are mostly manufacturing activities without intensive input of natural resources. We can identify only two projects in which local availability of natural resources is crucial to their operations. They are paper pulp and cement mills. Taiwan's relatively small firms do not command a demand for natural resources large enough to warrant the merit of internalizing the supply of raw materials. Buying from the market is more economical.

It is also worth noting that our sample consists of primarily indigenous Taiwanese firms. We can only identify one foreign-owned company in the sample. Multinational firms are unlikely to invest abroad from their Taiwanese base even when their counterpart indigenous firms do so vigorously under the same circumstances (Chen, Ku and Liu 1995). They may exit Taiwan and reestablish overseas, but the decision is likely to be made at the headquarters rather than the Taiwan subsidiary. In a few cases we observe that multinational firms made direct investment in a third country in a consortium with their Taiwanese joint-venture partners. This is to extend the business partnership established in Taiwan to new locations.

3.4 Motivations and Operational Characteristics

In addition to basic data on the parent firms, the survey inquires about the motivations for FDI, parent–subsidiary relations in various fields, and operational strategies concerning overseas production. Table 3.4 lists the 'pull' and 'push' forces named by the respondents as the motivational factors for FDI. It can be seen that low-cost labor in Southeast Asia is the predominant force driving Taiwan's FDI into the region. Out of 102 firms, 82 indicate that they invest in Southeast Asia in order to utilize low-cost labor in the host countries. The number surpasses all other motivational factors. The secondary motivational factor is market expansion. More than half of the respondents (61 out of 102) indicate that they invest in order to expand sales in local and third-party markets. Following these two major 'pulling' factors are two 'push' factors, namely to escape the high price of land and high currency value in Taiwan. Both 'push' factors and labor-seeking motives suggest that Taiwanese firms' investment in Southeast Asia is primarily a defensive reaction to wage hike, land-price increase, and currency appreciation in Taiwan. FDI is undertaken to defend their export markets in third-party countries. In fact, before an investor can 'expand sales' in the local market, it needs to protect current market position first. The potential to expand local sales, nevertheless, adds an extra incentive for the investor to choose that particular location. As we will see later, the local-market opportunity reduces the risk of labor-seeking FDI because this opportunity enables the investor to reduce dependency on the export market for the disposition of its products.

There are other relatively minor factors such as to avoid trade barriers and to secure the supply of raw materials. By trade barriers, we refer mainly to the difficulty of exporting from Taiwan as compared to Southeast Asian countries which are eligible for trade preferences such as GSP granted by the US and EC. Finally, there are only a few firms indicating that their FDI is part of a group action in which they follow the leaders in the group to venture abroad. This suggests that the Japanese type of collective FDI is uncommon among Taiwanese firms.

Table 3.4 also shows that there is little difference between large and small firms in terms of motivational factors for FDI. The ranking of motivational factors is identical except that, relatively speaking, small firms are more concerned about the land price than large firms, but less concerned about the currency value. This is probably because an increase in land price raises the amount of fixed capital requirement for a business operation in Taiwan which is tantamount to an entry barrier to small firms. Small firms are less sensitive to currency value because, as will be seen later, small firms sell a larger proportion of their products locally than large firms. Exporters are subject to more pressure from currency revaluation than local-oriented firms even if their products are incorporated into the final products of large firms destined for export. Note that the FDI motives reported here reveal the perspectives of parent firms who were in search of an overseas location to overcome the problems they faced in Taiwan.

Table 3.4 Motivational Factors for FDI

Motivational factors	Overall	Small firms	Large firms
To utilize low-cost labor in host countries	82	40	42
To expand sales in local and third-party markets	61	34	27
To escape high land price in Taiwan	45	27	18
To escape high currency value in Taiwan	41	19	22
To avoid trade barriers	23	12	11
To secure supply of raw materials	16	9	7
To follow FDI of other firms	8	7	1
Sample size	102	54	48

Source: This study.

Also noticeable is that seven small firms indicate that they invest by following in the footsteps of other firms while only one large firm indicates such an FDI pattern. It is self-evident that small firms are more likely to be subcontractors of other firms as compared to large firms. Subcontractors may follow their core firms in investing abroad as a package plan. The incidence, however, is not overwhelmingly commonplace. The majority of Taiwanese FDI is an independent action although investors may cluster in the same places due to agglomeration effect.

In the traditional FDI theory of Hymer and Caves, FDI is underlined by intangible asset of investing firms. Empirical research on Western multinationals often reveals technological superiority to be a manifestation of the intangible asset (Caves 1974; Horst 1972). Empirically, technological superiority is often measured by R&D expenditure as a percentage of sales. We list R&D intensity of Taiwanese investors in Table 3.5. It can be seen that Taiwanese parent firms, on average, spent 39.5 million NT (equivalent to approximately US$1.5 million in 1993) on R&D, or 2.2 percent of their sales. The ratio is substantially higher than the economy-wide private sector R&D ratio of 0.91 percent in 1992 (National Science Council, ROC 1994), suggesting that the average investors are technologically superior to their peers even though their FDI action is rather defensive.

There are, however, discernible differences in R&D intensity in terms of the host countries where they make investment. Those investing in Malaysia have the highest R&D ratio of 2.6 percent, followed by those investing in Thailand (2.2 percent) and Indonesia (2.1 percent), whereas R&D ratio for firms investing in Vietnam is only 0.7 percent. This suggests that firms choose their investment locations by matching their technological sophistication with local wages. Firms with relatively sophisticated technologies choose Malaysia in which supporting industries are also more sophisticated. Firms with relatively simple technologies choose Vietnam in which supporting industries are rudimentary. It also suggests that although Taiwanese firms invest in Southeast Asia mainly to take advantage of low-cost labor, lowest wages are not always most attractive. Although a substantial wage differential is needed to create benefits for division of labor, a large wage gap does not guarantee large benefits because it takes other supporting factors to facilitate the division of labor across national borders, such as supporting industries and skilled labor.

Also listed in Table 3.5 are royalties paid for foreign technologies by Taiwanese parent firms. The magnitude of the royalty payment indicates the degree to which the parent firms utilize modern foreign-sourced technologies. The pattern of royalty payments is similar to that of R&D expenditure; those investing in Malaysia pay the most and those investing in the Philippines and Vietnam pay none. This again suggests that the latter group employ standardized and probably indigenous technologies in home production. Nonetheless, they are still technologically more capable than their local counterparts in Southeast Asia to justify an FDI action. The superiority may arise from extensive production experience in Taiwan which enables them to master an old-fashioned technology to the extent that they may exploit it overseas. The last row of Table 3.5 lists the number of R&D personnel. The pattern is again similar to those of R&D expenditure and royalty payments. Those investing in Malaysia have the largest number of R&D personnel and those investing in the Philippines the smallest.

Table 3.5 R&D Expenditure and Personnel by Host Countries

	Overall	Thailand	Malaysia	Indonesia	Vietnam	Philippines
R&D expenditure (in million NT)	39.5	35.2	63.1	18.5	13.9	6.5
R&D as a percentage of sales	2.2	2.2	2.6	2.1	0.7	1.3
Royalty paid for foreign technology (in million NT)	6	6.3	9.8	1.3	0	0
R&D personnel (men)	27	32	36	14	9	9

Note: Survey is based on 1993 data.

Source: This study.

To understand the relationship between parent firms and their subsidiaries, we asked the parent firms to compare their products with those made by their subsidiaries. The results are tabulated in Table 3.6. It can be seen that out of 109 respondents, about half (51) of them indicate that products made in Taiwan and overseas are virtually identical. The other half indicate that products made overseas are either less sophisticated in technology requirement, lower in unit price, or more labor-intensive in the production process, or a combination of the above. There are only 17 cases in which products made overseas are vertically related to those in Taiwan, meaning that overseas products are intermediate goods used as inputs to Taiwanese production, or vice versa. This answer suggests that Taiwanese FDI in Southeast Asia is in pursuit of horizontal integration more often than vertical integration. In most cases, overseas products are identical to those produced in Taiwan or similar products differentiated by quality.

There is little discernible difference between large and small firms in terms of the strong inclination to pursue horizontal integration via FDI. Horizontal integration implies an extension or transplantation of domestic production to overseas locations, often serving the same national markets but different consumer groups. Horizontal integration allows the parent and subsidiary to complement each other with production capacities. With a broader range of product lines, the transnational firm improves its flexibility and widens the customer base. As we will see later, when the subsidiary establishes its independent marketing arm, it may swap orders with the parent to exploit scale economies.

Horizontal integration requires little adjustment in production technology. In fact, out of 109 respondents, 84 of them indicate that they employ identical technologies in home and overseas productions (not shown in the table). Vertical integration, on the other hand, usually requires a rearrangement of production processes both at home and overseas and a coordinating mechanism to integrate the bifurcated production processes into an efficient system to take advantage of division of labor. The cost of managing a vertically integrated cross-border operation is thus higher than that for a horizontally integrated operation.

Table 3.6 Comparison of Products Made by Parents and Subsidiaries (by number of firms)

Description	Overall	Small firms	Large firms
Virtually identical	51	29	22
Lower technology used in subsidiary production	45	21	24
Lower price for subsidiary products	47	26	21
Higher labor intensity used in subsidiary production	48	24	24
Vertically related	17	10	7
Others	11	5	6
Sample size	109	58	51

Source: This study.

To exercise control over the subsidiaries and to facilitate technology transfer, parent firms often send expatriate managers and technicians to the subsidiaries. The allocation of such expatriates reveals the management style of transnational operations. Table 3.7 tabulates the presence of Taiwanese expatriates in terms of their job responsibilities. It can be seen that out of 98 respondents, 75 of them send an expatriate to take the position of chief executive (president) or number two position (vice president) of the subsidiary. This is an apparent attempt to exercise control over the overall operations of the subsidiaries. Those which do not do so are usually minority equity holders. Nonetheless, the area in which Taiwanese expatriates are most prevalent is in the production departments where 78 firms send at least one technician to stations in the subsidiaries. This implies that production is the principal area of concern to Taiwanese investors in their overseas ventures. Most Taiwanese firms manufacture OEM products to serve Western markets. Ensuring smooth production overseas to earn the trust of their patrons is critical in maintaining the OEM business. When Taiwanese firms first locate abroad, they usually send a large number of production engineers and technicians to help transfer the technology needed to make the product quality up to the buyer's standard, often at a cost which is not sustainable on a long-term basis. But adjustment will not be made until the production line has been stabilized. As a result, the initial production method adopted by overseas subsidiaries is usually a copy of the parent firm with little regard to local conditions. Few managers are willing to take the risks of adjusting production methods, say to increase labor intensity, without first completing a successful transplantation of the production system from home.

Table 3.7 Presence of Expatriates in Different Departments of Operation (by number of firms)

Department	Overall	Small firms	Large firms
Chief executive or number two officer	75	37	38
Production	78	38	40
Finance	36	16	20
Marketing	36	14	22
R&D	23	11	12
Personnel	13	7	6
Others	11	6	5
Sample size	98	52	46

Source: This study.

In addition to production, expatriates are also quite visible in the areas of finance and marketing. More than one-third of the surveyed parent firms indicate the deployment of finance and marketing experts to the subsidiaries. There are also expatriates sent to the departments of R&D and personnel, but the number is relatively small.

The pattern of expatriate deployment is quite similar for small and large firms, indicating that their strategies in terms of controlling and managing overseas subsidiaries are similar. The only discernible difference is in the area of marketing in which small firms send a smaller number (in absolute and in relative terms) of expatriates than large firms. This is because the marketing function of the small firms is often assumed by the owners themselves and there is no need for additional expatriates to take charge of marketing responsibility in the subsidiaries.

The prevalence of expatriates in the production department also indicates that the 'intangible asset' of the Taiwanese firms lies with the production technology rather than brand name, management know-how or marketing expertise. This intangible asset is valuable when it is supported by a network of suppliers, subcontractors, traders, and so on. There is no market for such an intangible asset because network linkage is not marketable.

3.5 Localization of Taiwanese Firms

In this section, we compare our survey results with those from a survey conducted by the Council for Economic Planning and Development (CEPD) of the Taiwan government in 1991 (CEPD 1992). We found substantial variation in the pattern of Taiwanese companies' market orientation and sales strategy. Both surveys cover Taiwanese parent firms investing in Southeast Asia. They encompass a similar number of firms whose industry distributions are also comparable.[1] A simple comparison reveals a clear-cut change in three years' time. From Table 3.8, we can see that among the product markets of Taiwanese subsidiaries, the proportion of local sales increases substantially, from 33.0 percent in CEPD's survey of 1991 to 42.2 percent in our survey of 1994. This is accomplished mainly at the expense of exports to countries other than Taiwan (indicated as third-party country market in the table) whose share decreases from 52.7 percent in 1991 to 45.1 percent in 1994. Exports back to Taiwan also decrease, but to a lesser extent. Among subsidiaries' exports to Taiwan, intra-firm sales, which account for 13.1 percent of total sales in 1991, drop to 9.8 percent in 1994. Although overall exports still exceed local sales in 1994, the margin has shrunk to such a low level that it can easily be reversed in a few years.

If we compare small firms (defined as parent firms which employ fewer than 300 persons) with large firms (which employ 300 persons or more), we find that local market sales account for a larger proportion of sales among small firms. This seems to indicate that small firms are more eager than large firms to explore local markets, which suggests that small firms may be less capable of maintaining their competitiveness by cross-country operations. Therefore, tapping the local market is a survival strategy for small firms. Many host countries prefer export-oriented FDI over local-market-oriented FDI. Some host-country governments even impose an export performance requirement on foreign firms.[2] The backdrop of this policy preference is usually the existence of trade protection afforded to indigenous industries. Foreign firms, once they commence operations, soon realize that profit margins in the local market are higher than those in the export market, although risks in local sales are often also higher than in export sales due to possible buyer default and exchange rate fluctuation. If they can find suitable marketing channels, they are bound to exploit the local market, barring prohibitive government regulations. Of course, proximity to the local market gives them an advantage over competing imports.

Table 3.8 Product Markets for Taiwanese Subsidiaries in Southeast Asia (%)

Product destination	1994			1991
	Overall	Small firms	Large firms	
Sold in local market	42.2	44.2	39.9	33.0
Sold to the parent	9.8	10.8	8.7	13.1
Sold to other firms in Taiwan	2.8	3.5	2.1	1.2
Sold to third-party country market	45.1	41.6	49.2	52.7
Total	100.0	100.0	100.0	100.0
Sample size (number of firms)	96	52	44	100

Sources: 1994 data are from this study, 1991 data from CEPD (1992).

The reason underlying Taiwanese firms' eagerness to penetrate the local market is the precarious nature of their proprietary asset. A survey of Taiwanese firms in the electronics industry conducted in 1990 (Chen and Wang 1995) indicates that Taiwanese firms consider the primary advantage that enables them to invest abroad to be a guaranteed market for the products they intend to produce abroad (see Table 3.9). This refers to the lasting customer relationships which Taiwanese firms have built through their previous export experience which earned them a reputation as trustworthy manufacturers. In fact, the 'goodwill' advantage extends to other industries as well. Our interviews with Taiwanese shoe manufacturers indicate that their relocations to Southeast Asia are either initiated or supported by their major international buyers.[3] Patronage from buyers reduces the risk of FDI. In Chen and Wang's (1995) survey, the secondary advantage pinpointed by Taiwanese firms is their technological superiority over local firms. This superiority refers to their ability to manufacture products that meet quality requirements within a compressed time frame and at competitive costs. Brand names, R&D capability, and managerial know-how are not important proprietary assets for Taiwanese firms.

Table 3.9 Advantages Considered by FDI Firms

Advantage	Number of firms that identify with the advantage
Guaranteed market for the intended products	24
Technological superiority	22
Flexibility in production lines	12
Financial resources	8
Management know-how	8
R&D capability	8
Personal relations with the local government	5
Sample size	33

Note: Choice of advantages is multiple.

Source: Chen and Wang (1995), p. 221.

In other words, the type of oligopolistic firms that produce highly differentiated products envisaged by Hymer (1960) and Caves (1971) are conspicuously missing among Taiwanese investors. Instead, their main proprietary assets are their customer relationships, and the value of these assets is depreciating in Taiwan due to rising labor costs. It is their technological superiority that supports these relationships and enables Taiwanese firms to relocate overseas. The technology margin, however, is so thin that it easily evaporates through spillovers and as a consequence Taiwanese firms find the competitive pressure rising rapidly over time. The local market, therefore, is a natural alternative to help diversify market risk. Since the products are originally designed for consumers in industrialized countries, local sales usually entail some product modifications to meet demand specific to the local level of industrialization or the local taste. Localization seems to be more successful in countries where income is higher and the domestic market is larger. The higher the income, the less disparity between local taste and that in advanced countries. Hence higher-income countries requires less production modification. Meanwhile, larger market size provides scale economies for such a modification.

Theoretically, switching from the export to the local market is more likely for products designed for general usage rather than for a specific purpose. However, multinational firms which engage in the production of general-purpose products are often under export performance requirements which restrict their freedom of marketing. Taiwan's small affiliates usually produce niche products with a limited scope of market applications. But we still find a strong desire among these firms to embark on local sales. They often introduce a new product line, differentiated from the ones designed for the export market, to serve the local market. Although different in product characteristics, the technological superiority of Taiwanese transnationals often provides them with a competitive edge over their local peers. Moreover, the experience of local production allows transnational firms to accumulate local knowledge and establish local relationships which may create a new advantage for the company (Johanson and Vahle 1990). Sometimes, a product that they have never produced at home is introduced to the local market because they have the relevant technologies to manufacture it and the relevant knowledge about market demand.[4] As we will see later, this happens because the Taiwanese subsidiary maintains a capacity for product innovation independent of the parent firms.

It is important to note that, because of the lack of a proprietary asset that allows them to sufficiently differentiate their products from those of their peers, Taiwanese firms would have been unable to penetrate the host-country market through exports or licensing had they not made direct investment. Therefore, FDI is a vehicle that actually facilitates trade between Taiwan and the host countries although FDI is initially aimed at protecting export position in the third-party markets. Unlike the local-market-oriented FDI made by large multinationals in response to trade barriers, Taiwanese firms first invest to take advantage of low-cost labor, and then turn to the local market because complementarity between low-cost labor and technological superiority gives them a competitive edge in the local market. Trade barriers reinforce their incentive to exploit local markets, but trade barriers are not necessary conditions, neither for initial FDI, nor for their later drives to localization. In fact, in the highly protected industries in Southeast Asia, such as automobiles and consumer electronics, Taiwanese FDI is virtually nonexistent. Taiwanese firms usually invest in industries in which Southeast Asian countries are just beginning to develop a comparative advantage, and trade barriers are typically low in these industries. Only in the case of Vietnam, to which Western multinationals are still hesitant to enter due to international political uncertainty, several Taiwanese investment projects are aimed at protected local markets such as motorbikes and monosodium glutamate.

Reflecting the change revealed by the two surveys in Taiwanese firms' market orientation is the change in marketing strategy. We can see from the two sets of results compared in Table 3.10 that there is a dramatic shift of marketing responsibility from parent firms to subsidiaries. In the CEPD survey of 1991, parent firms assumed 49.2 percent of the marketing functions for their subsidiaries; this percentage was cut to only 36.9 percent by our survey of 1994. In contrast, subsidiaries had assumed over half of the marketing functions (54.7 percent) in the 1994 survey. There is no doubt that part of this increased responsibility is devoted to promoting local sales, but the marketing responsibility for exports also shifts over time.

Table 3.10 Marketing Channels of Taiwanese Subsidiaries in Southeast Asia (%)

Marketing channels	1994	1991
By subsidiaries themselves	54.7	43.6
Through local trading firms	3.0	3.8
Through foreign trading firms	6.4	3.4
Through parent firms	36.9	49.2
Total	100.0	100.0
Sample size (number of firms)	97	100

Source: Same as Table 3.8.

In general, Taiwanese subsidiaries allow their parent companies to dictate the marketing strategy at the beginning of overseas operations. The share as well as the destination of the export market to be served by the subsidiaries is decided by the parent firms. The sole responsibility of the subsidiary is to make sure the quality of the products meets the buyers' standard. Because of the predominant concern over quality, as discussed in the previous section, Taiwanese firms often transfer their production technology to overseas production intact, although a lower wage rate in the host country calls for a more labor-intensive production method. There are even cases in which machinery is used to substitute for labor, to avoid human mistakes. Most Taiwanese firms also bring machinery and equipment from Taiwan to eliminate risks arising from unfamiliarity of new machinery and equipment. After the quality target is achieved, the subsidiaries start to work on cost reduction. Market expansion and reorientation is the third phase of adjustment, occurring only after production efficiency has reached a satisfactory level.

In the early stages, many subsidiaries work for their parents as sub-contractors on a consignment basis and concentrate their effort on improving production efficiency. Under the subcontracting arrangement, almost all materials are shipped from the parents and all final products are destined for the export market designated by the parents. All efforts in the subsidiaries are devoted to making products 'right'. Subsidiaries embark on the course of marketing only if there are local sales to be handled. When local sales expand, their marketing responsibility also increases. Finally, subsidiaries will also begin to engage in export marketing when they develop their own market contacts independent of the parents or when the parents transfer part of the international market to be under their control. In Southeast Asia, new market development usually means forays into the regional markets.

Since subsidiaries normally produce the same products as their parents, market segmentation is based on quality of the products. That is, higher-quality and higher-priced products are manufactured in Taiwan, and lower-quality and lower-priced products in Southeast Asia. But division of labor is meaningful only if the quality gap is large enough to warrant the benefits of using different technology in production. For small firms that do not possess a technology spectrum large enough to meaningfully separate domestic and overseas production by quality, exploring local and regional markets using similar technology is an alternative option. Expansion of market reach enables the subsidiaries and parents to conduct parallel production of products differentiated only by local niches.[5] Only in the case of fairly large firms do we see market segmentation based on quality differentiation.

In addition to marketing, sourcing strategy also shifts over time. It can be observed from Table 3.11 that sourcing of raw materials, components and parts changed swiftly between 1991 and 1994. Local sourcing, in particular, increased from 22.4 percent to 34.3 percent in this period. Localization in this regard is attained mainly at the expense of sourcing through parent firms. This means that the number of semi-finished products that the parent firms used to send to the subsidiaries for further processing is now reduced in favor of locally made intermediate goods. It also means that some procurement that used to be arranged by the parent firms for their subsidiaries is now taken over by the subsidiaries themselves. This implies that the scale economies and informational advantage enjoyed by the parent firms in procurement shrink rapidly over time.

Comparison between large and small firms indicates that subsidiaries of small firms rely more on parent firms for procurement (28 percent) than those of large firms (22 percent), whereas the latter opt to buy more directly from other suppliers in Taiwan. When the two sources of supply are put together, small and large firms procure roughly an identical proportion of materials from Taiwan at 41–42 percent, down by 10 percentage points from the 1991 CEPD survey. Small firms' dependence on parent firms for sourcing is primarily a consideration for scale economies in procurement and access to market information. Even if the parent firms cease production in Taiwan altogether, they may still serve as procurement agents for their overseas subsidiaries. On the other hand, Table 3.11 also shows that subsidiaries of small firms buy more from third-party markets and less from local markets, as compared to those of large firms. This suggests that large enterprises are more capable of cultivating local suppliers than SMEs. They may bring subcontractors from Taiwan to join them in overseas production or solicit indigenous suppliers to become their subcontractors. On the other hand, SMEs are active in seeking international suppliers to supplant their needs in overseas production. This effort may be thwarted by their small size in overseas production, however, as will be seen in Chapter 4.

Table 3.11 Sources of Raw Materials, Components and Parts for Taiwanese Subsidiaries in Southeast Asia (%)

Product destination	1994			1991
	Overall	Small firms	Large firms	
Parent firms	25.8	28.4	22.3	37.9
Other firms in Taiwan	15.7	12.1	20.5	13.1
Local suppliers	34.3	32.4	36.8	22.4
Third-party country suppliers	24.2	27.1	20.4	26.6
Total	100.0	100.0	100.0	100.0
Sample size (number of firms)	96	55	41	89

Source: Same as Table 3.8.

Note that the procurement by parent firms is a manifestation of network advantage. Even if these components and parts are not produced in Taiwan, procuring them by the parent firms from advanced countries, say Japan, and then furnishing them to local subsidiaries in Southeast Asia may be cost-effective because parent firms can pool a large amount of orders to bargain for lower prices. Sometimes procurement by parent firms is more advantageous simply because parent companies are in a superior position to provide logistic support. One should not overlook the importance of logistic support provided by the parent companies from Taiwan. As an offshore assembly center for light manufacturers for many years, Taiwan has developed a closely knit network of supporting industries for export manufacturing. The network is so comprehensive and far-reaching that virtually all components and parts needed for assembly can be procured in Taiwan although many of them may be imported. This network lowers the transaction costs of material preparation and hastens the pace of production. In fact, Taiwanese small investors take full advantage of this network support to beat off local competition in terms of delivery time.

Parent firms may also perform a small function of adding value to the components and parts that they procure before sending them to the subsidiaries. The reason for performing simple assembly or adaptation work on components and parts is to ensure compatibility of goods produced at different sites, which is the essence of horizontal integration.

Synchronizing with the localization process is the shift in decision-making authority from the parent company to the subsidiary. Table 3.12 lists the distributions of decision-making responsibility in different fields. As of the time of our survey, parent firms dominated decision making in the fields of finance, marketing, and R&D. In these three fields, decisions are primarily made outright by the parent companies. In the areas of finance and R&D, the second most important mode of decision making is to have expatriate managers make decisions with regular influence from the parent company, whereas independent decisions, made either by expatriates or local managers in the subsidiaries, account for less than 30 percent of policy formation. In the field of marketing, although parent firms still dominate the decision making by outright orders and through their expatriate managers, a substantial proportion (41.3 percent) of decisions are made independently within the subsidiaries. In contrast, in the field of production and personnel matters (hiring, firing, and job assignment), decisions are largely made locally without the influence of the parent companies.

Parent companies' steadfast control over financial decisions is understandable because this is essential to rent appropriation. Their dominance in decisions relating to R&D and marketing functions is a manifestation of their technological superiority and their control over customer relationships. Both are extremely important because they are the predominant 'intangible assets' underlying Taiwanese FDI.

It is noteworthy, however, that parent companies' influence in decision making in all fields declines rapidly over time. As the survey results indicate, five years from the time of survey, parent firms are expected to have substantially cut the proportion of decisions made outright by headquarters in all fields. In lieu of decisions by the parent firms, more decisions are to be made by expatriate and local managers. The most noticeable change in the decision-making mode can be expected in the field of marketing, where independent decisions made by expatriate and local managers will dominate. Along with the major shift in decision-making mode in the field of marketing, substantial deepening of localization will also be observed in the area of production-related decisions. Independent decisions made within the subsidiaries, which accounted for 60.2 percent of production-related choices at the time of survey, will increase to 76.8 percent five years later. Intensified localization of production-related decisions means an increased degree of freedom for the subsidiaries to choose product lines, production technology, and sources of input. In fact, localization of marketing and production

Table 3.12 Decision Makers in Different Fields (%)

Decision maker	Field of decision									
	Finance		Marketing		Production		Personnel		R&D	
	Now	Five years later	Now	Five years later	Now	Five years later	Now	Five years later	Now	Five years later
The parent company makes the decision	48.1	36.0	38.5	21.9	10.7	2.1	7.7	3.1	51.0	30.5
Expatriate managers make the decision with regular influence from the parent company	26.4	32.0	20.2	25.0	29.1	21.1	29.8	21.6	18.6	28.4
Expatriates managers make independent decisions	8.5	18.0	22.1	30.2	39.8	38.9	35.6	42.3	14.7	24.2
Local managers make independent decisions	17.0	14.0	19.2	22.9	20.4	37.9	26.9	33.0	15.7	16.8
Sample size (number of firms)	106	100	104	96	103	95	104	97	102	95

Source: This study.

decisions are key to Taiwanese subsidiaries' success in their effort to integrate with the local economies. In both areas, availability of local manpower to assume new responsibilities and to facilitate the transition will determine the speed and success of localization. Those who fail to localize speedily enough face the real risk of extinction.

3.6 Technology Transfer

An important step in the process of localization is technology transfer. Generally speaking, technology will be transferred by parent firms whenever technological support across the border entails a transaction cost which is high enough to make the subsidiaries uncompetitive *vis-à-vis* their local peers. Technology transfer entails a resources cost among other things (Teece 1977), the magnitude of which depends on the absorption capacity of the host country. If the resources costs are so high as to make transfer of a needed technology uneconomical, the multinational firms will not survive.

Table 3.13 lists the survey results with regard to Taiwanese subsidiaries' technology transfers in various fields. As can be seen from the table, the extent of technology transfer varies according to functions of the technology. The highest degree of transfer takes place in the area of operation technology. Other technologies, ranked by the extent that they are transferred to the subsidiaries are, in order, quality control, maintenance, process technology, technological improvement, adoption of new technologies, product design, design of molds and tools, product innovation, and finally, design of machinery and equipment. The pattern reveals that the closer the functions are to production, the more likely it is that technology related to those functions will be transferred. Therefore, operations-related technology is to be transferred first in offshore operations, followed closely by technologies pertinent to quality control, maintenance of machinery and equipment, and process control. In these four areas, according to our survey, more than 70 percent of the related technology has been transferred to the subsidiaries. After these four categories is that of technological improvement of existing production methods. This refers to adoption, modification, and upgrading of production technology transferred from the parent company.

It is well documented in the literature that most parent firms transfer their production technology overseas virtually intact (Yeoman 1968; Lecraw 1979). But, as time goes by, subsidiaries will start to modify this technology to suit the local conditions (Morley and Smith 1974; Chen 1992b). Table 3.13 indicates that, within the Taiwanese overseas subsidiaries, over half of the technological improvement work is undertaken by local engineers and technicians. Meanwhile, adoption of new technologies, product design and innovations are mainly the responsibility of the parent firms; only a fraction of technology related to these functions has been transferred to the subsidiaries. In the last two technology categories, namely design of molds and tools, and design of machinery and equipment, technology transfer is even more sketchy. Note that in the areas in which technology transfer is less than half completed, cross-border technological assistance is relatively inexpensive compared to production-related technology support.

Table 3.13 Degree of Technology Transfer by Taiwanese and Japanese Subsidiaries (%)

Technology category	Taiwanese subsidiaries		Japanese subsidiaries
	Small firms	Large firms	
Operation technology	77.6	83.3	76.0
Quality control	75.6	82.5	66.1
Maintenance of machinery and equipment	72.0	81.3	71.0
Process control	72.1	80.4	69.5
Technological improvement	54.3	61.0	41.3
Adoption of new technologies	38.0	42.3	28.3
Product design	35.2	36.3	30.3
Product innovation	31.9	30.6	24.2
Design of molds and tools	32.7	31.1	39.9
Design of machinery and equipment	31.5	28.0	33.0

Sources: Data on Taiwanese subsidiaries are from this study; data on Japanese subsidiaries are from Urata (1993) which quoted the results of a survey conducted by Nikkei Research Institute of Industry and Market in 1992. The Japanese sample covers 133 subsidiaries in Southeast Asia, including ASEAN and newly industrializing countries. Listed in the table are the results of the ASEAN sub-sample whose size is not clear. Degree of technology transfer is generally higher in the newly industrializing countries of Taiwan, Korea, Hong Kong and Singapore.

If we compare small firms with large firms, we find that the latter group is consistently more advanced in making technology transfers in all areas except product innovation and design of production facilities (including molds, tools, machinery and equipment). The large firms do more innovation and design of facilities at home presumably because of the scale economies they enjoy at the parent company. Small firms also possess the same scale advantage at home, but to a lesser extent, because there is a higher probability among small firms that their overseas production surpasses domestic production.

Outside the areas of product innovation and facility design, why have large firms progressed further than small firms in transferring technology? It is not because large firms face greater pressure to localize. In fact, the opposite is true. Our contention is that large firms are more successful than small firms in accomplishing technology transfer because the division of labor is more refined within large firms. Job specification in large firms is more clearly and narrowly defined, making labor training easier. Product lines in large firms are also more stable. Repetitive production of the same products is conducive to learning-by-doing. Training and learning make technology transfer successful. In contrast, small firms require all-round skills in production, job assignment is less clear-cut, and product lines are frequently subject to change. All these characteristics make technology transfer more difficult. Teece's (1977) study of technology transfer also found that transfer costs decline with the size of transferee. He argues that transfer costs are higher for smaller transferees because they lack technical and managerial resources that can be called upon for assistance during the transfer process without interfering with normal production.

It is also interesting to compare our survey results with a similar survey of Japanese subsidiaries in ASEAN countries conducted in 1992 (Urata 1993). It can be seen from Table 3.13 that the degree of technology transfer to Japanese subsidiaries is generally lower than that to Taiwanese subsidiaries, but the pattern is similar. It seems to be a common practice for multinational firms in Southeast Asia to transfer production-related technologies first and most thoroughly, and to hold back on transferring innovation and design-related technologies. One explanation for Japanese firms' relatively slow progress in technology transfer is that Japanese firms possess more proprietary assets than Taiwanese firms. This advantage allows them to indulge in cross-border technological support which runs a lower risk of technology leakage. It is also possible that the costs of technology transfer are lower for Taiwanese firms than for Japanese firms. As Arrow (1969) argues, cost of communication is a fundamental factor influencing the worldwide diffusion of technology. Taiwanese firms are able to reduce this information cost using ethnically Chinese technicians and staff members as an intermediary for technology transfer. There are exceptions, however, especially in the areas of designing molds, tools, machinery and equipment, where Japanese subsidiaries have transferred more technology than Taiwanese subsidiaries. These exceptions may be related to the nature of proprietary Japanese products, which require a closer fit of facility design to local production to guard against product failure. As argued by Lecraw (1979), product failure is a predominant concern of subsidiary managers, especially those producing brand-name products.

To facilitate technology transfer, Taiwanese investors usually send workers from the subsidiaries to the headquarters for training. People selected as trainees are regular workers whose capability and working attitude are considered to merit advanced training by the parent companies. After training in Taiwan, these trainees are normally promoted to become low-echelon leaders at the subsidiary, such as foremen on the factory floor or section chiefs in the office. If their performance is further accredited, they may be sent to Taiwan for more training in preparation for further promotion. Through this process technology is gradually transferred to the subsidiaries.

Table 3.14 lists the fields in which training is conducted by Taiwanese firms. It can be seen that most training occurs in the areas of operation technology, quality control, maintenance of machinery and equipment, and process control. Training in non-production areas, such as marketing and finance, is sporadic. Note that there is little difference between small and large firms in terms of the fields in which training is offered. Substantial diversity is observable, however, in terms of training intensity. Our survey results as shown in Table 3.15 indicate that while that two groups of firms send a roughly equal proportion (about 10 percent) of white-collar workers for training in Taiwan, small firms train a substantially larger proportion (about 10 percent) of blue-collar workers than large firms (about 6 percent). This reflects the scale economies enjoyed by large firms in training blue-collar workers as their average employment of blue-collar workers is about three times that of small firms.

Table 3.14 Training Provided by Parent Companies (by number of firms)

Field of training	Number of firms providing training	
	Small firms	Large firms
Operation technology	27	27
Quality control	27	30
Maintenance of machinery and equipment	22	26
Process control	24	25
Marketing	7	10
Financial management	7	10
Sample size	37	36

Source: This study.

Table 3.15 Training Intensity

Training intensity	White-collar workers Small firms	White-collar workers Large firms	Blue-collar workers Small firms	Blue-collar workers Large firms
Average number of workers trained (persons)	3	25	10	43
Average training hours per worker (hours)	56	41	102	65
Average employment (persons)	30	249	126	753

Source: This study.

The most intriguing aspect of training intensity is the average number of hours spent by each trainee at the parent firms. For white-collar workers, trainees from small firms go through 56 hours of training while those from large firms only undergo 41 hours. For blue-collar workers, the difference is even more dramatic: 102 hours for workers from small firms versus 65 hours for those from large firms. In other words, small-firm trainees, especially for production workers, go through more intensive training. More training is needed for them because small firms' workers must acquire skills in a wide spectrum of operations. Division of labor within small firms is limited due to the small number of workers. Therefore, small firms' workers, especially those assuming leadership roles, have to perform multiple functions and longer training is hence necessary. More intensive worker training notwithstanding, small firms still fall behind large firms in technology transfer as previously revealed in the statistics.

3.7 Conclusion

Speedy localization is a common feature observed among Taiwan's small- and medium-sized multinationals. Limited managerial resources make cross-border operation very costly for them, forcing Taiwanese subsidiaries to quickly become independent of their parent firms in terms of sourcing and marketing. Their competitive edge over local firms is based on technological superiority and market access, but this edge is so thin that it quickly evaporates over time, forcing them to localize. Firms that are more adaptive to the local environment have a better chance of succeeding in overseas operations.

The localization drive is reflected in the growing importance of local sales, local procurement, and speedy transfer of technology. Market potential and resource availability in the host country support the transformation and growth of Taiwanese subsidiaries. It is not uncommon for Taiwanese subsidiaries to grow to exceed the size of their parent firms in a short period of time. The center of the transnational firm's operations may thereafter shift to the subsidiary, leaving the corporate parent in Taiwan as little more than an information-collecting agency or a marketing arm for the subsidiary.

Notes

1. The Council for Economic Planning and Development (CEPD) survey covers 107 firms investing in Southeast Asia, including two firms investing in Singapore which is absent from our survey. The CEPD sample is also drawn from the FDI projects approved by the Taiwan government and dominated by 58 firms in the electronic and electrical products industry.
2. Sometimes foreign firms are committed to export a certain proportion of their products in order to qualify for fiscal incentives such as tax holidays or exemption from import duties on imported materials and capital goods.
3. In some cases, the international brand-name distributors, such as Nike, initiated a relocation of the whole production network encompassing OEM manufacturers, inspectors, and local procurement agents from Taiwan to Southeast Asia. This ensures a smooth transplantation of the whole system which has been working well in Taiwan.
4. Johanson and Vahlne (1990) called the creation and shifting of advantage in the internationalization process the 'advantage cycle'.
5. Differentiation by quality is sometimes referred to as vertical differentiation and differentiation by varieties as horizontal differentiation.

4. Economic Effects of Taiwanese FDI on Host Countries

Ying-Hua Ku

4.1 Introduction

In this chapter, we will discuss the economic effects of Taiwanese FDI on host countries, emphasizing the differences attributable to the size of the affiliates. We will address four areas of economic effects: employment, trade, linkage effect, and technology transfer.

It is generally believed that small- and medium-sized transnationals are more labor-intensive in production techniques than their larger counterparts; therefore their investment is more conducive to job creation. Small- and medium-sized transnationals, by definition, also commit a smaller amount of capital, however. In the end, whether small or large transnationals are more effective in generating local employment is unclear. The composition of jobs created must also be considered in the discussion of employment effects, because providing job opportunities for skilled labor may be very different from providing job opportunities for unskilled labor. In most developing countries, skilled labor is in short supply while there is a surplus of unskilled labor. Therefore, FDI that requires more unskilled labor tends to bring more employment benefits to the host country. FDI that intensively utilizes skilled labor will only bid up wage rates for the group, which is usually already fully employed, and may even worsen income distribution in the host economy. However, if the increased demand for skilled labor accelerates investment in human capital, it will bring long-term benefits. Therefore, it is also important to examine whether FDI contributes to human resources development.

There has been a long debate as to whether FDI is a substitute for or a complement to trade (Mundell 1957; Schmitz and Helmberger 1970). Kojima (1973) asserts that the answer depends on the country-origin of FDI and the industrial structure in that country. He argues that Japanese FDI is trade-enhancing because Japanese investors operate in competitive industries, while American FDI is trade-reducing because it emanates from oligopolistic industries at home. Markusen (1983), meanwhile, demonstrates that whether trade and FDI are substitutes or complements depends on production technology, market structure and tax policy, among other things. Disregarding the theoretical contradistinction, empirically it is essentially the market orientation of FDI that determines the pattern of trade between the source and host countries. A recent survey by the United Nations on small- and medium-sized multinationals (UNCTAD 1993) indicates that small transnationals are more export-oriented than large transnationals. If they also source more from home countries due to their reliance on domestic production networks, then small transnationals will be more conducive to trade creation between the source and host countries. But the generalization may not be universally applicable. Debates notwithstanding, from the viewpoint of host countries, the ultimate objective of attracting foreign investment is to accelerate economic growth. What matters is not the volume of trade resulting from FDI, but whether this trade linkage can enhance the host country's international competitiveness or enable it to realize economies of scale in production.

One of the major concerns of development economists regarding FDI is the linkage of multinational firms to the host economies. Overseas subsidiaries are often criticized for operating in 'enclaves' and lacking such linkages (Weisskoff and Wolff 1977; Dietz 1985). Theoretically, if FDI is the chosen mode of entering a foreign market (alternative modes being exporting and licensing) with the main purpose of internalizing proprietary assets (Buckley and Casson 1976), linkage to host economies will be limited to the areas where production does not involve such proprietary assets. For example, a study of Japanese multinationals in the electronics industry found that maintaining exclusive production of major components within the parent firm is a strategy for maintaining the competitive edge of Japanese overseas affiliates (Kotabe and Omura 1989). We may then infer that the more firm-specific the production process is, the less likely it is that this production process will be localized and hence the smaller chance of linkage effects. If small- and medium-sized firms possess an intangible asset which is less firm-specific than large multinationals, they will be more inclined to localize production and create linkage effects. They are also under greater pressure to localize because of their managerial constraints, as argued in Chapter 3. This is the demand side of linkage effects.

On the supply side, the capability of host economies to provide such linkages also matters. Recent studies on industrial development have emphasized the role of agglomeration. Industrial agglomeration is found to be a key factor in locational choice of foreign direct investment (Wheeler and Mody 1992). In essence, the area where an industry concentrates tends to attract more foreign investment in that industry. This makes life miserable for the countries with little industrial base to begin with which want to attract FDI. Some authors also argue that the linkage effect is related to the market orientation of overseas subsidiaries. In particular, export-oriented operations tend to be enclave-prone because their production runs are subject to tight control by the parent firms, and their products and associated technology are subject to constant change in an effort to meet international demand (Lall 1979).

Finally, technology transfer is one area where small- and medium-sized transnationals receive few favorable comments. Small- and medium-sized transnationals are considered to be less able to transfer technology because their management and production procedures are often personalized and difficult to formalize in blueprints or put in written form. Due to their limited technological and managerial manpower, they are also less able to send technical experts to overseas affiliates to transfer technology. When they do transfer technology, they usually prefer oral instruction and personal demonstration to written manuals. They are also less likely to transfer their best technologies to host countries (UNCTAD 1994, pp. 16–17).

This argument needs to be accepted with caution, however. Precisely because the technology possessed by small- and medium-sized transnationals is personalized, technology transfer by these firms often takes informal channels and may be underestimated when formal indices are used to gauge the extent of technology transferred. Although small- and medium-sized transnationals may not send as many technical experts to overseas affiliates as do large multinationals, the most crucial technology is probably known by owners who themselves are stationed in the single overseas subsidiary. Lack of expatriate technicians may actually pressure owners to transfer technology more thoroughly to local employees. Furthermore, it is the unsophisticated technology owned by small transnationals and suited for small-scale production that may be more easily transferred. Such technology requires less adaptive effort and incurs less resources cost on the part of transferees (Teece 1977). The aforementioned United Nations survey indeed found that it takes fewer years for local affiliates of small- and medium-sized transnationals to achieve technological mastery, compared with affiliates of large multinationals (UNCTAD 1994, p. 17).

4.2 Nature of the Sample

The analysis presented in this chapter is based on the survey of Taiwanese subsidiaries in Thailand, Malaysia, Indonesia, Vietnam, and the Philippines. The same sample is used in the country studies presented in the following chapters. The purpose of this chapter is to provide an overall assessment of economic effects of these subsidiaries on host countries, which will be followed by the detailed country-specific studies. Comparison and contrast will be made between subsidiaries of different sizes and between subsidiaries located in different host countries. We will again define small- and medium-sized subsidiaries to be those employing fewer than 300 workers and denote them 'small affiliates' hereafter. The rest are called 'large affiliates'. Although small affiliates do not always correspond to small parent firms, the degree of correlation is high.

There is a total of 287 subsidiaries in our sample, including 65 subsidiaries in Thailand, 125 in Malaysia, 48 in Indonesia, 22 in Vietnam and 27 in the Philippines. As shown in Table 4.1, small affiliates dominate large affiliates in every host country. Overall, there are 190 small affiliates versus 97 large affiliates in our sample. This differs from the parent-firm sample that we studied in Chapter 3 in which small and large parent firms are about equal in number. The subsidiary sample contains many Taiwanese subsidiaries which did not obtain official approval from the Taiwanese government for investing overseas, and is therefore useful in providing information to supplement the parent-firm sample which seems to be biased towards large enterprises.

Table 4.1 Sample Firms by Country and Size

	Thailand	Malaysia	Indonesia	Vietnam	Philippines	Overall
Small firms	39	95	26	12	18	190
Large firms	26	30	22	10	9	97
Total	65	125	48	22	27	287

Note: Small firms are subsidiaries which employ fewer than 300 workers; others are called large firms.

First, Table 4.2 summarizes the year of establishment of all subsidiaries in the sample. It can be seen that among 270 subsidiaries providing such information, more than half (141 firms) were established after 1990, and only a few (7 firms) were established before 1980; the rest were established in the 1980s, primarily the second half of the 1980s. As indicated earlier, Taiwanese outward FDI took off after 1986. In the group of subsidiaries founded in the second half of 1980s, the number of small affiliates (59) is about the same as large affiliates (56). In the group founded in the 1990s, however, the sample is dominated by small affiliates. This suggests that many small affiliates were established in the 1990s following in the footsteps of pioneer investors who embarked on FDI in the 1980s and created a viable market in the host countries for these latecomers. This is apparently similar to the Japanese pattern, in which small subcontractors followed large firms to invest overseas with some time lag (Adachi 1991). Note, however, that Taiwanese small firms act more independently than their Japanese counterparts because Taiwanese firms belong to a network which is only loosely connected as compared to Japan's tightly knit *keiretsu* web. There are also many independent Taiwanese small firms which invested abroad long before large firms did.

Table 4.2 Distribution of Firms by Year of Establishment (by number of firms)

Decade of establishment	Small firms	Large firms	Total
1960s	2	1	3
	(1.1)	(1.1)	(1.1)
1970s	2	2	4
	(1.1)	(2.2)	(1.5)
1980–85	5	2	7
	(2.8)	(2.2)	(2.6)
1986–89	59	56	115
	(33.1)	(60.9)	(42.6)
1990–94	110	31	141
	(61.8)	(33.7)	(52.2)
Sample size	178	92	270
	(100.0)	(100.0)	(100.0)

Note: Figures in parentheses are percentages.

Source: This study.

Table 4.3 lists the industrial composition of the sample. It can be seen that among 278 firms that provide information on the industry to which they belong, the electrical and electronic machinery industry has the largest number of subsidiaries (74) in the sample, followed by, in order, textiles (26), fabricated metal products (24), clothing (23), plastic products (18), and wood products (17). Although the sample does not perfectly reflect the industrial composition of Taiwan's FDI as approved by the host countries, it is fairly close. Among our sample firms, electronics and electrical machinery top the industry list in Malaysia and Thailand. Textiles and clothing combine to top the industry list in Indonesia, Vietnam, and the Philippines, and are equal in number of firms in electronics and electrical machinery in Thailand. Miscellaneous industrial products (mainly sporting goods and toys) are also important in Thailand. Firms in the fabricated metal industry concentrate in Malaysia, while those in the wood products industry spread over Malaysia and Indonesia. Altogether, the electronics and electrical machinery industry has the largest samples, followed by textiles and clothing combined, and then by fabricated metal.

Table 4.3 Distribution of Industries (by number of firms)

Industries	Thailand	Malaysia	Indonesia	Vietnam	Philippines	Overall
Food manufacturing	1	0	2	1	0	4
Beverages and tobacco	0	0	0	0	0	0
Textiles	3	4	9	3	7	26
Clothing and accessories	8	0	5	7	3	23
Leather, fur and products	2	0	1	2	1	6
Wood products, bamboo products and non-metallic furniture	0	11	5	1	0	17
Paper and paper products; printing and publishing	3	3	4	0	0	10
Chemical materials	0	1	4	1	2	8
Chemical products	3	3	1	1	1	9
Petroleum and coal products	0	0	0	0	0	0
Rubber products	2	3	0	1	2	8
Plastic products	6	8	3	1	0	18
Non-metallic mineral products	1	1	0	0	1	3
Basic metal industries	1	5	1	1	0	8
Fabricated metal products	5	16	3	0	0	24
Repair of machinery and equipment	2	2	0	0	0	4
Electronics and electrical machinery	11	51	8	0	4	74
Repair of transport equipment	4	0	2	0	1	7
Precision instruments	2	0	0	1	1	4
Miscellaneous industrial products	11	3	0	0	3	17
Others	0	7	0	0	1	8
Sample size	65	118	48	20	27	278

Source: This study.

Since we use employment as the criterion to distinguish small affiliates from large affiliates, it will be useful to see how the value of transactions and registered capital corresponds to this classification. Table 4.4 lists the average turnover and average turnover per employee of Taiwanese affiliates in 1993. It can be seen that, overall, the average turnover of Taiwanese affiliates is US$14.7 million and average turnover per employee is US$39 900. Affiliates with 300 and more employees (large firms) report an average turnover of US$32.9 million, while those with fewer employees than 300 (small firms) report an average turnover of US$4.0 million. Small affiliates, however, report a much higher turnover per employee than large affiliates – 60 percent higher (US$46 300 versus US$28 800). Although a higher per capita turnover does not necessarily mean a higher productivity, this result seems to point toward supporting the conclusion of the UN survey (UNCTAD 1994) which reports that small transnationals produce more value added per unit of input (p. 16).

Table 4.4 Average Turnover and Average Turnover per Employee

	Small firms	Large firms	Total
Turnover (US$ '000)	4 049	32 924	14 717
Turnover per employee (US$ '000/person)	46.3	28.8	39.9
Sample size	128	75	203

Note: Statistics are based on 1993 data.

Source: This study.

In fact, as will be seen later, since large affiliates engage in large-volume production for export, while small affiliates specialize in niche products destined for diversified markets, small affiliates may obtain a higher value added out of each dollar of turnover than large affiliates. This would make the productivity ratio even higher than the per capita turnover ratio, in favor of small affiliates.

The pattern for the distribution of registered capital is slightly different. As we can see from Table 4.5, most small affiliates (81.7 percent of the total) have a registered capital of not more than US$3 million. Only a few small affiliates (3.8 percent of the total) have registered capital exceeding US$10 million. This suggests that those affiliates which are small in terms of employment are also generally small in capital commitment. The distribution of registered capital for large firms is more diverse. Most large firms (91.8 percent of the total) commit more than US$1 million of capital, but the range of distribution is wide. This suggests that some firms which are large in terms of employment are also labor-intensive in production and thus relatively small in terms of capital commitment. These affiliates typically serve as offshore platforms for export, producing labor-intensive goods for their parent firms which are generally also large.

Table 4.5 Distribution of Registered Capital (by number of firms)

	Small firms	Large firms	Total
Less than US$1 million	74 (39.8)	8 (8.2)	82 (29.0)
US$1 million–3 million	78 (41.9)	29 (29.9)	107 (37.8)
US$3 million–5 million	12 (6.5)	14 (14.4)	26 (9.2)
US$5 million–10 million	15 (8.1)	20 (20.6)	35 (12.4)
US$10 million and more	7 (3.8)	26 (26.8)	33 (11.7)
Sample size	186 (100.0)	97 (100.0)	283 (100.0)

Note: Figures in parentheses are percentages.

Source: This study.

It has become increasingly evident to economists that capital injection is not the major contribution that host countries should expect from foreign investment. Instead, it is mainly in technology, market access, and superior management that foreign investors will benefit host economies. In fact, the actual inflow of capital from multinational firms may not be very large. For example, US-based multinationals as a whole provided only 12 percent of the total value of expenditures on capital investment and profit remittances of overseas subsidiaries in 1966–70, the rest coming from locally earned and reinvested profits and local savings (Lall and Streeten 1977). Moreover, there are alternative sources of capital for developing countries, such as international aid and loans, which are generally cheaper than private direct investment (Lall and Streeten 1993). In Southeast Asia, however, the amount of equity commitment is still used by host-country governments as a criterion for project screening and awarding incentives. This practice may boost initial capital inflow, but there are always hidden channels, notably transfer pricing, that allow investors to repatriate capital. Therefore, equity commitment is not exactly an accurate indicator of investors' financial contribution to the host country. Moreover, there is investment in the form of machinery and equipment which adds little cash to the host country. Some host countries, notably Vietnam, also encourage investment in the form of 'cooperative operation' in conjunction with state-owned enterprises. In this arrangement, foreign investors provide only working capital and modern technology to manage and operate the existing facilities owned by state companies. Saving the need to purchase land and the part of machinery and equipment which are still usable, capital requirement for foreign investors is reduced.

Let us now turn to the issue of ownership structure. It is not surprising that most overseas investors prefer majority ownership over minority ownership. For example, Hill (1988) quoted Indonesian data and reported that more than 90 percent of the proposed FDI cases approved in 1967–76 by the Indonesian authority had majority foreign equity (p. 67). As can be seen in Table 4.6, only 16.2 percent of Taiwanese investors take a minority position in the ownership of overseas affiliates. Insistence on majority ownership is evident, especially with regard to small affiliates. In fact, over half (50.5 percent) of Taiwanese investors maintain whole ownership in small affiliates. This is a manifestation of small investors' concern about their ability to control the operation and the coherence of management.

In fact, a sizable portion of our sample cannot really be called transnational firms at all. They are Taiwanese-owned firms in Southeast Asia, but are unaffiliated with a parent firm in Taiwan. They were either invested in by Taiwanese individuals or by one-time Taiwanese firms which disappeared from Taiwan after such investment. In the case of individual investment, it represents an establishment of new business on foreign soil rather than a relocation or duplication of an existing business with a proprietary asset. Investment by individuals across national borders is possible only when the host countries are psychologically close to the investing individuals. Many of these individuals have worked in the host countries for many years as technical experts or managerial consultants and developed good connections with local economies. As can be seen from Table 4.7, approximately a quarter (25.2 percent) of the affiliates in our sample belong to this category. Parent-less (free-standing) subsidiaries account for an even higher proportion (28.4 percent) of the sample among small affiliates. Lack of parent firms does not necessarily mean lack of linkage to Taiwan, however. Individual owners of these affiliates still use their personal connections in Taiwan for material sourcing, technician recruitment, and information collection. They may maintain an office in Taiwan for this kind of logistic support, taking orders from overseas 'affiliates'. Naturally, this reversal of parent–subsidiary relations occurs more often in SME investors than large enterprises.

Table 4.6 Distribution of Firms by Taiwanese Ownership (by number of firms)

Extent of Taiwanese ownership	Small firms	Large firms	Total
Less than 50%	29	16	45
	(15.8)	(17.0)	(16.2)
50% or more	62	40	102
	(33.7)	(42.6)	(36.7)
Fully Taiwanese	93	38	131
	(50.5)	(40.4)	(47.1)
Average (%)	81.3	77.3	79.9
Sample size	184	94	278
	(100.0)	(100.0)	(100.0)

Note: Figures in parentheses are percentages.

Source: This study.

Table 4.7 Is there a Parent Company in Taiwan? (by number of firms)

	Small firms	Large firms	Total
Yes	131	77	208
	(71.6)	(81.1)	(74.8)
No	52	18	70
	(28.4)	(18.9)	(25.2)
Sample size	183	95	278
	(100.0)	(100.0)	(100.0)

Note: Figures in parentheses are percentages.

Source: This study.

Finally, let us examine the mode of investment as summarized in Table 4.8. Due to the large transaction costs involved in FDI, we may presume that many investors would choose to acquire, merge, or join existing overseas operations instead of starting a new company, particularly small investors. To our surprise, an overwhelming majority (over 90 percent) of Taiwanese affiliates in our sample start with green-field projects (new startups), regardless of the size of employment. This attests to the notion that investors are keen on building overseas subsidiaries in their own 'image', such that the firm-specific asset can be transferred intact. This will reduce the costs of adaptation in the early stage of operation and keep the overseas operation within the domain of competence (Morley and Smith 1977).

Table 4.8 Mode of Investment (by number of firms)

	Small firms	Large firms	Total
Started new company	173 (91.1)	90 (92.8)	263 (91.6)
Acquired, merged or joined existing company	10 (5.3)	6 (6.2)	16 (5.6)
Other	7 (3.7)	1 (1.)	8 (2.8)
Sample size	190 (100.0)	97 (100.0)	287 (100.0)

Note: Figures in parentheses are percentages.

Source: This study.

4.3 Employment Effect

Employment is an indisputable contribution that FDI can bring to host countries. For countries plagued by unemployment, this means job creation; for countries where full employment prevails, this means higher labor productivity and higher wages. For most developing countries open to foreign investment, these two effects usually occur simultaneously. FDI creates jobs which were nonexistent before and, at the same time, replaces existing jobs with similar ones at higher wages. According to a United Nations estimate, multinational firms had created two million jobs by 1970, if only direct employment is considered. This amounts to roughly 0.2 percent of total active population of the LDCs (Sabolo 1975).

Table 4.9 shows the employment data of the Taiwanese affiliates in our sample. It can be seen that, on average, each affiliate employs 403 workers, with small firms employing an average of 117 workers each and large firms 962 each. It is interesting to note that the average employment of small affiliates is virtually the same in all host countries while the average employment of large affiliates varies greatly. The average employment of large affiliates is largest in Indonesia, where each firm employs an average of 1459 workers. Average employment of large affiliates in Malaysia also exceeds 1000. In contrast, average employment for large affiliates is only slightly above 600 in Thailand and Vietnam. The large average number of employees in Indonesian affiliates is attributable to several large-scale Taiwanese FDI operations in paper and shoe-making industries there. In Malaysia the high average is mainly due to some large-scale offshore assembly operations in the electronics industry.

Altogether, the subsidiaries in our sample alone employ approximately 115 000 workers in the five Southeast Asian countries. The actual employment is higher because our sample only covers a fraction of investment projects. If we take the corporate membership of the local Taiwanese Investors' Association as a proxy for the total population of Taiwanese affiliates in the host countries, then as of 1994 there were approximately 600, 400, 200, 200, and 100 Taiwanese affiliates in Thailand, Malaysia, Indonesia, Vietnam, and the Philippines respectively. Assume that those out-of-sample subsidiaries are all small affiliates. Multiplying the number of out-of-sample subsidiaries by the average employment of small affiliates and adding it to the in-sample employment gives a total employment of approximately 84 000 workers in Thailand, 72 000 in Malaysia, 56 000 in Indonesia, 30 000 in Vietnam, and 19 000 in the Philippines. All told, Taiwanese subsidiaries create about 261 000 jobs in the five Southeast Asian countries.

Table 4.9 also reveals the composition of these jobs. It can be seen that, proportionately, small affiliates create more jobs for white-collar workers than do large affiliates. On average, 15.4 percent (18 out of 117) of jobs created by small affiliates are for staff members and R&D personnel. In comparison, only 8.8 percent (85 out of 962) of jobs created by large affiliates are for white-collar workers. Among blue-collar jobs, small affiliates also slate a larger proportion for skilled workers. The average ratio of skilled to unskilled workers is 0.81 for small affiliates and 0.54 for large affiliates. Here we define skilled workers as those whose jobs require training for three months or longer. Since this definition is rather lax, some may prefer to call them semi-skilled workers. In any event, the contradistinction between the skilled and unskilled ratio may be attributable to three possible factors. First, there are scale economies in managing labor in general, and unskilled labor in particular. As the size of employment increases, the proportionate need for supervisory staff members decreases. Second, the technology employed by small affiliates generally has a larger tacit portion (requiring judgment by operators) which requires proportionately more skilled labor to handle. Third, small affiliates are subject to shorter production runs which require proportionately more skilled labor to provide flexibility. The results suggest that, although a large pool of unskilled labor is attractive to foreign investors, availability of sufficient white-collar workers and skilled labor is indispensable for a successful overseas operation, especially for small-scale subsidiaries.

Table 4.9 Employment at Taiwanese Subsidiaries (persons)

	Thailand			Malaysia			Indonesia			Vietnam			Philippines			Overall		
	Small firms	Large firms	Total	Small firms	Large firms	Total	Small firms	Large firms	Total	Small firms	Large firms	Total	Small firms	Large firms	Total	Small firms	Large firms	Total
Total no. of employees	118	612	316	103	1124	348	135	1459	742	122	713	391	159	493	271	117	962	403
	[39]*	[26]*	[65]*	[95]*	[30]*	[125]*	[26]*	[22]*	[48]*	[12]*	[10]*	[22]*	[18]*	[9]*	[27]*	[190]*	[97]*	[287]*
Staff	16	53	30	14	89	31	16	102	57	14	33	23	17	26	20	15	71	33
R&D personnel	3	10	6	3	21	7	3	17	10	3	7	5	1	0	1	3	14	6
Skilled labor	45	159	90	32	377	113	46	387	208	34	270	140	123	395	214	46	318	136
Unskilled labor	60	402	194	58	665	200	80	1028	542	61	336	185	19	71	36	57	586	233
Sample size	31	20	51	89	27	116	21	19	40	11	9	20	18	9	27	170	84	254

Note: [ ]* is sample size used in calculating total number of employers, which differs from the sample size shown in last row.

Source: This study.

A study of the offshore assembly activities of foreign affiliates in Taiwan's electronics industry showed that skilled and unskilled production workers are substitutes while white-collar workers are complementary to both (Chen and Tang 1987). In other words, production processes can be remodeled in the host economy to accommodate more unskilled labor and so cope with a shortage of skilled labor. We often witness this kind of adaptation in overseas affiliates. For example, jobs are divided and refined to reduce the need for manual skills and judgment, less sophisticated machinery is used in lieu of modern equipment to make it manageable by inexperienced workers, and the like.

On the other hand, a shortage of white-collar workers often poses a more serious problem since these workers are irreplaceable. Foreign investors often have to call upon expatriate managers and technicians to fill the gap, resulting in cost increases. The problem is particularly acute for SMEs, since they are short of managerial and technical experts available for dispatch abroad, and they are in need of a higher proportion of such expert workers. Making the situation worse, small transnationals are also at a disadvantage in hiring those experts even if they are available locally. Jobs provided by small transnationals are usually considered insecure and lack prestige. Those who have the option to work somewhere else will work for these small transnationals only if the pay is substantially higher. Therefore, the presence of a large number of small transnationals often quickly bids up the wage rates for white-collar workers and skilled labor in developing countries. For Taiwanese investors, this effect is particularly evident for white-collar workers who are bilingual. For host countries where white-collar and skilled labor are already in short supply, FDI actually makes the market even tighter. This, however, may serve as an inducement for more investment in education and set the course for a virtuous circle of economic development in which human capital has been recognized as a core impetus (Lucas 1989). In Malaysia, Thailand, and Vietnam, for example, we have observed renewed interest in learning the Chinese language. Part of the motivation for this comes from job market opportunities created by Taiwanese FDI.

Moreover, as shown in Chapter 3, small transnationals in need of capable staff members in their overseas subsidiaries, but unable to send expatriates, are keen on training overseas staff. Although compared to large enterprises they train a smaller number of overseas workers, their training is usually more intense and long-lasting. This is undoubtedly conducive to human resources development in the host country.

The inability of SME investors to send expatriate managers also allows local staff to play greater roles in the management of subsidiaries, particularly with regard to technical aspects of the operation. Table 4.10 shows the number and responsibilities of Taiwanese expatriates in overseas subsidiaries. It can be seen that, on average, there are only three expatriate managers or technicians stationed in small affiliates as compared to nine in large affiliates. The average number of expatriates in the overall sample, five, is also small by international standards, considering Taiwan is not far from Southeast Asia. Wells and Warren (1979), for example, reported that the average number of expatriates of Japanese subsidiaries in Indonesia is eleven, and that of American and British affiliates five and six respectively. American and British multinationals sent fewer expatriates because costs are much higher due to distance. The same study reported an average of 14 expatriates for 'Chinese' (including Hong Kong, Singapore, Taiwan) originated projects, which is close to the average number of expatriates in our survey of Taiwanese large affiliates in Indonesia, 15. At the time when Wells and Warren conducted the survey, FDI by Taiwan's SMEs was still sparse.

Table 4.10 Number of Expatriate Employees from Parent Companies

	Small firms	Large firms	Total
Total number of expatriates from parent company	3 [139]*	9 [81]*	5 [220]*
President or vice president	117 (86.0)	75 (91.5)	192 (88.1)
Finance department	48 (35.6)	36 (43.9)	84 (38.7)
Marketing department	42 (31.3)	41 (50.0)	83 (38.2)
Production department	93 (68.9)	66 (80.5)	159 (73.3)
Planning or R&D department	35 (25.9)	26 (31.7)	61 (28.1)
Personnel department	11 (8.1)	16 (19.5)	27 (12.4)
Other	8 (5.9)	16 (19.5)	24 (11.1)
Sample size	135	82	217

Note: [ ]* is sample size used in calculating total number of expatriates. Figures in parentheses are percentages.

Source: This study.

Looking at positions and responsibilities of expatriates, it can be seen that they primarily serve as presidents (or its equivalent, managing directors, in a British-style corporate structure) or vice presidents; secondly they are in charge of production departments. There is little doubt that wherever they are placed, they are the top manager of that department. Because of the larger number of expatriates sent to large affiliates, the presence of expatriate managers is more common among large affiliates compared with small affiliates. Presidency or vice presidency is an exception, where expatriates are equally visible (about 90 percent) in both small and large establishments. In production departments, the difference is still small, with expatriates present in 80.5 percent of large affiliates and 68.9 percent of small affiliates. Schann (1983) demonstrated that parent firms tend to seek control over specific 'strategically important activities' of the subsidiaries rather than the whole range of activities. Geringer (1986) also found that parent firms use their resources parsimoniously and contingently in controlling their overseas ventures. The principles of selective control and contingent usage of resources are closely adhered to by Taiwanese SMEs who face stringent resources constraints. General management and production are two priority areas for Taiwan's small transnationals which give strategic importance to controlling the production functions and making their products competitive in the world market. In other areas, small transnationals demonstrate their apparent shortage of expatriate personnel. They are behind large firms in terms of sending experts to marketing, finance, R&D, and personnel departments. The absence of expatriate managers implies more responsibilities for local managers, and hence, more opportunities for learning-by-doing.

4.4 Trade Effect

The trade effect of FDI depends on the market orientation and sourcing strategy of the subsidiaries. Table 4.11 lists the market distribution of product sales of Taiwanese affiliates in our sample. It can be seen that the market orientation of small affiliates is distinctively different from that of large affiliates. In general, large affiliates are ostensibly export-oriented, selling an average of 10.4 percent of their products back to Taiwan and 69.4 percent outside of both Taiwan and the host country (that is, third-party market). Only the remaining 20.1 percent are sold locally. On the other hand, small affiliates divide their products almost evenly between the local and export market, with the local market holding a slight edge at 51.6 percent. Whereas large affiliates are uniformly export-oriented in all of the host countries studied, the market orientation of small affiliates varies by host country. In Malaysia and Indonesia, small affiliates sell a majority of their products locally, while in Thailand, Vietnam, and the Philippines, they sell the majority abroad. In Malaysia and Indonesia, a substantial proportion of these local sales are of partially finished products which are incorporated into final products, however, and are exported eventually. In other words, these small affiliates are supporting industries of export businesses. These include, for instance, producers of electronics parts and components in Malaysia and textile-related supporting firms in Indonesia. Although it has been documented elsewhere that FDI originating in developing countries tends to be more domestic-market-oriented than in others (Hill 1988; Hasan 1981), Taiwanese affiliates seem to be exceptionally export-oriented.

Table 4.11 Distributions of Sales by Market (%)

	Small firms	Large firms	Total
Local market	51.6	20.1	41.0
Third-party country market	39.7	69.4	49.7
Parent company	6.2	7.8	6.7
Other firms in Taiwan	2.5	2.6	2.6
Sample size	187	95	282

Source: This study.

Compared to local sales and exports to third-party markets, the proportion of the products of Taiwanese affiliates sold back to Taiwan is relatively small. On average, large affiliates sell 10.4 percent of their products back home, and small affiliates only 8.7 percent. The majority of these sales take the form of intra-firm transactions, meaning selling to their parent firms for further processing or direct marketing in Taiwan.

The promotion of exports is a contribution that most developing countries expect from multinational firms, and they have generally lived up to this expectation. Nonetheless, multinational firms are by no means the most important agents of the developing countries' dynamic comparative advantage (Lall 1993, pp. 16–17) as local firms are equally, if not more, important in a successful export expansion drive. Since most products of Taiwanese affiliates are either directly or indirectly exported, Taiwanese FDI must have contributed to the export expansion of host countries, including export to Taiwan. The contributions of Taiwanese investment to the export expansion of the host economies, although less noticeable than FDI from major industrial nations, are nonetheless significant.

Taiwanese investment came to Southeast Asia at a time when Japanese companies were also launching a big wave of FDI aimed at establishing an export base in the area in the wake of the sharp yen appreciation which started after the Plaza Accord of 1985. Taiwanese investors are thus overshadowed by big-ticket investors from Japan and other industrial nations. For example, while it is well known that Malaysia became the third largest exporter of TV sets and semiconductors in the world, largely due to investment by Japanese and American multinationals, few people notice that Malaysia is also now a major exporter of computer monitors in the production of which Taiwanese affiliates play a large role. Japanese investors, among others, have made textiles the largest export item for Thailand (Yoshihara 1994). Few people notice that Thailand is also now a major exporter of luggage, sporting goods, and handbags, in the production of which Taiwanese investors are active players.[1] In Indonesia, Taiwanese investors have contributed to exports of textiles, shoes, and furniture. Textiles have become the largest manufactured export for Indonesia. In Vietnam, Taiwan is by far the largest foreign investor, helping Vietnam build links to the external world in its early stages of economic reform with exports of garments, toys, and other light manufactures.

In fact, linking the host country to the international market may be a more significant contribution of FDI than export promotion. Market access is a valuable asset that multinational firms bring to host countries. As described in Chapter 3, Taiwanese investors have identified market access as their most important advantage in competing with local firms. Once multinational firms establish an export base in the host country, indigenous competitors can easily take advantage of the market accessibility by offering themselves as alternative suppliers. Equipped with the same inputs and aided by an informational advantage, indigenous competitors can win the competition as long as relevant production technology can be acquired. The development experience of Taiwan and Korea has exemplified this spillover effect.

Contrary to product sales, which may be export-enhancing, the procurement of raw materials, components, and parts by foreign subsidiaries inevitably increases imports to the host country. Imports can increase so much that FDI actually creates trade deficits for the host country, at least in the early stage (Petri 1992).

Table 4.12 lists the sourcing strategies of Taiwanese affiliates. It can be seen that, in the overall sample, Taiwanese affiliates procure 37.8 percent of materials, components, and parts from local sources; the rest (62.2 percent) is imported. About two-thirds of the imports are from Taiwan, the other one-third is from the rest of the world, such as Singapore, Japan, and the US. On average, small affiliates procure slightly more from Taiwan than large affiliates, and large affiliates procure slightly more from local sources. Since all affiliates procure a substantial proportion of intermediate goods from Taiwan, Taiwanese FDI will undoubtedly contribute to increased imports from Taiwan for each host country.

Note that the survey of subsidiaries shows that small affiliates import more from other suppliers in Taiwan and less from third countries when compared to large affiliates, while the survey of parent firms reported in Chapter 3 indicates that small parent firms procure more from third countries and less from suppliers in Taiwan when compared with large parent firms. The apparent contradiction suggests that the scale of overseas operations determines the scope of material sourcing. When the overseas subsidiary is small, it does not pay to spend extra search costs to explore international (third-country) suppliers as Taiwanese suppliers are easily accessible through Taiwanese networks. Small parent firms procure more from international suppliers than their large counterparts because they are less likely to have fixed suppliers and subcontractors in Taiwan and diversification in the sources of materials increases the flexibility of small operators.

Table 4.12 Sources of Components and Parts (%)

	Small firms	Large firms	Total
Procurement from local suppliers	37.6	38.2	37.8
Import from third countries	18.8	22.0	19.9
Import from other suppliers in Taiwan	26.5	21.4	24.7
Import from the parent company	17.1	18.8	17.7
Sample size	179	95	274

Source: This study.

In addition to intermediate goods, Taiwanese affiliates also import a substantial proportion of machinery and equipment from abroad. As can be seen from Table 4.13, the overall import ratio of machinery and equipment is 89.7 percent, of which 72.1 percent is from Taiwan. The import ratio varies somewhat from country to country: Vietnam has the highest import ratio at 98.8 percent and Thailand the lowest at 85.2 percent. Large affiliates have a higher equipment import ratio overall, but small affiliates import a larger proportion from Taiwan. Their dependency on Taiwan-made machinery and equipment indicates that small affiliates try to exploit their competitive edge embodied in this machinery and equipment which is unavailable elsewhere. This competitive edge may have been based originally on some generalized technology originating from industrialized countries but adapted to the special production environment in Taiwan. For example, it may be particularly designed for small-scale production, low-precision operations, or for use with electric power flawed with unstable voltages. Because they do not have standardized equipment, small affiliates have to obtain them from Taiwan. In comparison, large affiliates use more standardized (and probably more advanced too) equipment which is available from alternative sources.

In fact, there are many cases attesting to the existence of some equipment-embodied technology which gives rise to a competitive edge for Taiwanese affiliates. One Taiwanese affiliate producing paper told us that they achieve a high level of productive efficiency by using Taiwan-made, inexpensive, and low-precision machines while their competitors struggle with more expensive and sophisticated (and more delicate) machines imported from advanced countries. The key is that human skills in the host country are inadequate to handle the high-precision machines, resulting in frequent failures.[2] Another Taiwanese affiliate producing socks told us they beat off competitors by introducing a Taiwan-made, computer-controlled sewing machine which can handle more sophisticated configurations than traditional machines. In this case, the more advanced machine does not require much human attendance.[3]

Table 4.13 Sources of Machinery and Equipment (%)

	Small firms	Large firms	Total
Procurement from local suppliers	11.7	7.7	10.3
Import from third countries	14.0	24.3	17.5
Import from suppliers in Taiwan	64.0	50.8	59.4
Old machinery relocated from the parent company	10.3	17.3	12.7
Sample size	182	96	278

Source: This study.

Dependence on Taiwan-made machinery gives Taiwanese subsidiaries in Southeast Asia extra costs of maintenance and replacement, however. Taiwanese machinery makers are mostly small- and medium-sized and hence unable to establish service posts in Southeast Asia despite a large outflow of Taiwan-made machinery to the region. We have witnessed Taiwanese investors travelling with briefcases filled with machine parts made in Taiwan to furnish the replacement needs of overseas factories. Importation of these machine parts may be subject to duties and delay by customs procedures. Extra costs of cross-country maintenance burdens the small affiliates so much that they eventually have to seek local replacements.

Statistical analysis of Taiwan's trade with Malaysia, Indonesia, Thailand, and the Philippines in recent years has shown that trade in both directions is positively correlated with Taiwan's outward investment in these countries (Lin 1995). Table 4.14 summarizes Taiwan's trade with these countries, plus Vietnam in the areas where Taiwanese FDI is active. It can be seen that bilateral trade between Taiwan and each of these countries increases several times between 1986 and 1996 (for Vietnam, between 1990 and 1996).

Taiwan's export of machinery to every host country increased, but exports to Thailand and Malaysia were the largest in 1996, indicating that these two countries were major recipients of Taiwanese FDI. Machinery exports to Indonesia and the Philippines were also sizable, exceeding 10 billion NT (about US$0.14 billion) in 1996.

In other areas, the increase in Taiwan's exports to a host country is largely commensurate with the amount of Taiwan's outward investment. For example, when textiles and clothing are combined, the largest increase occurs in Indonesia and the Philippines, reflecting the fact that these two countries are major recipients of Taiwanese FDI in the textile and clothing industries. For electrical and electronic products, Malaysia and Thailand show the largest increase in Taiwanese exports entering those countries, again suggesting their dominant share in Taiwan's FDI in this industry. Likewise, Malaysia and Thailand are also major importers of plastic and rubber products from Taiwan and major recipients of FDI in those industries.

FDI-induced trade apparently dominates trade originating from pure comparative advantage. For example, in 1986, Indonesia imported from Taiwan more electrical and electronic products than all other countries in the list; then, by 1996, its imports were overtaken by all countries except Vietnam. Indonesia has received only a small share of Taiwanese FDI in the electronics industry since 1986, hence a small increase in imports from Taiwan. A qualification needs to be made for the textile industry, however, where the Philippines has seen the largest increase (in terms of value) of imports from Taiwan from 1986 to 1996. Although the Philippines also received substantial FDI from Taiwan in the textile industry, the rapid increase in textile imports from Taiwan was partially attributed to the relatively weak spinning and weaving industries in the Philippines. The booming garment production in the Philippines, partly aided by FDI, resulted in a rising demand for fabrics and yarn, in which Taiwan was a very competitive supplier.

The pattern of exports from the host countries to Taiwan was less systematic, although it also showed a general upward trend. The increase in the exports of wood products from Malaysia and Indonesia was apparently FDI-related. The increase in the exports of electrical and electronic products from Malaysia and Thailand may also reflect the effect of investments from Taiwan. The association of FDI and exports to Taiwan was not apparent for other items.

Nonetheless we can still identify a clear trend of an increase in intra-industry trade between Taiwan and Southeast Asian countries since the mid-1980s. Table 4.15 lists the change of intra-industry trade index as defined by Grubel and Lloyd (1975) between Taiwan and six ASEAN countries (including Singapore, excluding Brunei) in 1989 and 1994. It can be seen that intra-industry trade increased from 1989 to 1994 for each manufacturing industry

Table 4.14 Bilateral Trade between Taiwan and Southeast Asian Countries (in millions NT)

	Taiwan's Exports									
Items	To Malaysia		To Thailand		To Indonesia		To Philippines		To Vietnam*	
	1986	1996	1986	1996	1986	1996	1986	1996	1986	1996
Plastic and rubber	393	6 383	432	5 644	411	3 802	1 167	4 088	65	2 420
Wood products	41	144	6	95	9	52	13	43	0	44
Textiles	1 153	7 706	1 786	8 056	1 190	11 666	3 348	14 084	867	9 769
Clothing	153	513	71	200	94	365	246	595	16	562
Machinery	853	16 722	2 046	19 800	2 701	12 304	706	10 898	338	5 377
Electrical and electronic products	1 472	27 128	1 128	19 912	2 451	7 317	1 198	7 504	59	1 324

	Taiwan's Imports									
Items	From Malaysia		From Thailand		From Indonesia		From Philippines		From Vietnam*	
	1986	1996	1986	1996	1986	1996	1986	1996	1986	1996
Plastic and rubber	59	2 015	16	2 980	4	1 713	6	262	28	510
Wood products	1 293	13 722	58	350	4 957	10 989	2	342	660	1 492
Textiles	194	3 719	134	1 811	16	2 582	42	213	121	337
Clothing	0	204	9	1 215	1	729	1	404	12	1 453
Machinery	7	8 244	52	8 409	34	1 708	1	4 110	0	53
Electrical and electronic products	2 596	48 784	255	14 799	25	1 556	70	11 730	0	61

Note: * Data on trade with Vietnam are available only from 1990. Direct trade with Vietnam was prohibited before 1990.

Source: *Monthly Statistics of Exports (Imports)*, Ministry of Finance, ROC, December issues, 1986 and 1996.

without exception. For industries in which Taiwanese FDI was active, such as textiles and clothing, electronics and machinery, leather (shoes and handbags), paper and pulp, intra-industry trade indexes all increased by large percentage points. Intra-industry trade reflects the exchange of parts and components for semi-finished goods or the cross-hauling of differentiated products. FDI is conducive to intra-industry trade whether the investment results in horizontal or vertical integration between home and overseas production. Examples are Southeast Asia's shipment of gray fabrics to Taiwan in exchange for finished fabrics, or Taiwan's shipment of large-size computer monitors to Southeast Asia in exchange for small-size computer monitors. Intra-industry trade may in fact take the form of intra-firm trade, which is a typical transaction of multinational firms.

Table 4.15 Intra-Industry Trade Index between Taiwan and Southeast Asia

Industry	1989	1994
Foods	17.1	28.7
Chemicals	25.1	33.3
Plastics and rubber	17.4	28.9
Leather	25.8	60.0
Wood products	2.7	3.5
Paper and pulp	29.4	44.3
Textiles and clothing	4.8	26.4
Footwear and clothing accessories	5.9	14.0
Non-metal minerals	40.2	47.2
Jewelry and precious metal	19.0	27.7
Basic metal	19.6	24.8
Electronics and machinery	29.9	52.3
Vehicles	28.7	36.0
Precision instruments	36.3	42.0
Miscellaneous manufactures	17.8	32.6

Note: Southeast Asia includes Singapore, Malaysia, Thailand, Indonesia, Philippines, and Vietnam.

Source: Chung-Hua Institution for Economic Research (Taiwan), *How to Strengthen Ties with Southeast Asian Countries and Organizations on the Basis of Political and Economic Development in Taiwan*, project report, Taipei, 1996.

4.5 Linkage Effect

Multinational corporations can have various types of linkage with local firms. The most important types are backward linkages to local suppliers of parts, components, raw materials, and services. The other types include forward linkages to distributors and sales agents, indirect linkages stemming from local suppliers, and spillover effects (Lall 1993, p. 19). Some researchers have suggested that, in an unconstrained environment, multinational firms would prefer to retain linkages overseas, rather than undertake extra costs of developing local suppliers (for example, Hill 1985). They subcontract locally only under government pressure (Thee 1985). However, when compared with home operations, retaining linkage overseas also incurs extra costs in terms of coordination and communication across national borders, in addition to administrative barriers in the form of tariffs, customs procedures and local content regulations. Therefore, procurement of components, parts and the like depends on many factors, including the availability of local suppliers and the capability of multinational firms to maintain overseas networks which, in turn, may be related to firm size.

The conventional literature based on comparative statistics has yet to offer convincing evidence as to whether large or small affiliates generate stronger linkage effects, however. We argue in this section, based on the dynamic perspective obtained through our survey, that because of pressure to localize, small affiliates tend to offer stronger linkage effects to host economies in the long run. In the short run, large affiliates may source more materials locally because of scale economies in local procurement and because they use standardized components and parts that enable alternative sourcing.

Table 4.16 details the sourcing strategies of Taiwanese affiliates in our sample based on size and year of establishment. Although we are unable to follow the same set of affiliates over time, comparing affiliates established in early years to those established recently gives us some idea about the change of sourcing strategies over time.

It can be seen that older affiliates (those established before 1990) procure more materials, components, and parts from local suppliers than younger affiliates (those established in 1990 and thereafter). For affiliates established in the 1990s, small operators procured less locally than large operators; for affiliates established before 1990, the opposite is true. This suggests that local experience encourages local sourcing, and the effect is stronger for small operations.

Both groups increase procurement from third-party countries, but large affiliates increase this purchase more substantially. Large affiliates are apparently more 'multinationalized'. Again, this is because their components and parts are more standardized.

Table 4.16 Sourcing of Materials, Components, and Parts by Size and Year of Establishment (%)

Sources	Established before 1990		Established 1990–94	
	Small firms	Large firms	Small firms	Large firms
Local suppliers	40.0	38.4	36.5	38.1
Suppliers in third countries	21.7	24.1	17.5	17.2
Suppliers in Taiwan	31.5	20.8	25.8	19.6
Parent firm	6.8	16.7	20.3	25.2
Sample size	60	61	107	29

Source: This study.

Both groups cut their supply from parent firms over time, but small affiliates made more substantial cuts. This is because they grow more independent of their parent firms over time – some even lost their parent firms altogether. When parent firms in Taiwan stop sourcing for the subsidiaries, subsidiaries turn to procuring from suppliers in Taiwan directly. This is reflected in an increase of sourcing from Taiwanese suppliers by older small affiliates. The result indicates that although the parent firm fades away in its supporting role of overseas operations, Taiwan's networks remain a crucial source of support to Taiwanese subsidiaries. An independent affiliate lacking global sourcing capability and losing support from Taiwan's parent also deepens the degree of localization by sourcing more and more locally.

A similar pattern can be observed for the procurement of machinery and equipment (Table 4.17). Older affiliates purchase slightly more machinery and equipment from local sources than younger affiliates. The increase in local procurement over time is particularly rapid among small affiliates; again a manifestation of localization. Older affiliates also procure more machinery and equipment from third-party countries and cut importation from Taiwan. The shift is particularly fast among large affiliates; again a manifestation of their capability for alternative sourcing. For Taiwanese subsidiaries established before 1990, small affiliates purchase an average of 16.7 percent of machinery and equipment from local suppliers, more than twice the proportion of local sourcing by large affiliates. This indicates small affiliates' inclination and ability to adapt to locally available equipment. With some adaptative efforts, machinery and equipment used by small firms is more likely to be partitioned and made interchangeable with parts available locally whereas that used by large affiliates is more likely to be integrated and indivisible. On the other hand, large affiliates established before 1990 procure an average of 27 percent of machinery and equipment from third-party countries, substantially higher than the proportion of third-party purchases by small affiliates. Large affiliates' links to the outside world are apparently stronger because they use modern and standardized machinery. They are also adaptive, but not particularly to the local environment. They pursue a globabilization strategy with worldwide suppliers in mind.

Table 4.17 Sources of Machinery and Equipment by Size and Year of Establishment (%)

Sources	Established before 1990		Established 1990–94	
	Small firms	Large firms	Small firms	Large firms
Local suppliers	16.7	7.5	7.9	7.7
Suppliers in third countries	17.0	27.0	13.6	20.2
Suppliers in Taiwan	58.8	48.9	66.9	56.9
Parent firm	7.5	16.7	11.7	15.1
Sample size	63	61	107	31

Source: This study.

Small affiliates lead large affiliates in the speed of localization in the area of production, but lag behind large affiliates in the area of financing. Financial constraints often limit the risk-taking capacity of small transnationals. Table 4.18 shows the sources of financing for Taiwanese subsidiaries. It can be seen that local financial institutions and parent firms are two major sources of financing for Taiwanese subsidiaries. Compared with younger affiliates, older affiliates are financed substantially more by local financial institutions and substantially less by parent firms. The switch from parent financing to local financing is particularly striking among large affiliates where local financial institutions account for 35.8 percent of the financing for those established since 1990, but account for 58.9 percent of the financing for those established before 1990. A similar pattern is observed among Japanese multinationals where larger multinationals and older affiliates are found to be financed more by local financial institutions and less by parent companies when compared with smaller and younger counterparts (Mukai 1990, pp. 107–10). Large affiliates are also more successful in tapping international financial markets, as shown by the fact that a higher proportion of their financing sources are third-party countries. Small affiliates, on the other hand, draw a fraction of funds from informal financial markets, such as borrowing from shareholders, suppliers, subcontractors and friends. Large affiliates are less involved in the informal sector. Small transnationals are not only disadvantaged in the institutional loans market, but they are also generally excluded by the local equity market. Financial constraints force small transnationals to rely on internal funds. Therefore, there is little chance for them to remit overseas earnings back to the parent firms. They may also be forced to seek a financially resourceful local partner although they would otherwise prefer a wholly owned equity structure.

Table 4.18 Sources of Financing by Size and Year of Establishment (%)

Sources	Established before 1990		Established 1990–94	
	Small firms	Large firms	Small firms	Large firms
Local partners	10.6	3.2	2.4	10.5
Local financial institutions	47.6	58.9	43.3	35.8
Financial institutions in Taiwan	8.1	4.8	3.8	5.0
Financial institutions in third countries	2.1	5.8	1.3	6.7
Parent firm	29.0	27.0	44.9	39.7
Informal financial sources	2.5	0.3	4.4	2.3
Sample size	63	59	104	30

Source: This study.

In essence, compared with large affiliates, small affiliates are more inclined to localize and are less able to internationalize. Over time they tend to procure more and more materials, components, and parts from local suppliers, and to integrate more and more locally available machinery and equipment into their production facilities. They are less able to seek alternative sourcing in international markets partly because they lack scale economies and expertise in international procurement. Inability to tap into international resources and the decline of support from their parent firms force small transnationals to localize.

Localization implies adaptation to the local environment to maximize the usage of local resources. Adaptation involves modification of production technology to suit the characteristics of local factors. This often necessitates an increase of in-house production and a reduction of capital intensity and skill content in production processes to take advantage of the abundant supply of labor in general and unskilled labor in particular (Chen 1992b). Increasing in-house production reduces outsourcing of materials, particularly those which must be imported, thus increasing the possibility of local linkage.

The key to local linkage is the availability of subcontractors. Taiwanese SMEs which are spoiled by the flexibility of the subcontracting system in Taiwan often find themselves in a dilemma when they venture abroad. Given the limited supply of subcontractors locally, Taiwanese affiliates either have to subcontract back to Taiwan or produce the needed components and parts internally. The former solution increases managerial costs and the latter increases capital commitment and risks. Small transnationals are too lacking in managerial and financial resources to accept either solution on a sustained basis. They need to find local subcontractors or to create new ones. In addition to searching for local subcontractors, they sometimes encourage their employees, partners or friends to establish subcontracting firms. They also subcontract to local affiliates of other Taiwanese or Japanese investors.

4.6 Technology Transfer

Small transnationals are sometimes said to transfer less technology to their overseas affiliates because they lack the ability to formalize their technologies (UNCTAD 1994, pp. 16–17). Our survey of Taiwanese transnationals, as presented in Chapter 3, found this assertion less than convincing. In Taiwan's case, the degree of technology transfer by small transnationals is very similar to that of their larger counterparts.

In fact, because of localization efforts, overseas affiliates of small transnationals are technologically more independent from their parents, compared with those of large transnationals. The technology may originally be embodied in owners and key expatriate experts, but it stays within the overseas affiliates and will be transferred to indigenous managers and technicians when they assume the responsibilities for operating the firms. Therefore, technology transfer in small affiliates may be slow but sure. These firms will even develop their own technology specifically adapted to the local environment and distinctive from that which originated from Taiwan. Once they achieve that status, they are capable of spawning their own affiliates abroad.

To demonstrate the existence of this process, Table 4.19 shows the technology sources for new product innovation in Taiwanese overseas subsidiaries. It can be seen that although Taiwanese affiliates draw technology most frequently from their parents, local R&D also provides an important source of product innovation. There is little difference between small and large affiliates in terms of local R&D effort; but large affiliates depend on their parents for technology support more than their smaller counterparts. Like multinational firms from developed countries, large Taiwanese affiliates tend to centralize their innovation at home and use internalized technology markets to maximize economic rents accrued from their know-how (Lall 1993, p. 5). Therefore, their overseas affiliates can always import technology from the parent firms. On the other hand, small affiliates produce more imitations of the products of their peers and are more active in acquiring technology from other advanced countries. All this suggests that small affiliates are more independent than their larger counterparts in sourcing technology. Technology independence means an ability to transform themselves and possibly develop indigenous technology which is intrinsically different from that of their parents.

Table 4.19 Technology Sources of New Product Innovation by Taiwanese Subsidiaries (by number of firms; %)

Technology source	Small firms	Large firms	Total
Through own R&D	71	39	110
	(39.2)	(41.9)	(40.1)
Imitate other companies	44	14	58
	(24.3)	(15.1)	(21.2)
Acquire technology from other advanced countries	32	11	43
	(17.7)	(11.8)	(15.7)
Technology transfer from the parent company	109	67	176
	(60.2)	(72.0)	(64.2)
Others	6	4	10
	(3.3)	(4.3)	(3.6)
Sample size	181	93	274

Note: Choices are multiple.

Source: This study.

Large transnationals are perceived to make more extensive technology transfers because they conduct more formal training, while small transnationals transfer technology mainly through on-the-job training. We have argued above that although training by small transnationals is less extensive, it is more intensive. Furthermore, in the area of on-the-job training, skilled workers in small transnationals are exposed to multiple job functions, whereas those in large multinationals often are limited to single-function training. Even for Japanese foreign affiliates, job rotation is a rare undertaking although it is a standard practice in Japan (Sato 1994). Skilled workers in large foreign affiliates, therefore, have few opportunities of learning enough to enable them to start their own business by imitating their former employers, compared with those working for small foreign affiliates. More commonly, these skilled workers practice 'job-hopping' to increase their pay but usually end up in another foreign-owned company.

4.7 Concluding Remarks

Small transnationals do not necessarily contribute more or less than large multinationals to host economies. They simply contribute in a different manner, and may cover some areas where large multinationals are absent. Our survey of Taiwanese affiliates in Southeast Asia shows that small affiliates employ an average of 117 workers each, which is dwarfed by large affiliates' average employment of 962 per firm. In terms of composition of employment, small affiliates hire proportionately more white-collar workers and skilled blue-collar workers. Large affiliates, on the other hand, are more unskilled-labor-intensive. Therefore, small affiliates may contribute more than large affiliates to increasing the wages of white-collar workers and skilled laborers, but are less effective in job creation for unskilled labor. For countries plagued with unemployment of unskilled workers, large-scale Taiwanese investment seems to be more beneficial. For countries seeking to enhance human resources development, however, small investors from Taiwan may provide a more effective impetus.

Both small- and large-scale Taiwanese FDI ventures contribute to export expansion in the host countries, as well as trade between Taiwan and the host countries in both directions. Large Taiwanese affiliates contribute to host-country exports with mass production of standardized products. Small Taiwanese affiliates contribute to the export of niche products and intermediate goods that go on to further production for eventual export. Production technology of small affiliates is also more firm-specific, making them more dependent on Taiwanese supply of equipment, components and parts, compared with large affiliates.

However, because of their inability to pursue a truly global strategy in sourcing and production, and their inability to overcome managerial deficiencies in maintaining connections with production networks in Taiwan, small Taiwanese transnationals are under pressure to localize. Localization enhances linkage to local economies, manifested by increasing local sourcing of materials, machinery, and equipment.

Localization also leads to technological independence from the parent firms. This implies that small affiliates stand a better chance of developing indigenous technology, which may become a base for dissemination of that technology locally and to neighboring countries. The drawback is that the technology of small affiliates is usually personalized and embodied in key persons in the company, and thus more difficult to transfer.

Notes

1. According to US Customs Statistics, in the first six months of 1994, Thailand occupied a 5.7 percent share of the US import market for sporting goods, a 3.5 percent share for luggage, and a 3.8 percent share for leather cases and handbags.
2. Interview in Jakarta, Indonesia, 15 September 1994.
3. Interview in Bandung, Indonesia, 20 September 1994.

5. Noneconomic Elements of Taiwan's Foreign Direct Investment

Homin Chen and Meng-chun Liu

5.1 Introduction

Taiwanese firms have been characterized as weak organizations with strong linkages. Strong linkages allow these weak organizations to transcend their inherent limitations in operating scale and managerial resources. The strength of these linkages is manifested by their strategic adaptability, which rests upon their flexibility, low cost, and breadth of choice (Redding 1991). In other words, strong network ties are essential to the viability of Taiwan's small- and medium-sized firms. Within the network, independent firms basically make 'arms-length' transactions where transaction costs are reduced by personal trust. In certain industries, this structure is more efficient than hierarchical structures in meeting market fluctuations. Hence, small- and medium-sized firms prevail.

It is doubtful that network strength is sufficient for a successful foreign direct investment; it takes some other organizational strength to establish overseas operations. Furthermore, the 'personal trust' machine which works so well in Taiwan may turn rusty overseas, even within the overseas Chinese community. In fact, mistrust between Taiwanese investors and their overseas Chinese partners often contributes to the failures of Taiwanese overseas investments. More importantly, although linguistic and cultural proximity reduces the transaction costs, Taiwanese firms' efforts in building production networks overseas are severely constrained by the industrial structure of the host country. In many host countries, the nurturing of subcontractors is hindered by lack of capital and entrepreneurship. As a result, Taiwanese firms are usually more hierarchical in their overseas operations than they used to be in home operations.

This chapter analyzes Taiwanese firms' interactions with local communities in general, and with overseas Chinese business networks in particular. Our analysis is based on interviews with local managers of Taiwanese firms in various countries as well as the survey of parent firms as described in Chapter 3.

5.2 Startup Concerns

Foreign direct investment entails startup costs in searching for potential locations, conducting feasibility studies, obtaining government approvals, building factories, installing machinery and equipment, hiring workers, and so on. For small firms, these startup costs may present an insurmountable barrier to overseas investment. Taiwanese small firms overcome this barrier by relying on their local connections, notably those based on shared Chinese ethnicity.

Due to their small scale, Taiwanese firms rarely undertake a comprehensive survey of potential foreign locations before they decide to make an overseas investment. It is not uncommon for Taiwanese firms to commit themselves to investing in a particular location on their first trip abroad to explore FDI opportunities.[1] Many investment decisions are made incidentally, with initiatives originating from friends, peers, governments, related firms, and so on. Table 5.1 lists the sources of FDI initiatives for Taiwanese firms. Although many firms claim their FDI decision is self-motivated, local connections also provide important initiatives. These connections include local sales agents, local suppliers, local users, and so on. The most important connections, however, are overseas Chinese. Roughly one-fourth of FDI by Taiwanese firms is partially initiated by local Chinese in host countries. This 'Chinese connection' is particularly common among small firms, where 17 out of 59 FDI projects made by sampled firms were instigated by local Chinese. Large firms, in contrast, are more self-motivated; invitations from overseas Chinese, nonetheless, still play a non-negligible role in their FDI decisions (12 out of 51 cases). While private connections are vital, initiatives provided by host-country as well as home-country governments are relatively unimportant.

There are only a few cases of group investment actions taken by competitive firms in the same industry or by a consortium of suppliers and users to extend the core–satellite working relationship from home base to abroad. This implies that attempts to transplant Taiwan's production networks abroad are rare undertakings. Instead, Taiwanese firms use local connections to establish new networks abroad or to link to existing local networks. This provides impetus for Taiwanese firms to integrate with local industries.

Once Taiwanese firms decided to invest abroad, they usually expedited the legal procedures and other preparatory work in order to commence operations within the shortest time possible. Our survey indicates that, on average, Taiwanese firms took only one year to commence operations after they filed an application for foreign investment. In countries where approval of foreign investment license is known to be time-consuming, such as Indonesia and Vietnam, many Taiwanese firms disguised themselves as local investors in order to save time in legal proceedings. Our interviews with Indonesian subsidiaries of Taiwanese firms revealed that quite a few firms acquired local Indonesian establishments and used their legal status to start overseas operations while they awaited foreign investment approvals. Some used their partners' names to establish local firms first and then switched to foreign-firm status when the investment license was obtained. Of course, some retained the local-firm status permanently.

Table 5.1 Sources of FDI Initiatives (by number of cases)

Sources of initiatives	Small firms	Large firms
Urged by local sales agents	8	5
Urged by local suppliers	9	3
Urged by local users	6	3
Urged by other local firms	5	3
Urged by core firm (to invest as a subcontractor)	2	0
Group actions by firms in the same industry in Taiwan	4	3
Urged by Taiwanese government	1	3
Urged by overseas Chinese	17	12
Induced by host-country government	3	5
Self-motivated	26	30
Others	2	4
Sample size	59	51

Source: This study.

Expedience, however, is costly at times. Registering equity or property under somebody else's name risks losing this asset altogether if the local collaborators break the faith and come to claim legal ownership. The cheater, normally ethnically Chinese, may go unpunished in the overseas Chinese community because the Taiwanese firm, as a newcomer to that network, lacks the credentials to make the charge trustworthy. Ironically on these occasions, Taiwanese firms often mobilize the judiciary power of the host country to win back their property. For example, they ask the police department or prosecutors' office to 'persuade' the local dummy owners to return the property with a threat that the officials will otherwise pursue a conspiracy case. In spite of high risks, expediting setup procedures through collaboration with local Chinese is particularly useful for small- and medium-sized firms in reducing transaction cost in a society where legal procedures are subject to administrative discretion. Large multinational corporations can exert pressure on local governments through their home-government agencies or through their own economic influence to overcome bureaucratic barriers. Small- and medium-sized firms from Taiwan do not have this kind of pressure apparatus at their disposal.

Moreover, the decision makers in Taiwan's small- and medium-sized firms believe that early entry is essential to the profitability of their overseas operations. This belief is largely extrapolated from their experience of operating in Taiwan. Low entry barriers in Taiwan often dispel abnormal profits existing in any industry in a short period of time. There is a popular saying in Taiwan's business world: 'No industry in Taiwan prospers beyond three years.' Therefore, in Taiwan, rushing to a new business opportunity before the industry gets crowded is an important strategy for profit making and survival. Taiwan's small- and medium-sized firms tend to approach overseas investment with the same conviction. But they soon realize that entry barriers in Asia's other developing countries are much higher than those of Taiwan, and they end up competing more with other Taiwanese subsidiaries than with indigenous firms.

5.3 Local Partners

Local partners may help foreign investors overcome informational barriers and provide resources that complement foreign investors' proprietary assets. But local participation also reduces the hierarchical authority of the parent firms and hinders the managerial efficiency of multinational operations. Thus, Stopford and Wells (1972) described the choice of ownership structure as a trade-off between a foreign investor's 'need for resources' and its 'need for control'. In general, the more firm-specific the proprietary assets are, the more likely it is that multinational firms will choose whole ownership over joint venture. Also, the more firm-specific know-how and technology are susceptible to being learned and emulated, the less likely it is that multinational firms will accept local partners. In the case of Taiwanese firms, however, we do not find firm specificity of the proprietary asset and prevention of technology spillover to be important concerns for the choice of ownership structure. It is the consideration of managerial coherence and efficiency that dominates the decision on ownership structure, particularly among small- and medium-sized firms. A crucial competitive edge for small- and medium-sized firms is their ability to make prompt decisions in response to shocks and opportunities. They are able to do so because the owners of these firms are trusted family members or friends, and the managers are either the owners themselves or intimate friends of the owners. The coherent ownership–management structure reduces the 'principal–agent' problem to a minimum. The overriding principle in Taiwanese firms' choice of local partners is to avoid undermining the managerial coherence and efficiency based on this structure.

Table 5.2a summarizes the choice of partnership by Taiwanese investors. It can be seen that ownership structure is strongly affected by market orientation. Among export-oriented firms, about half of them choose not to have any local partners. For the other half choosing to have some local partnership, most opt for majority ownership. Small- and medium-sized firms, in particular, are reluctant to hold minority equity positions: only two out of 26 firms surveyed chose to have minority ownership. As can be seen in Table 5.2b, the average equity share of export-oriented SMEs who chose to have some local participation is 68 percent, much higher than the 55.8 percent average of large firms. This contradicts Stopford and Wells's (1972) assertion that SMEs are more inclined to favor joint venture than leading firms because of their compelling need for resources. Taiwan's SMEs tend to place the need for managerial integrity to maintain flexibility as top priority and then to access needed resources through personal connections and industry-based networks. In other words, their needs for resources are largely met by arms-length transactions with the transaction costs reduced by personal connections and industry networks. Being able to do the latter is crucial to SMEs for otherwise they will be forced into a joint venture that will undermine their agility. And precisely for this reason, SMEs usually locate in 'familiar' host countries which are within the perimeters of their networks. Gomes-Casseres (1989) has also shown that multinational firms prefer whole ownership over joint venture in 'familiar' host countries.

As for local-market-oriented investors, their ownership structure is often affected by government regulations. With the exception of Malaysia, one hundred percent foreign ownership is either prohibited outright, or disqualified from fiscal incentives in Southeast Asia. Regulations notwithstanding, among 22 Taiwanese small- and medium-sized firms, only seven choose to have minority ownership. In contrast, among 16 large firms, eight choose to have minority ownership. This suggests that small- and medium-sized firms are more wary of local participation than large firms. Many of them are forced to provide some degree of local ownership by government regulations. Among the small- and medium-sized firms that we interviewed, if they are majority-owned by Taiwanese, almost without exception, local partners are not allowed to participate in day-to-day management decisions. Local partners may sit on regular meetings of the board of directors, but daily management is subject to the discretion of presidents or vice presidents, who are normally expatriate managers from Taiwanese parent companies. A similar pattern can be seen from Table 5.2b where on average Taiwanese investors own 45.5 percent equity share of overseas ventures that are local-market-oriented while they own 62.4 percent equity share of export-oriented ventures. There is virtually no difference between large firms and SMEs in terms of equity ownership if the overseas venture is local-market-oriented. Among the export-oriented ventures, however, SMEs hold a larger average equity share than large firms.

Table 5.2a *Ownership Structure of Taiwanese Subsidiaries (by number of firms)*

Size	Local-market-oriented	Export-oriented
Large firms	Total: 16	Total: 26
	Wholly Taiwanese: 0	Wholly Taiwanese: 13
	Majority Taiwanese: 8	Majority Taiwanese: 9
	Minority Taiwanese: 8	Minority Taiwanese: 4
Small firms	Total: 22	Total: 26
	Wholly Taiwanese: 4	Wholly Taiwanese: 12
	Majority Taiwanese: 11	Majority Taiwanese: 12
	Minority Taiwanese: 7	Minority Taiwanese: 2

Source: This study.

Table 5.2b *Average Equity Share of Taiwanese Investors in Joint-Venture Projects (%)*

Size	Local-market-oriented	Export-oriented
All firms	45.5	62.4
Large firms	45.4	55.8
Small firms	45.5	68.0

Source: This study.

The backgrounds of local partners, listed in Table 5.3, reflect the strategic choices of Taiwanese firms. We can see from the table that local manufacturers provide most partners to Taiwanese firms. These manufacturers are usually in industries related to those in which the Taiwanese firms operate. Many Taiwanese firms form joint ventures with local firms in the upstream or downstream industries. Before forming a joint venture, they normally have traded with each other for some time and have developed a sense of mutual trust. This type of joint venture enables local partners to be vertically integrated with Taiwanese subsidiaries, whereby both gain market strength. Taiwanese firms also form joint ventures with local firms which manufacture products of related industries. For example, a Taiwanese firm specializing in rubber shoes may form a joint venture with a local firm producing leather shoes, or a shrimp-culture firm from Taiwan may form a joint venture with a local chicken farm. This type of joint venture allows Taiwanese investors to reduce training costs since the local partners already possess similar technologies which allows economies of scope to be exploited by the new business entity. It is rare to observe two firms producing identical products entering a joint venture for the purpose of producing the same products. Apparently, apart from capital, complementarity of technology is an important factor contributing to the formation of partnerships. In fact, many overseas Chinese conglomerates have access to a large pool of international capital; therefore what they seek from Taiwanese investors is technology rather than capital (Yoshihara 1994).

Table 5.3 Background of Local Partners (by number of firms)

Background	Small firms	Large firms
Government	4	5
Local manufacturing firms	16	20
Local sales agents	4	4
Local financial institutions	2	3
Individuals	14	7
Multinationals	5	3
Others	0	1
Sample size	35	33

Source: This study.

What is striking in Table 5.3 is the popularity of inviting local individuals who have no previous experience of owning business to be local partners. The popularity of this practice is especially high among small- and medium-sized Taiwanese firms, where 14 out of 35 sampled firms have such individuals as local partners. This arrangement is aimed at taking advantage of these individuals' knowledge of the local market and their linkage to local society and government without sacrificing managerial integrity. These individuals are usually allotted an equity share large enough to secure their allegiance to the company, but small enough to prevent them from interfering with daily decision making. Many of these individuals are capable persons who are otherwise unable or unwilling to launch business ventures on their own. As noted earlier, entry barriers in many of Southeast Asia's developing countries are much higher than in Taiwan, so these individuals may never have an opportunity to start their own businesses without the aid of some established firms. Many owners of Taiwanese firms have been nurtured by established entrepreneurs on their way to success. They believe that cultivating talented young individuals and making them partners of the company is not only beneficial to the long-term growth of the business group, but is also a virtue *per se*.

In addition to manufacturing firms and individuals, Taiwanese firms also form partnerships with local government, sales agents, financial institutions, and other multinationals. The motive for teaming up with local government and financial institutions is self-evident. The motive for teaming up with sales agents is usually to promote local sales. However, the small number of cases in which sales agents are sought as local partners indicates that local sales are not the predominant concern of Taiwan's investors at the time of investment. In fact, Taiwanese firms prefer establishing their own local marketing network over relying on a few local trading agents. One characteristic of Taiwanese small- and medium-sized firms is the inseparability of production from marketing functions. Taiwan's small manufacturers maintain full authority to make spontaneous price decisions. Their thorough knowledge of technical details and ability to set production priorities give them an advantage in sales negotiations. Knowledge of buyers' needs and market conditions also helps manufacturers adjust production capacity and shipment priority whenever needed (Seetoo 1994). Owing to this background, Taiwan's small- and medium-sized firms prefer to establish their own local marketing channels through the assistance of local partners, but they rarely delegate the entire marketing responsibility to local partners.

There are also a few cases in which Taiwanese firms form joint ventures with multinationals. These include cases where Taiwanese firms are themselves affiliates of multinationals or entrusted subcontractors of multinationals. The investments are usually organized by multinational corporations and Taiwanese investors only take a minor position in a third-country venture. The arrangement is made to facilitate the transfer of Taiwanese technology which is deemed to be more appropriate for the host country than the 'modern' technology owned by the multinationals. For Taiwanese investors, the joint venture allows them to stand on the shoulders of a giant in attempting to crack open an unfamiliar market. Usually, multinational firms provide most logistic supports and bear most financial risks of the joint ventures.

Table 5.4 lists the previous relationship of Taiwanese firms with their major local partners. It is surprising to find from the table that almost half of the sampled Taiwanese firms indicate that they have no history of business with their local partners. In other words, it is common for Taiwanese firms to form partnerships with someone who is foreign to their industry and sometimes totally unknown to them as a person. In this case, Taiwanese firms usually cement the partnership through personal connections to common friends. Personal trust forms the basis of working relations. Of course, the collaboration does not always go smoothly. In our interviews, we were repeatedly reminded by Taiwanese owners that choice of proper partners is crucial to the success of overseas operations. Many interviewees drew this conclusion from painful lessons. Mismarriage between Taiwanese investors and local partners occurs largely because Taiwanese investors want a quick entry into the host country without accumulating enough 'internationalization' experience to do so. According to Johanson and Vahlne (1977), internationalization is an evolutionary process whereby firms take a small step at a time within the neighborhood of their domain of competence. Each step of internationalization allows firms to accumulate some strategic assets which in turn enables them to take the second step. Many Taiwanese firms, particularly those small and medium-sized, do not follow the 'evolutionary' process. Their FDI is a spontaneous action in response to sudden changes in operational environment. They need to invest in a country they have never had experiences of exporting to, licensing with, or technical cooperation with before. And they need to do it quickly before the market gets crowded with competitors. Under these circumstances, they do not have many options. In essence, Taiwanese firms pick partners from a shallow pool of candidates. They want their partners to be helpful in overcoming their foreignness to the local society, but they also do not want to be dominated by their partners. Exactly what kind of functions do they want their local partners to perform?

Table 5.4 Business Relations with Partners (by number of firms)

Business relations	Small firms	Large firms
No previous business relations	17	14
Some previous business relations	18	18
Average length of previous business experience with partners (years)	6.5	8.3
Sample size	35	32

Source: This study.

Table 5.5 lists the contributions of local partners as assessed by Taiwanese investors. It can be seen from the table that the most-mentioned contribution of local partners is their governmental and business connections. In other words, those who are able to connect Taiwanese firms with the host-country government and business community are the most sought-after partners. Although local manufacturers are in a good position to provide such connections because they are in a business related to that of the Taiwanese investors, certain local individuals may also possess such 'intangible assets' worthy of being internalized by a joint venture. These individuals include retired government officials, family or distinguished staff members of the local elite business group, political leaders of the local Chinese community, and so on. This explains why many Taiwanese investors form partnerships with local individuals.

Table 5.5 Contribution of Local Partners (by number of firms)

Contribution	Small firms	Large firms
Providing financial support	14	16
Providing technological support	3	4
Providing marketing support	20	17
Providing governmental and business relationship	23	25
Personnel recruitment and management	14	19
Others	2	2
Sample size	35	32

Source: This study.

In addition to governmental and business connections, providing marketing and financial support and helping in personnel recruitment are also considered important functions of local partners. In general, small- and medium-sized firms mentioned marketing support more often than financial support and recruitment assistance, whereas large firms mentioned recruitment and managerial assistance more often than marketing and financial support. The difference, however, is not very large. It is noteworthy that although Taiwanese firms are not enthusiastic about forming joint ventures with local marketing firms, they do earnestly seek marketing support from their local partners. Local partners may offer Taiwanese firms access to their own marketing networks or help Taiwanese firms become connected with local networks. Taiwanese firms rarely manufacture brand-name products; therefore networking is a more practical approach to potential buyers than delegating the marketing function to specialized agents, especially when their customers are industrial users rather than the general consumers.

Recruitment and managerial assistance is also an important function of local partners. The local labor market may be very different from Taiwan's. Thus, selection and management of local workers may be hindered by informational barriers which make assistance from local partners very useful. In Taiwan, selection of management staff is often based on educational status. Educational status provides important information on an applicant's aptitude and capability. Taiwan's well-developed vocational education system prepares a pool of skilled labor resources for Taiwan's small- and medium-sized firms (Lin 1994). In most Southeast Asian countries, vocational education is largely neglected. Higher education is highly selective, but the quality of students is hard to ascertain. Given this background, recruitment can hardly be done without the assistance of local experts. Jedel and Kujawa (1976) also reported that most foreign subsidiaries in the US had considerable autonomy from their parent firms in terms of employment decisions.

Although local partners are expected to perform many different functions, there are only a few cases in the survey in which Taiwanese firms noted that they want technical support from their local partners. In other words, Taiwanese firms generally believe they have the technological superiority and are prepared to capitalize on its value in overseas production. Local partners are sought to provide other functions to make this aspiration a reality.

5.4 Relations with Local Chinese Communities

In all the countries that we studied, ethnic Chinese form a non-negligible portion of the local society. With the probable exception of Vietnam, Chinese business groups also dominate the local economy. The degree of assimilation of ethnic Chinese into local society varies. In Thailand, it is very difficult to distinguish ethnic Chinese from indigenous Thai. In Malaysia, Chinese are distinctive from Bumiputras and ethnic Indians. Nonetheless, cultural and linguistic proximity bring Taiwanese firms into contact with local Chinese at various fronts of business functions.

In general, we found that the business culture embraced by overseas Chinese in Southeast Asia is very different from that embraced by Taiwanese businesspeople in spite of the fact that they share commonalities in other aspects of general culture. At the risk of oversimplifying, we may say that Taiwanese business culture is embedded in 'industrial capitalism' which characterizes the postwar economic development of Taiwan, while the business culture of overseas Chinese is only beginning to be affected by this set of ideas. In 'industrial capitalism', technological innovation underlies the structural change of industries, where human skills and ingenuity are the most valuable assets. Capital deepening is a necessary condition for enhancing the labor productivity on which economic growth depends, but not a sufficient one (Fei 1989). Private firms, as production units in industrial capitalism, derive their strength from an organizational structure that encompasses such human skills and ingenuity. This strength, together with an interfirm network consisting of many small operators, accounts for Taiwan's success in industrialization. Capital is fungible and can be employed at a market cost.

Taiwan's industrial capitalism carries a special flavor, as it is seasoned by the international division of labor and disciplined by the forces of global markets. This comes from its long history of export-oriented economic development. Taiwanese investors are interested in establishing a lasting organization which combines productive resources to make competitive products. This organization enables them to continue to serve their customers in third-party markets even if they move to a foreign location.

Overseas Chinese merchants, on the other hand, mostly still operate under a 'refugee mentality'. Their business aim is to accumulate personal wealth, particularly in the form of tangible assets. They are keen on keeping their portfolio highly liquid, so that they can move their wealth away from hazardous locations with ease. As Suehiro (1991, p. 10) said of Chinese conglomerates in Thailand, they are: (1) a closed system dominated by family members; (2) reluctant to invest in risky manufacturing ventures, preferring to invest in projects with a short investment horizon, looking to recover capital investment in three to four years; (3) inclined to move profits overseas rather than reinvest them; and (4) inclined to invest in building relations with politicians in order to protect personal security and wealth or to seek privileges from such relations.

The first characteristic may be intrinsic to Chinese culture. The second and third characteristics are conditioned by the 'refugee mentality'. The fourth characteristic is a survival strategy conditioned by local politics. Since many overseas Chinese thrive in economies where political power interferes with market forces, they value political privilege more than market competitiveness. They would rather devote resources to rent-seeking activities than development of human resources within the firm. If they need certain skills to perform specific functions, they usually hire the talent from abroad. In short, they place little value on organizational strength.

Due to these sharp differences in managerial philosophy, co-management of the joint-venture business is a rare undertaking if Taiwanese firms hold the majority of equity shares. If Taiwanese investors hold a minority equity share, expatriate managers from Taiwan usually take charge of the production sector and probably participate in financial decisions, allowing local partners to make the decisions in the other areas. In the case of minority Taiwanese-owned subsidiaries, contributions of Taiwanese investors are normally in the area of technology. These ventures are usually capital-intensive and engage in mass production. They are usually geared toward the local market which is the domain of local Chinese. It is interesting to note that minority Taiwanese-owned subsidiaries usually hire more expatriate technicians from Taiwan than majority Taiwanese-owned subsidiaries, because the former are less willing to invest in training. On the other hand, minority Taiwanese-owned subsidiaries are more likely to purchase brand-new and advanced machinery, whereas majority Taiwanese-owned subsidiaries may even use second-hand machinery from Taiwan for production.

In general, Taiwanese investors refrain from entering sectors in which local Chinese businessmen possess vested interests. Businesses owned by local Chinese in Southeast Asia are primarily domestic-market-oriented, while Taiwanese investors are mainly export-oriented. Taiwan's domestic industry is characterized by a dichotomized structure where large firms dominate the domestic market and small- and medium-sized firms prevail in the export markets (Chou 1988). We have observed that Taiwan's small- and medium-sized firms have little trouble joining local industries in Southeast Asia because they present no conflict of interests with local Chinese-owned businesses. Export-oriented Taiwanese firms are inclined to maintain a wholly owned equity structure (see Table 5.2a). In comparison, Taiwan's large firms face significantly higher entry barriers when they try to establish overseas subsidiaries in Southeast Asia because they pose a greater threat to local establishments. Entry barriers are even higher in industries whose products are consumed locally than those for which products are indirectly exported. For example, large Taiwanese investors are visible in the production of synthetic fiber, yarn, and fabrics throughout Southeast Asia, but they are relatively scarce in the area of consumer electronics and food products. Local-market-oriented Taiwanese investors usually prefer to establish a joint venture with local Chinese interests and allow local partners to assume the leading role in marketing. This arrangement avoids direct confrontation with local rival groups.

Consciousness of the domain of local Chinese interests has led to a symbiotic structure between Taiwanese investors and local Chinese businesses. In the area of low-technology end products such as apparel and footwear, for example, we have observed that Taiwanese subsidiaries concentrate on export markets and refrain from entering the domestic market which is the domain of local Chinese interests. In the upstream industries, such as yarn, fabrics, and shoe-making materials, Taiwanese subsidiaries take advantage of the booming local markets to establish local operations. They sell to downstream users, many of which are Taiwanese subsidiaries. Their products present little threat to local competitors because local competition is either in a different class of production or simply nonexistent. For example, fabrics used in local clothing may be different from those used in apparel destined for the US and European market.

In the case of high-technology products aimed at local consumers, overseas

Chinese conglomerates usually prefer working with internationally renowned multinationals. Taiwanese firms have little chance of penetrating this field. Therefore, despite the formidable economic power possessed by Southeast Asian Chinese, Taiwanese producers of consumer electronics, motorcycles, or even food products fail to penetrate Southeast Asian markets by linking to this power house.

In fact, overseas Chinese identify themselves with the regions of China from which they came. Major points of origin of overseas Chinese include Canton, Fujian, Teochew, and Hainan. Different groups cluster in different regions of Southeast Asia. Overseas Chinese conglomerates in Thailand are mainly from Teochew and Hainan,[2] those in Malaysia came mainly from Canton and Fujian, and those in Indonesia came mainly from Fujian. Overseas Chinese networks are mainly united by commonality of homeland (*tong-shian*). Taiwanese investors are perceived by overseas Chinese as new immigrants from a new location which is only semi-Chinese. Taiwanese investors maintain some distance from all major groups of overseas Chinese, but are closer to Fujianese than others because they share common dialects.[3] Clusters of Fujianese ethnics, like Penang in Malaysia, attract more Taiwanese FDI than other parts of the region. Taiwanese expatriates in Southeast Asia prefer sending their children to local American schools over Chinese schools. They also have recently established their own schools (normally called Taipei schools) in Kuala Lumpur, Penang, Bangkok, and Jakarta to retain educational links with Taiwan.

Most overseas Chinese in Southeast Asia speak multiple dialects and encounter no communication barriers in dealing with Taiwanese investors, but inherent suspicion often clouds their business relationships. Taiwanese investors complain about rip-offs by local Chinese on land deeds, and registration of company licenses and trademarks. Disputes in land transactions are particularly commonplace because Taiwanese firms often acquire land using local Chinese as dummy owners when there are restrictions on foreigners' land ownership. Some also engage in property speculation through this route. Meanwhile, local Chinese often complain about their Taiwanese partners' overvaluation of used machinery when it is used as part of capital contribution to a joint-venture company.

Taiwanese firms also complain about the local Chinese merchants' opportunistic approach to business relationships. This reminds us of Western multinationals' complaints about Taiwanese suppliers in earlier years. Local Chinese merchants are perceived to adopt a 'hit-and-run' strategy of maximizing the opportunity wherever it arises, and being uninterested in developing a long-term working relationship with Taiwanese firms. Many Taiwanese subsidiaries choose to internalize the production of components and parts which they normally contract out in Taiwan because of the frustration of dealing with local Chinese merchants. As suppliers, local

Chinese merchants are considered to be lacking in quality consistency; as customers, they are considered to be lacking in loyalty. Many of these problems arise because local Chinese merchants are unaccustomed to export business or because of their dominance in the domestic market.

The indisputable contribution of local Chinese communities to Taiwanese subsidiaries is in the supply of managerial staff. Traditional Chinese value the merits of education. Relatively well-educated ethnic Chinese form the backbone of the management team of virtually every Taiwanese subsidiary in Southeast Asia. Cultural proximity plays an important role here, in the sense that it reduces the training costs and communication barriers. Almost every Taiwanese investor in our survey relied on local Chinese interpreters as his/her communication bridge in the early stages of operation. Many of the managerial staff of Taiwanese subsidiaries had even received higher education in Taiwan. Easy-to-train ethnic Chinese local staff members are not only good substitutes for expatriate managers from Taiwan, but also serve as good conduits for technology transfer to indigenous workers.[4] An important reason that Malaysia attracts the largest investment from Taiwan among Southeast Asian countries is its sizable Chinese labor force. Throughout our interviews, we have heard many complaints about local Chinese merchants as business counterparts, but few complaints about local Chinese staff, except for their high turnover rates.

In our survey questions, we asked Taiwanese investors about the roles of local Chinese in their offshore operations. The results are summarized in Table 5.6. It can be seen that providing information is most frequently mentioned by all firms alike. This is followed by offering managerial assistance and helping building relations with local government, with small- and medium-sized firms ranking the former ahead of the latter, and large firms vice versa. This suggests that ethnically Chinese local staff are valued more by small- and medium-sized firms than by large firms. Smaller firms are less capable of dispatching expatriate managers from Taiwan because they are short of such managerial resources. And even if they do, high costs of expatriates are burdensome for the small-scale operations. To retain their advantage of production flexibility, small- and medium-sized firms need staff members who are adaptive, responsive, and compatible with the personalized style of management that most Taiwanese firms adopt. Only local Chinese workers conform to these qualifications.

In addition to managerial staff, local Chinese accountants are also in high demand. Many small- and medium-sized firms like to keep accounting books in two languages, Chinese in addition to the local language. Some also like to maintain two versions of accounting - one for tax officials, and one for shareholders.

Also frequently mentioned are roles played by local ethnic Chinese in serving as partners, helping to establish marketing channels, and helping with customer relations. At least one-quarter of the sampled firms recognized contributions by local Chinese in these areas. In contrast to the aforementioned contributions, local Chinese are only sporadically mentioned as helping to supply raw materials, serving as subcontractors, or providing finance. This suggests that Taiwanese firms only occasionally try to build their overseas networks among local Chinese communities. More often, they utilize local Chinese connections to link up to local government, local consumers, and local supporting firms. In short, local Chinese help reduce the problems of being foreign to local society and accelerate the pace of localization. But Taiwanese firms do not form an enclave within local Chinese communities.

Table 5.6 Roles of Local Chinese (by number of firms)

Role	Small firms	Large firms
Providing information	33	35
Serving as managerial staff	31	21
Helping establish marketing channels	20	16
Supplying materials	7	8
Providing financial support	8	8
Serving as partners	20	17
Building relations with the government	25	28
Helping establish subcontracting network	5	3
Building relations with customers	14	17
Others	1	2
No role whatsoever	3	4
Sample size	56	51

Note: Choices are multiple.

Source: This study.

5.5 Labor Relations

Taiwanese firms are used to harmonious labor relations. Strikes and other forms of labor disputes are rare among Taiwan's small- and medium-sized firms. Taiwanese owners and managers build friendship with their workers. They motivate workers to work overtime by this friendship when they have to meet extra demand or tight shipping schedules. This working relationship is pivotal to the flexibility of Taiwan's small- and medium-sized firms (Seetoo 1994). Many owners of Taiwan's small- and medium-sized firms were blue-collar workers when they were young. They made their way to ownership of a firm basically by hard work. This type of owner, known as 'dirty-hand' bosses in Taiwan, treat their workers more like family members than subordinates. They are used to the managerial style of leading by actions. They themselves are the hardest workers of the whole company and often expect their workers to behave the same way. This group of owners are particularly frustrated when they find it difficult to motivate their workers by either pecuniary or non-pecuniary incentives. They are surprised by some Southeast Asian workers' reluctance to work overtime even if they are paid two or three times more than their regular wages. Unlike in Taiwan, where overtime work is an adjustment mechanism to accommodate demand fluctuations, overtime work in some Southeast Asian countries needs to be planned and scheduled well ahead of the time of implementation; otherwise it is unacceptable to local workers. This, of course, reduces flexibility. Where possible, such as in the apparel industry, Taiwanese firms pay their workers by job accomplishment rather than by hours. This reduces the likelihood of job shirking and improves labor productivity. In this case, workers usually end up earning higher wages per hour compared to their counterparts in rival firms.

Taiwan's small- and medium-sized firms are not used to unionization. They lack the experience in collective bargaining. Labor strikes in countries like the Philippines and Indonesia have scared away many Taiwanese investors. Since labor supply in the strike-prone countries is normally in surplus, Taiwanese firms have learned to pay high wages to accommodate workers' demands, but ask for high work intensity in return. This combination helps weed out unproductive and irritating workers. High work intensity requires stringent discipline which, however, needs to be implemented with extreme care. Any perceived mistreatment of local workers may incite nationalistic sentiment against foreign owners. When a labor movement is tinted with nationalism, the labor relationship is doomed to fail. Taiwanese managers approach local workers with an extraordinarily low profile. The president of a computer firm in Malaysia said that he invited the union representatives to the best restaurant in town to introduce himself when he first took over the position. Most of these representatives had never been to this prestigious restaurant before and were undoubtedly appreciative of the favor. To support his demand that workers report to work on time, he regularly arrives at the workplace one hour earlier than his workers.[5]

Strikes do arise, but are usually short-lived among Taiwanese firms. The reason is that union representatives can negotiate directly with the owners who can make spontaneous decisions at the negotiation table. Union leaders know that the offer made on the table is enforceable, so negotiations usually proceed with efficiency. If the owners or their surrogates threaten to close down the operations, the threat is also credible.

One thing that sets Taiwanese investors apart from local firms is their egalitarian approach to colleagues. It is common to observe Taiwanese owners and expatriate managers eating together with local workers in the factory dining hall. In cases where meals are not served at the factory, Taiwanese firms usually provide facilities for dining. Some also provide dormitories for their workers. Breaking down class distinctions within the firm by Taiwanese investors contributes to harmonious labor relations. One Taiwanese owner said that he equipped each of his Indonesian salespeople with a sedan while he himself drove a pickup truck to work.[6] Highly motivated salespersons work hard and respect their boss. Most interviewees reflected that the key to a successful labor relationship is fairness. They concluded that the friendship approach may not always work in Southeast Asia, but setting clear-cut rules and faithful implementation of such rules can go a long way. In order to enhance labor productivity, some undesirable working habits among local workers have to be broken. In such cases, local staff play an instrumental role in enforcing the change. They need to be converted first. Taiwanese firms usually send their local staff to Taiwan for training, through which they understand why some changes in working habits are crucial for productivity enhancement.

Then, the carrot and the stick are mixed to gradually induce the change in working habits. Unlike the approach adopted by many Taiwanese subsidiaries in China, conducting military-type exercises to increase workers' inclination to accept discipline was unheard of in Southeast Asia. There was an apparent awareness of the danger of xenophobia. Enforcing discipline through local staff, with pre-enforcement consensus building, is a safe way to achieve the goal of reform without provoking nationalistic sentiment.

Although job-hopping is a common problem, Taiwanese firms' investment in staff training does not seem to be discouraged. After all, there is no alternative. Some firms indicated that they did examine the aptitude of potential trainees when selecting workers for training at the parent firm. The selection takes the probability of job-hopping into account. Capable and ambitious workers were sometimes encouraged to establish their own businesses and become subcontractors of Taiwanese firms to avoid loss of firm-specific know-how to competitors. Through financial and technological support provided by Taiwanese owners, these employees-turned-subcontractors usually become strong supporters of Taiwanese firms. Some anecdotal cases indicate that firms which acquire skilled labor by bidding away workers from their competitors instead of training are prone to failure.

5.6 The Image of Taiwanese Investors

Most local people are impressed by the industriousness and dedication to work of Taiwanese investors. Generally speaking, there are two types of investors: small- and medium-sized firms where the owner (or one of the owners) or a member of his family, usually a son or son-in law, is in charge of the overseas operation; and large firms where one of the most capable, well-rounded high-level managers is in charge.

Owners who moved to Southeast Asia in person were usually in their 40s and 50s, and had started their businesses in the 1970s in Taiwan and became well established by the mid-1980s. At that point in time, there was a sudden change of macroeconomic conditions in Taiwan - the Taiwanese currency appreciated rapidly and wage rates rose dramatically. The competitiveness of their products was eroded and they were forced to move operations to Southeast Asia to regain their competitive edge. For them, FDI is the second chance to start a new business. They approach it in the old-fashioned hard-working way. The only difference this time is that they have a substantial amount of capital at their disposal.

Owners of small- and medium-sized firms who are too old to go abroad in person usually send one of their sons or sons-in-law. If the home operations remain in place, FDI is tantamount to a pluralization of the family business where brothers may compete for their father's recognition or for a strategic position in the family business. The second-generation owners, although inexperienced in establishing a new business, are usually compensated with a high level of education, sometimes in Western countries. They are equipped with modern technology or management know-how. In their overseas venture, they are often accompanied by an older manager entrusted by the first-generation owners to ensure a successful transfer of firm-specific advantage. Having their apparent bequest at stake, these second-generation owners usually work hard.

Large-firm managers who are dispatched to establish subsidiaries are the cream of the company's staff. They are usually promoted to the presidency of the subsidiary from the lower ranks in the parent firm. They are delegated substantial authority over local operations to ensure accountability. These expatriate managers are usually young, energetic, and aggressive. They are eager to succeed once they obtain the opportunity to be their own boss. Partially due to their appreciation of the owner's vote of confidence, partially due to their personal drive for excellence, these overseas chiefs will demonstrate nothing but dedication.

Unlike expatriate managers of giant Western multinationals who are dispatched overseas to manage a firm, Taiwanese expatriate managers are dispatched to create a firm from scratch. Resources at the disposal of Taiwanese managers are much more limited. It is common for Western managers to stay and work in classy tourist hotels while monitoring the construction of factories (even after the commencement of operations). This practice is almost unheard of among Taiwanese expatriate managers. They stay in rented apartments (houses) and work in temporary offices to prepare for the commencement of operations. Many Taiwanese firms commence operations using rented factories while their own factories are under construction. These pilot runs are used for recruiting and training workers. Although expatriates are paid bonuses for working abroad, their workload is often twice as heavy as that of their home counterparts, especially during the early stage of overseas operations. Once they succeed in setting up an overseas subsidiary, expatriate managers tend to stay on the job, being rewarded with equity shares in the company. They may also extend their domain of influence by engineering new investments into neighboring countries.

When we asked the investors to evaluate themselves, aggressiveness stands out as the characteristic which draws the highest degree of consensus. Table 5.7 lists various statements with which we asked investors to express their degree of concurrence. A Likert scale was assigned to their answers: those who strongly agree with the statement are assigned a value of six, those who agree with the statement, five, those who somewhat agree, four, somewhat disagree, three, disagree, two, and strongly disagree, one. Table 5.7 shows the average Likert value of each statement. It can be seen that all statements got responses between 'somewhat agree' and 'agree'. The statement that Taiwanese investors are aggressive earns the highest degree of agreement, however. This indicates that working hard toward their goals is a principle to which most Taiwanese investors subscribe.

Table 5.7 Taiwanese Investors' Own Assessment (unit: Likert scale)

Statement	Large firms	Small firms
Concerned about workers' well-being	4.4	4.5
Emphasizing safety in workplace	4.5	4.5
Active in public and community affairs	4.1	4.0
Producing good-quality products	4.7	4.7
Aggressive and hard-working	4.9	5.1
Introducing new products regularly	4.4	4.2
Having a globalized business view	4.6	4.4
Having an excellent management system	4.5	4.8
Having strong R&D capability	4.6	4.5
Having excellent after-sales services	4.3	4.4
Having relatively few cases of labor disputes	4.4	4.4

Source: This study.

Taiwanese investors and their expatriate managers not only work hard themselves, but they also demand that their workers work hard. They have to do so because they often strive to earn a thin profit margin in the competitive export market. If they fail to achieve a high level of productivity, the profit margin can easily turn negative. Local ethnic Chinese conglomerates in Southeast Asia who are used to abnormal profits in protected domestic markets dubbed Taiwanese managers as '*gen-cho*', a Fujian-dialect phrase meaning 'working for the sake of work (not for money)'. Because of the pressure to enhance labor productivity, Taiwanese managers push workers harder than their local counterparts. Naturally, they also pay higher wages than their competitors.

The second common image of Taiwanese firms is that they are invisible. Taiwanese firms are among the largest group of investors in Vietnam, Malaysia, Thailand, and Indonesia. Except for Vietnam, in which some billboards advertising Taiwanese food products and motorcycles are visible in the nation's capital, Taiwanese firms are mostly unknown to the general public in host countries. This is because Taiwanese firms are mostly export-oriented and produce under OEM (original equipment manufacturer) arrangements rather than their own brand names. Therefore they remain anonymous in the host country even if they are famous among OEM buyers. For example, in Thailand, Cal-Comp is the largest exporter of the whole nation, specializing in calculators, but few people in Thailand know that the Casio, or Citizen, calculators they bought may be products of this Taiwanese subsidiary located outside Bangkok. In Indonesia, Pochen is the largest manufacturer of sports shoes for Nike, making 45 000 pairs of shoes per month and employing some 8000 workers, but the name Pochen is equally unknown in Indonesia. A few of Taiwan's largest electronics firms operate in Malaysia, but few people know that ACER Peripheral Co. in Penang produced more monitors than its parent firm in Taiwan, just as many overseas Japanese subsidiaries do with TV sets and air conditioners.

Anonymity has advantages and disadvantages. One of the major advantages is the avoidance of exposure when the firm runs into trouble with labor. Lack of publicity enables the firm to solve the labor dispute quietly without inflaming public opinions. In a country like Thailand where unionization is normally orchestrated by union movement activists outside the firm, anonymity also makes Taiwanese firms less likely to be targeted. The major disadvantage of anonymity for a firm is the difficulty of getting government attention when it needs administrative assistance. Taiwanese firms seek to overcome this disadvantage by building personal relations with government officials, particularly with local government officials. They regularly contribute to charity, but they do not want that fact to be publicized because publicity may draw too many requests for donations to be accommodated by their small capacity. They like to work things out without public attention because they lack the celebrity status to tilt public opinion in their favor. Although some Taiwanese tourists like to show off their wealth in Southeast Asia (and often end up in misery), Taiwanese manufacturers usually hide their wealth. Their lack of a nationally known name is often offset by intimate relations with local government and community officials. Some Taiwanese subsidiaries located in remote rural areas provide electricity and water free of charge to their neighborhood for public relations reasons. It is also common for them to donate to military establishments nearby or to the police department in their jurisdiction.

The third common image of Taiwanese investors is their speedy assimilation to local society. This is particularly true among owners who directly manage the overseas operations. Sometimes, Taiwanese owners are eager to be naturalized in order to share privileges reserved for citizens, such as land ownership. Aside from state-sanctioned privileges, assimilation brings other economic benefits. First, it is conducive to good labor relations and may even reduce the labor cost. One naturalized Taiwanese investor in Thailand said workers demanded lower wages when he became a Thai.[7] That foreign firms pay higher wages seems to be a rule in developing countries. Second, as described in Chapter 3, assimilation is part of the localization process of Taiwanese firms. Assimilation helps break down the barriers to local networks, including the ethnic Chinese network.

As expatriate managers of Western multinationals come and go, Taiwanese owners of small- and medium-sized firms usually stay permanently in the host country. They may send their children to Taiwan or Western countries for education, but they themselves do everything to integrate with the local society. This behavior resembles that of older Chinese immigrants. If these small- and medium-sized firms do not maintain sizable operations in Taiwan, their FDI is tantamount to industrial migration, whereby both the capital and its owner will be absorbed by the host country.

5.7 Concluding Remarks

Taiwan's small- and medium-sized firms excel in exploiting linkages to offset their organizational weakness. Once they go abroad, they also strive to build up local linkages, but with only limited success. In the end, their overseas operations are usually much more integrated than their operations at home.

One factor that limits their local linkage is the difficulty of getting established in the local ethnic Chinese networks. This is partly due to the differences in business culture which underline different market orientations, and partly due to lack of personal trust between the two groups. In the end, Taiwan's small- and medium-sized firms benefit more from local ethnically Chinese individuals than from established local Chinese business groups. In fact, Taiwanese firms consciously refrain from intruding on the patch of local Chinese businesses, namely their vested interests in the domestic market.

Since most small- and medium-sized firms are export-oriented and engage in stiff price competition, labor is their bread and butter. Taiwanese firms are keen on maintaining good labor relations and maximizing labor productivity. Their low-profile approach to labor disputes shortens the duration of confrontations with labor. Nonetheless, they are often defeated by labor strikes since they are under tremendous time pressure to export goods.

Taiwanese owners and expatriate managers treat their overseas investment project as a personal endeavor to establish a new business. They work with extreme industriousness and aggressiveness. Taiwanese firms are keen on establishing and maintaining harmonious relations with labor while trying to squeeze labor productivity to the maximum. They use high wages, fringe benefits and, above all, friendship and care to win the loyalty of labor. Their flexible production depends upon workers' willingness to work flexibly. They usually rearrange production processes and job assignments to enhance labor productivity. Sometimes, discipline is used to reinforce the effort and they are generally successful in this regard.

Notes

1. Buckley, Newbould and Thurwell (1988) found similar phenomena in British small firms' overseas investment. Among 43 small firms they surveyed, only 15 at any stage considered an alternative country to the one in which they in fact established production subsidiaries.
2. According to Suehiro (1991, p. 36), out of 25 major business conglomerates in Thailand, 23 are owned by Chinese families. In terms of their origins, 13 came from Teochew, two from Hainan, two from Fujian, one is Hakka, and five are unknown.
3. For example, in Malaysia, Penang receives the largest number of Taiwanese investors because Fujianese form the majority of local residents. Even in Klang Valley, Taiwanese firms prefer to locate in areas close to Fujianese communities. The inclination is particularly obvious among small firms.
4. Enos, Lall and Yun (1996) reports similar findings among the banking industry where overseas Chinese banks in Singapore, Hong Kong and Taiwan are more effective than Western banks in transferring software technologies to Chinese-owned banks in Southeast Asia.
5. Interviews in Penang, Malaysia, 17 August 1994.
6. Interviews in Bandung, Indonesia, 19 September 1994.
7. Interviews in Bangkok, Thailand, 18 January 1995.

6. Taiwanese Investment in Indonesia

Mari Pangestu

6.1 Introduction

Taiwanese investment has been important in Indonesia and has increasingly become so in the last few years since the relocations undertaken by Taiwanese firms in order to stay competitive in the face of appreciation of the NT (Taiwanese currency) and rising costs, especially labor costs. By late 1989, the NT had appreciated by more than 40 percent from its 1985 level and during the 1985–91 period wages valued in US dollars almost tripled in Taiwan. Furthermore, foreign investments from Taiwan have increased since 1986 when foreign exchange controls were abolished by the ROC government in recognition of Taiwanese firms' need to relocate. The main difference between Taiwanese investment and investments from the other major investors, such as Japan, the US and some of the European countries, is that most of Taiwan's overseas investments are undertaken by small- and medium-sized firms.

In theory, a firm will undertake foreign direct investment if it possesses some firm-specific intangible asset. It is hypothesized that the intangible asset of small- and medium-sized Taiwanese firms is their ability to conduct small-scale, flexible production. In their home country, Taiwan, these firms could afford to specialize and do so efficiently since there is a network of such specialized producers. What happens when they invest overseas? How do they maintain their intangible firm-specific assets? Another advantage of Taiwanese investment is their know-how in production and marketing of mass-produced items (see Hayashida 1993). Why does this advantage matter in Taiwan's FDI?

A Taiwanese firm investing overseas can maintain its advantage by keeping a close connection with the existing network in Taiwan as well as internationally. All it is doing is relocating all or part of its production (and related services) to the host country. It will in turn export from the new location back to the home country or directly to third markets. This could lead to trade between host and home country, both in terms of exports and imports.

To the extent that there is direct exporting to third markets from Indonesia, it should also promote trade to third-country markets. The technology used is often the same or similar to that used originally in the home country. There is less linkage to the local economy in this case.

Alternatively the overseas subsidiaries establish a similar network in the host country, possibly with other Taiwanese firms with which they had alliances in the home country or with local firms. The overseas subsidiaries may provide technical assistance and even capital to the local firms. Furthermore, the technology used is often adapted to local conditions. The employment and domestic investment effects could also be larger since there are presumably more linkages to the local economy.

In reality the situation will be somewhere in-between, and the trade, technology, employment and linkage effects are likely to differ depending on the characteristics of the investing firm (large, medium or small), nature of the product, structure of the market and whether they are export- or domestic-oriented.

The aim of this chapter is to analyze the characteristics of Taiwanese investments and their postulated effects on Indonesia. The methodology adopted was to conduct a survey based on questionnaires as well as interviews with Taiwanese investors in the manufacturing sector.

6.2 Background and Overview

6.2.1 Policy Environment

The policy environment faced by firms in Indonesia has undergone substantial changes in the last 25 years (see Table 6.1). In the first two decades of its independence under President Sukarno (1949–66), the Indonesian economy was characterized by a growing inward orientation and state control. The economy stagnated, and in 1966 inflation reached 660 percent per annum. The New Order Government that came into power in 1966 restored macroeconomic stability and altered the course of the economy from state control to a greater reliance on market forces. Dramatic changes were introduced in the trade and incentive regime and a more favorable stance adopted towards private investment, including foreign investment, rehabilitated the economy.

During the oil boom years of the 1970s, the economy became dominated by oil to such an extent that during the peak year of 1980–81, oil and LNG (liquified natural gas) accounted for 75 percent of export earnings and 70 percent of budget revenues. Indonesia also followed an import substitution industrialization strategy which included state participation, especially in the basic industries. The incentive regime became progressively inward-oriented and complex in nature, imparting a substantial anti-export bias and a distorted

Table 6.1 Changes in Indonesian Policy Direction and External Conditions

Period	Changes in external environment	Macroeconomic policy	Trade and industrial policy	Ownership
1958–65 Guided Economy		Growing instability ending with hyperinflation; foreign exchange control	Strongly inward-oriented	Nationalization; state-dominated economy; strict control over private domestic and foreign investment
1967–73 New Order Rehabilitation & Stabilization		Successful stabilization; open capital account	Moderately outward-oriented (beginning of import substitution policy)	Liberalization of domestic and foreign investments; some rationalization of state-owned enterprises (SOEs)
1974–81 Oil Boom	Sharp increase in oil prices 1973, and non-oil commodity boom 1975–79; second oil price increase 1979	Maintenance of macroeconomic stability, although some inflation from lack of sterilization of oil rev.	Growing inward orientation (increasing import substitution)	Increasing share of public investment and SOEs; growing restrictions on foreign and domestic investments
1982–85 First External Shock	Decline in oil prices; decline in primary commodity prices	Macroeconomic stabilization: fiscal austerity, devaluation and tight monetary policy	Strongly inward-oriented: proliferation of non-tariff barriers	Continued reliance on SOEs and regulation of market economy
1986–88 Second External Shock	Sharp decline in oil prices and continued decline in primary commodity prices; yen appreciation: shock on external debt	Continued macroeconomic stabilization: devaluation, tight monetary policy and balanced budget	Shift to outward oriented economy	Deregulation of customs and imports; relaxation of foreign and domestic investment regulations; reduced reliance on SOEs and public investment
1988–now Non-Oil-Led Recovery	Stable oil prices; further decline in primary commodity prices	Maintenance of macroeconomic stability	Further shift to outward-oriented economy	Deregulation extended to investment, finance, maritime and other areas; initial steps towards SOE reform; substantial relaxation of foreign investment restraints

Source: Update of Table 3 in Bhattacharya and Pangestu (1993).

incentive structure. The distortions in the trade regime were reinforced by growing controls on investment and finance, in the form of investment licensing and restrictions, as well as credit allocation at subsidized interest rates.

At the same time, spending of oil revenues led to high domestic inflation, averaging 20 percent per annum and leading to a substantial real exchange rate appreciation (that is, the Dutch Disease). To offset the adverse effects of the Dutch Disease and encourage non-oil exports, the rupiah (Indonesian currency) was devalued by 50 percent in November 1978; a duty drawback system (*Sertifikat Ekspor*) was also introduced in 1978;[1] and a subsidized export credit scheme implemented in 1982. Textile and garment exporters were the main beneficiaries of the duty drawback scheme, and exports of these two products increased rapidly in 1978 and even more so after 1982. The export surge after the 1978 devaluation proved to be short-lived due to the subsequent inflation after the second oil price increase in 1979.

Import substitution industrialization which was followed up to the early 1980s led to rapid industrial growth and the structural transformation of the economy. The share of manufacturing increased from 7 percent to 13 percent of GDP and manufactured exports grew at an average rate of 14 percent per annum during the 1969–80 period.

There was also rapid structural change within the manufacturing sector as the share of output of the more labor-intensive and light consumer goods industries, such as the food and textile industries, declined in relative importance, while the more capital-intensive and intermediate goods industries, such as the chemicals and the basic metals industries, and the capital goods industries, such as the metal goods industries, gained in relative importance.

Unlike the other East Asian economies, Indonesia is a late starter in adopting an outward-oriented policy. The oil windfall and large domestic market allowed Indonesia to follow an import substitution strategy for longer than most countries in the region. The Indonesian government was only forced to embark on adjustment and reform measures in response to major external shocks during the 1982–88 period. The shocks were caused by the fall in the price of oil and other primary commodities in 1982, the steep decline in oil prices in 1986, and the rapid depreciation of the US dollar *vis-à-vis* other major currencies in 1985, which led to a substantial increase in its debt service.

Appropriate macroeconomic stabilization measures undertaken included two large devaluations (amounting to 50 percent in rupiah terms) in March 1983 and September 1986; a reduction of the fiscal deficit through expenditure cuts; and a prudent monetary policy. Furthermore, since 1988 the government has also maintained the competitiveness of the real effective exchange rates by a combination of keeping inflation low and continuously depreciating the rupiah against the US dollar. This has been recognized as an important factor for pushing exports. At the same time, the government initiated structural reforms in a number of areas, including comprehensive financial and tax reforms, and made major efficiency improvements in customs, ports, and shipping.

More substantial outward-oriented reforms were only introduced in 1986 after the rapid decline in the price of oil and the sharp appreciation of the Japanese yen. The reforms were aimed at stimulating non-oil exports and investment by reducing trade restrictions and other regulations that have led to a 'high-cost' economy. The main reforms undertaken were: (a) simplification of the cumbersome investment licensing system, especially for export-oriented investments; (b) a series of trade reform packages to replace non-tariff barriers with tariffs as well as a reduction in tariffs; (c) financial sector deregulation that built on the 1983 reforms by reducing entry barriers and increasing competitive pressure; and (d) deregulation in other bottleneck areas such as the maritime sector.

As a result of these comprehensive measures, the economy recovered with growth averaging 6.8 percent annually in the 1988–94 period, while non-oil exports, especially manufactured exports, rose rapidly. Export growth has led to continued strong growth of the manufacturing sector which averaged 11 percent annually during the 1986–90 period and at close to 10 percent during the 1990s. The manufacturing sector comprised 21 percent of GDP in 1993, making Indonesia a semi-industrialized economy.

6.2.2 Foreign Investment Policy

Right after independence, in the old order period under Sukarno, the economy became increasingly guided by the state and there were strict controls over private domestic and foreign investment. There was a strong sense of nationalism rooted in anti-colonial and anti-Chinese sentiment. Dutch enterprises were nationalized as state enterprises.

Indonesian policy towards foreign investment has shifted like a pendulum from being liberal to being restrictive, depending on external conditions as well as availability of resources to undertake development since then (see Table 6.1). The latter has been influenced by the size of government oil revenues as well as the size of foreign investment inflows themselves. Nationalist sentiments have also influenced foreign investment policy.

In the rehabilitation period at the beginning of the new order period under Suharto, one of the earliest reforms undertaken was to adopt an open-door policy towards foreign investment (Foreign Investment Law 1967) in an attempt to get the economy back on track. It was recognized that Indonesia needed foreign capital and technology for economic development. However, nationalistic tendencies still prevailed and a divestment requirement for transfer of ownership from the foreign owners to Indonesian ownership was introduced in the 1967 Foreign Investment Law. In the 1967–74 period, the law was interpreted liberally in the sense that 100 percent foreign ownership was allowed and the divestment requirement was not quantified or made mandatory.

Foreign investment increased substantially in these early years, much of it going to import substitution manufacturing such as textiles, consumer electronics, food and beverages, chemicals and pharmaceuticals. Japanese investments dominated in the manufacturing sector and led to a backlash in the anti-Tanaka riots of 1974. After this incident foreign investment policy became increasingly restrictive, especially given the fact that these were also the oil boom years so the government had plentiful resources to undertake development on its own and the share of public investment and state-owned enterprises in the economy became more significant. Divestment requirements were mandated whereby transfer of ownership to Indonesian majority had to take place within ten years, 100 percent foreign ownership was no longer allowed, and a complicated system of priority investment listing was introduced. Foreign investment deregulation did not take place until 1985, with relaxation of ownership and equity restrictions being linked to non-oil export orientation. This is of course in line with the growing outward-oriented adjustment and reform process in the wake of falling oil prices. Since then the foreign investment restrictions have been gradually relaxed. First during the 1986–87 period the allowable level of foreign ownership was increased up to 95 percent for export-oriented projects and extension of the divestment period to 15 years. Then in 1989 the complex priority list was replaced by a negative list, 100 percent foreign ownership was allowed in Batam, a duty-free zone located near Singapore, and the minimum capital requirement for certain industries was lowered from US$1 million to US$250 000.

Major deregulation, however, began in 1992, culminating in the June 1994 deregulation package. In 1992, 100 percent foreign ownership was allowed for investments greater than US$50 million or located in Eastern Indonesia, and foreign divestment was not required for some types of investment. In 1993, 100 percent foreign ownership was allowed for investments in export-bonded zones and for investments with a minimum paid-up capital of US$2 million and in supporting industries. The divestment requirement became stricter again, although the period of divestment was extended to 20 years.

It was only in June 1994 that most of the restrictions on foreign investment were removed. The rationale for the most recent deregulation has been increased competition from China and a realization that restrictions and divestment requirements did not automatically bring more benefits and effective Indonesian participation. In fact it discouraged technology transfer and some types of investments.

The main foreign investment policy changes in the June 1994 package were: equity restrictions are only in place for public sectors opened for foreign investment; 100 percent foreign ownership is allowed with the requirement that some (not mandated) divestment is to take place after 15 years; joint ventures are no longer required to undertake divestment; the minimum capital requirement of US$1 million (US$250 000 for some service sectors) was eliminated; and the nine public goods sectors such as electricity, that were previously closed, are now open to foreign investment.

6.2.3 Role of Foreign Investment in the Economy

The 1967 Law Concerning Foreign Investment reflected the view that the role of foreign investment was to supplement domestic investment or capital and that foreign participation would be phased out, by including the requirement that foreign investors must allow for national participation within a certain period of time. This is the main reason for earlier policies which closed sectors to foreign investment, and set various equity restrictions and divestment requirements. Up to the more recent deregulation Indonesia has thus had an ambivalent attitude towards foreign investment, on the one hand welcoming it and on the other requiring Indonesianization of a majority of those investments.

Nevertheless growth of foreign investment has been quite rapid, although by most estimates the contribution of foreign investment to capital and exports has not been significant (see Hill 1988; Thee and Pangestu 1998). Due to the abundance of oil revenues and official capital flows, the share of foreign direct investment in net capital inflows based on balance of payments data is not large (see Table 6.2). Approved foreign investment is lower than approved domestic investment, but then the latter has a lower realization rate so that the difference may not be as large as indicated by approved data. Based on balance of payments data, it can be seen that around US$2 billion of the almost US$5 billion net capital inflows are sourced from foreign investment. The role of foreign direct investment and the role of other capital flows from borrowing and other portfolio investment have been increasing, while the role of official capital flows has declined as the amount of new borrowing has remained around the same in the last few years while amortization has continued to go up.

Based on data from the Central Bureau of Statistics' (BPS) Survey of Industries, a rough indication can be obtained about the role of foreign investment in contributing to value-added production in the manufacturing industry (see Table 6.3). As of 1991, for example, foreign investors are important in beverages, footwear, chemicals, basic metals, and precision instruments. 'Important' is defined as comprising 40 percent or more of the share of value-added production in the sector.

Foreign investment has only recently begun to contribute to exports. The main investors in the major non-oil export products, such as textiles, garments, and plywood and wood products, are mainly domestic. For instance in 1991, foreign investors accounted for 24 percent of value-added production in

Table 6.2 Development of Investment Approvals and Capital Flows, 1980–94 (US$ million)

			Net capital		
	Domestic investment approvals	Foreign investment approvals	Foreign direct investment	Official capital flows	Other capital flows
1980	4 493	1 074	140	2 069	184
1981	3 626	707	142	2 712	207
1982	5 471	2 417	311	4 085	162
1983	7 124	2 471	193	4 783	998
1984	2 056	1 097	245	2 227	254
1985	3 363	853	299	1 788	273
1986	3 438	847	252	3 343	980
1987	6 356	1 520	544	1 526	1 165
1988	8 423	4 411	585	2 825	(796)
1989	11 070	4 714	722	1 830	(147)
1990	30 662	8 751	1 424	924	4 432
1991	21 066	8 778	1 531	1 418	2 602
1992	14 454	10 323	1 705	915	2 579
1993	18 976	8 144	1 971	1 063	2 677
1994	24 551	23 700	n.a.	n.a.	n.a.

Sources: Approved investment data are from the Board of Investment (BKPM), and balance of payments data are from the Annex to the President's Independence Day Speech, various years.

textiles, 15 percent of value-added production in garments, and 9 percent of value-added production in wood and wood products. It is also estimated that in 1991, 30 percent of textile exports, 20 percent of garment exports, and 12 percent of wood and wood product exports are accounted for by foreign investors. There are several sectors where the contribution of foreign investors to exports is estimated to be above 40 percent; they are food products, footwear, publishing and printing, plastic and non-mineral products, metal products, non-electrical machinery, electrical machinery, precision equipment and transportation equipment. None of these product groups are major contributors to non-oil exports as yet; however two product groups, footwear (that is, mainly sports shoes) and electrical machinery (that is, consumer

Table 6.3 Share of Value-Added Production in Industry by Ownership, 1985–91 (%)

	1985			1991		
	Government	Foreign	Domestic	Government	Foreign	Domestic
311 Food processing	38	9	54	28	8	64
312 Other foods	18	25	57	9	31	60
313 Beverages	0	72	29	0	57	44
314 Tobacco	0	7	93	0	4	95
321 Textiles	10	32	59	5	25	70
322 Garments	1	3	96	0	15	85
323 Leather and products	5	30	65	8	8	84
324 Footwear	0	63	37	0	39	61
331 Wood, rattan and bamboo products	15	13	72	2	9	89
332 Household appliances from wood	0	6	94	1	15	83
341 Paper and paper products	33	12	55	22	34	44
342 Publishing and printing	11	4	84	20	2	78
351 Chemicals	70	17	14	43	39	17
352 Chemical products	4	40	56	5	32	63
354 Petroleum and coal products	0	23	77			
355 Rubber products	10	10	80	25	27	48
356 Plastic products	0	58	42	1	11	88
361 Ceramic, porcelain, clay and other products	1	5	94	1	26	73
362 Glass and products	4	81	15	8	0	92
363 Cement and related products	34	34	33	57	19	24
364 Clay products	7	11	82	5	0	95
369 Other non-mineral products	7	0	93	2	5	92
371 Basic steel and iron	72	19	9	53	15	32
372 Basic metals	0				45	55
381 Metal products	10	27	62	4	28	66
382 Machinery, except electric	35	39	26	21	29	49
383 Electric machinery	11	43	46	12	33	47
384 Transportation equipment	13	20	67	5	33	61
385 Precision instruments	0	33	67	0	40	60
390 Others	3	41	56	0	35	65

Source: Central Bureau of Statistics, *Annual Industrial Survey*, several years.

electronics and telecommunication equipment such as hand sets), are experiencing rapid growth.

6.2.4 Taiwanese Investment in Indonesia

A general picture of foreign investment in Indonesia, highlighting the role of Taiwanese investment, can be obtained from published data sources. The main source of published data on foreign investment is the Indonesian Board of Investment (BKPM). The main deficiency of the data is that most are based on approved investment rather than realized investment. It should be noted that data from the Board of Investment also do not include foreign investment in the oil and financial services sectors. Careful interpretation of the data is needed due to the level of aggregation and the fact that it is based on approved investment. Another data source is the list of Taiwanese firms collected by the Taipei Economic and Trade Office (TETO) in Indonesia.[2] At best the following general tendencies can be observed from existing published sources.[3]

As indicated above, Indonesia began to relax its foreign investment policy in the mid-1980s as part of its overall policy adjustment and reform process in the wake of falling oil prices. The strongly outward-oriented policy and more conducive investment policy environment succeeded in pulling a significant amount of investment into the Indonesian economy beginning in the late 1980s. Approved foreign investments jumped from under US$1 billion prior to 1986, to US$4.7 billion in 1989 and US$10 billion in 1992. A record of US$23 billion in approved investment was reached in 1994. The rising amount of approved foreign investments can be attributed to the substantial relaxation of foreign investment restrictions and a number of large projects in infrastructure, petrochemicals, paper and pulp, and oil refining.

The improved investment climate in Indonesia since the mid-1980s coincided with the timing of push factors that led to a large outflow of Taiwanese investments after the liberalization of Taiwan's capital outflows policy in 1986. The appreciation of the Taiwanese NT, rising labor costs, increased trade friction with the major trading partners, and facilitation in the form of liberalization of capital outflows contributed to the growth in Taiwanese investments overseas. Of course previous controls on foreign exchange meant that many Taiwanese firms probably invested overseas in Indonesia and other Southeast Asian countries, but not openly, and so were often registered as domestic investment (Thee 1991, p. 61).

The coincidence in timing of push and pull factors explains a large part of the story of the strong growth of Taiwanese investment in Indonesia. Since the 1965 aborted communist coup in Indonesia, Chinese schools and literature have been banned. There were also restrictions on entry and stringent visa requirements for visitors from Taiwan and China. For instance, entry had to be through Jakarta and no other entry point. However, the Indonesian government has relaxed some of these policies in order to encourage foreign investments from capital-rich countries such as Taiwan. The Taiwanese have been allowed to set up a Chinese school for their nationals.

Most Taiwanese investments came after 1988. Based on data recorded by the Taipei Economic and Trade Office, only a few firms are recorded as being established before 1988, one of the biggest ones being the joint venture P.T. Indah Kiat Pulp and Paper Corp. (in which the Taiwanese are a minority partner).

Since 1988 a large number of Taiwanese firms have been recorded by the Taipei Economic and Trade Office. The main industries are: textiles, synthetic yarn, textile chemicals, garments, sports shoes, rattan and wood products and furniture, shrimp hatcheries, feed production and farming, food processing (for instance, canned mushrooms and tuna, canned pineapples), some electrical goods (white goods such as air conditioners, fans) and consumer electronics, and miscellaneous light manufacturing (for instance, umbrellas, toys, plastic housewares, bicycles).

As Thee (1991) noted, Taiwanese investment in Indonesia has risen significantly only since 1988. Based on Board of Investment data, approved foreign investments from Taiwan to Indonesia have fluctuated since 1989, but have continued to be relatively high. In fact approved investment from Taiwan is often higher than that from the US and Europe. In 1994, due to a slowdown in overall Japanese investments to all countries, approved Taiwanese investment was even higher than approved Japanese investments. Approved foreign investment from Taiwan, along with approved investments from the other Asian Newly Industrialized Economies (ANIEs) such as Hong Kong, South Korea and Singapore, are clearly important for Indonesia. As a group the ANIEs and Japan are the dominant investors compared with the other major investors from the US and Europe. It should be borne in mind that the approved data from the Board of Investment exclude the oil and financial services sector. When one includes those two sectors, US investments would also be large.

Another observation that can be made is that the average size (as measured by value of investment divided by the number of projects) of approved foreign investment from Taiwan is smaller than the investment from Korea, Japan and other major investor countries (see Table 6.4).

Table 6.4 provides a comparison of approved and realized foreign investment by investor country. On a cumulative basis approved Taiwanese investment amounted to US$6.5 billion in 1994 or 7.1 percent of total approved foreign investment. However, realized Taiwanese investments accounted for US$0.8 billion or 2.9 percent of realized investments.

Realized investments from Taiwan comprise only 12.2 percent of approved investments compared with the average realization rate of 30 percent and much higher rates of realization for other countries. Only South Korea has a lower

Table 6.4 Approved and Realized Foreign Investment by Source Country

	Approved 1967–94*				Realized 1967–94*				
	Number of projects	Value (US$'000)	Value/ project	Share of total value (%)	Number of projects	Value (US$'000)	Value/ project	Share of total value (%)	Realization rate (%)
USA	172	4 555.4	26.5	5.0	119	2 290.4	19.2	8.3	50.3
Europe									
Switzerland	45	643.3	14.3	0.7	21	165.8	7.9	0.6	25.8
Holland	116	2 760.5	23.8	3.0	58	1 466.8	25.3	5.3	53.1
UK	144	5 635.2	39.1	6.1	86	1 346.8	15.7	4.9	23.9
West Germany	65	2 025.1	31.2	2.2	44	504.0	11.5	1.8	24.9
France	39	466.5	12.0	0.5	25	336.2	13.4	1.2	72.1
Asia									
Japan	642	15 487.8	24.1	16.9	458	8 914.8	19.5	32.3	57.6
South Korea	289	11 983.9	41.5	13.1	155	846.9	5.5	3.1	7.1
Hong Kong	314	5 376.6	17.1	5.9	197	3 105.4	15.8	11.2	57.8
Taiwan	309	6 561.2	21.2	7.1	116	803.4	6.9	2.9	12.2
Singapore	325	5 352.6	16.5	5.8	110	1 153.0	10.5	4.2	21.5
Others	427	6 190.6	14.5	6.7	224	3 404.1	15.2	12.3	55.0
Joint countries	205	24 746.6	120.7	27.0	91	3 268.9	35.9	11.8	13.2
Total	3 092	91 785.3	29.7	100.0	1 704	27 606.5	16.2	100.0	30.1

Note: * Up to October 1994; cumulative value is the addition of new investment, expansion and change of status.

Source: Board of Investment (BKPM).

realization rate. These figures need careful interpretation, however. The lower realization rate is most likely due to the fact that a large sum of the approved Taiwanese investment, over one third, occurred in 1994 and thus a lower realization rate is recorded given the lag between approval and realization. The smaller size of Taiwanese investments is also once again evident from the lower than average size of Taiwanese approved and realized value per project.

Some rough indication of employment generated from foreign investments by source countries can be observed in Table 6.5. Taiwanese investment is estimated to contribute close to 200 000 jobs for Indonesians based on approved investments up to 1994, or 12 percent of total employment generated from approved foreign investment up to that point. On a realized basis, the number of jobs created from Taiwanese investment is slightly more than 10 percent, at 23 527 workers or 4.6 percent of total employment generated from the realization of foreign investment.

Based on approved investment data, there is some rough indication that Taiwanese investments tend to be more labor-intensive. The average number of workers per planned project is 644, which is higher than the average for all investments and higher than US and Japanese investment. The value of capital invested per worker is also lower in the case of Taiwanese investment compared with other countries; only investment from Hong Kong has a much lower value. However, when one looks at realized numbers, the number of workers per project in the case of Taiwan is in fact lower than the average and lower than most other countries. Since there is a lag between approved and realized investment, the tentative conclusion one reaches is that the more recently approved projects tend to be larger or more labor-intensive. In terms of value of capital invested per worker, the realized value for Taiwan is also lower than for all other major investors, except for South Korea. These figures of course only provide a very rough picture of tendencies; a better picture can be obtained if a sectoral breakdown can be provided, since labor use and size of investments will vary across sectors also.

Table 6.6 provides data, by source country, on the number of projects that are export-oriented, defined to be projects wherein 65 percent or more of the production is exported. The value of planned exports is also provided. It is clear that a majority, 91 percent, of approved Taiwanese investment is export-oriented. Only South Korea has a higher percentage, with 99 percent of projects being export-oriented. Once again careful interpretation is needed since the main reason for a lower percentage of Japanese approved investments that are export-oriented is that Japanese investments have been coming to Indonesia since the early 1970s, when a large number of the investments were for import substitution purposes. The higher export orientation ratio for the newer investors such as South Korea and Taiwan is not surprising since most of the new projects are export-oriented, strongly motivated by the need for low-cost labor in order to stay competitive. It is

Table 6.5 Approved and Realized Workforce Employed by Foreign Investor (persons)

	Approved 1967–94*			Realized 1967–94*			
	Workforce Indonesian	Workforce foreign	% share in total (Indon.)	Workforce Indonesian	Workforce foreign	% share in total (Indon.)	% realized out of approved (Indon.)
USA	65 331	2 048	4.0	38 683	1 117	7.6	59.2
Europe							
Switzerland	8 389	480	0.5	2 542	386	0.5	30.3
Holland	55 834	1 159	3.4	13 486	317	2.6	24.2
UK	95 260	1 593	5.8	30 941	491	6.1	32.5
West Germany	17 920	615	1.1	11 082	243	2.2	61.8
France	9 050	437	0.6	3 470	200	0.7	38.3
Asia							
Japan	254 917	7 534	15.5	129 511	2 641	25.4	50.8
South Korea	294 022	5 432	17.9	70 803	1 096	13.9	24.1
Hong Kong	281 342	6 777	17.2	72 867	1 375	14.3	25.9
Taiwan	199 007	5 492	12.1	23 527	511	4.6	11.8
Singapore	107 338	4 308	6.5	21 883	427	4.3	20.4
Others	126 768	4 982	7.7	61 156	1 000	12.0	48.2
Joint countries	124 606	4 170	7.6	29 490	550	5.8	23.7
Total	1 639 784	45 027	100.0	509 441	10 354	100.0	31.1

Note: * Up to October 1994; cumulative workforce calculated from new investment, expansion and change of status.

Source: Board of Investment (BKPM).

*Table 6.6 Approved Foreign Investment by Export Orientation and Planned Exports, 1967–94**

	Number of projects	Number of export-oriented projects	Share of export-oriented projects (%)	Planned export value (US$ mil.)	Share in total planned exports (%)
USA	172	82	47.7	2 782.8	6.5
Europe					
Switzerland	45	27	60.0	208.5	0.5
Holland	116	56	48.3	677.5	1.6
UK	144	58	40.3	4 209.8	9.8
West Germany	65	47	72.3	382.5	0.9
France	39	17	43.6	223.6	0.5
Asia					
Japan	642	424	66.0	7 295.2	17.0
South Korea	289	287	99.3	4 939.3	11.5
Hong Kong	314	179	57.0	6 166.3	14.4
Taiwan	309	282	91.3	4 912.5	11.5
Singapore	325	200	61.5	2 882.5	6.7
Others	427	200	46.8	2 701.3	6.3
Joint countries	205	117	57.1	5 415.4	12.7
Total	3 092	1 976	63.9	42 797.2	100.0

Note: * Up to October 1994; cumulative value is the addition of new investment, expansion and change in status.

Source: Board of Investment (BKPM).

quite likely that if one isolates investments from most of the major investor countries, especially from Asia, for the years since the late 1980s, a higher export orientation ratio would be found. As of 1994, planned exports from foreign investment amounted to US$43 billion or almost double the value of non-oil exports at that time. Even if a 30 percent realization rate is applied, the amount would still be large at US$14.3 billion or around 50 percent of total non-oil exports. The high export orientation of Taiwanese investments also means that its share out of total planned exports is relatively high, at 11.5 percent, compared with its share of total approved investments of 7 percent.

The export orientation of Taiwanese investments is not surprising as they have the firm-specific advantage of business relations with buyers in developed-country markets. When they relocated, this advantage was brought by the owners and senior management to Indonesia.

Based on approved investment data, Taiwanese investment is concentrated in a few subsectors: manufacturing, coal mining, and transport. Given that Taiwan does not have much in the way of natural resources, an important motivation of Taiwanese investment is to secure raw material supply; hence its large investments in coal mining. Other motives for Taiwanese investments are to raise the parent firms' profitability by exploring host-country markets and to facilitate exports from Indonesia. Taiwanese investments that came to Indonesia prior to 1989 were mostly export-oriented ones, with only a few for import substitution.

6.2.5 Objectives of Study and Methodology

As outlined in the introductory chapter, the objective of this study is to analyze the characteristics of Taiwanese investment in Southeast Asia and to postulate its impact on the local economy.

Primary data collected in Indonesia are in the form of questionnaires sent to Taiwanese subsidiaries. The number of respondents amounted to 49, including questionnaires filled in by parent companies in Taiwan about their subsidiaries in Indonesia. The survey was carried out during September to October of 1994. A sample of the firms filling in the questionnaire was interviewed in the host countries and in some cases the interview was also conducted by the Taiwanese researchers with the parent company in Taiwan.[4] The interviews were undertaken to gain additional insights beyond what was obtainable from the questionnaire.

The results of the survey and interviews are analyzed below, first with regard to the motivations and determinants of Taiwanese FDI, and second with respect to the postulated effects of Taiwanese FDI on the local economy. The chapter concludes with a presentation of the major conclusions arising out of the analysis and the main policy implications.

The questionnaire is provided in the Appendix. The definition of small and large firms is based on employment, with small firms being defined as firms employing fewer than 300 persons, and the definition of an export-oriented firm is that exports comprise 60 percent or more of its sales; the remaining firms are considered to be selling mainly to the domestic market.

6.3 Motivation and Determinants of Taiwan's FDI

The main motivation of all interviewed firms for investing in Indonesia was to take advantage of low labor costs (84 percent) and to expand sales in local or third-country markets (63 percent). The low cost of labor was much more important for large firms compared with small firms, while the market motivation was more important for small firms compared with large firms.

Appreciation of the NT was next in importance (47 percent), with a similar degree of importance for both small and large firms. Around 20–30 percent of respondents, both small and large firms, were also motivated by the low cost of land, securing raw material supply, avoiding trade restrictions, and the low cost of energy and water resources. The other factors were not considered important by all firms, although a larger number of small firms than of large firms invested to avoid environmental regulations, to undertake joint actions with other firms, or to collect market information.

Not surprisingly the two main reasons that stand out for the choice of Indonesia for investment location rather than the other Southeast Asian countries are the good potential of the local market (56 percent) and cheap labor (73 percent). Indonesia has the largest population and potential market size in the region and, other than Vietnam, it also has the lowest labor cost at present (Table 6.7).

The only other significant reason is good personal connections through familiarity with local entrepreneurs and people. The interviews reveal that the local network built up by Taiwanese investors often relates to past business relations as a supplier or in some cases as a technical consultant. This finding is consistent with the observation made by Thee (1991, p. 60) that 'the presence in Indonesia of a large Chinese business community obviously facilitated the establishment of trade and investment links between the Chinese NICs and Indonesia'.

The other factors identified that could influence the decision to invest in Indonesia compared with other countries in Southeast Asia were not thought to be important by the respondents. Only 35 percent thought that Indonesia fared better relatively in terms of political stability; the percentage was much higher in other countries. Furthermore only 25 percent chose Indonesia because of its favorable status for exporting to third-party countries, for instance to utilize GSP status, textile quotas and so on. Most of the Taiwanese firms (83 percent of the sample) also did not invest in other Southeast Asian countries once they invested in Indonesia. This is another distinguishing

Table 6.7 Firms' Reasons for Choosing to Invest in Indonesia rather than Other Southeast Asian Countries (by number of firms)

	Small firms	Large firms	Total
Also invest in other Southeast Asian countries	6 (23.1)	2 (9.1)	8 (16.7)
Cheap labor	17 (65.4)	18 (81.8)	35 (72.9)
Political stability	8 (30.8)	9 (40.9)	17 (35.4)
Good infrastructure	3 (11.5)	4 (18.2)	7 (14.6)
Sound legal framework and commercial practices	1 (3.8)	0 (0.0)	1 (2.1)
Racial homogeneity	1 (3.8)	0 (0.0)	1 (2.1)
Good supporting industries	2 (7.7)	4 (18.2)	6 (12.5)
Good potential for local market	19 (73.1)	8 (36.4)	27 (56.3)
Have familiar entrepreneurs or people	10 (38.5)	12 (54.5)	22 (45.8)
High level of education	0 (0.0)	0 (0.0)	0 (0.0)
Attractive fiscal incentives	3 (11.5)	2 (9.1)	5 (10.4)
Favorable status for exporting to third-party countries	6 (23.1)	6 (27.3)	12 (25.0)
Little government intervention	3 (11.5)	3 (13.6)	6 (12.5)
Others	1 (3.8)	3 (13.6)	4 (8.3)
Sample size	26 (100.0)	22 (100.0)	48 (100.0)

Note: Figures in parentheses are percentages.

Source: This study.

feature of Taiwanese investments. Since most of the investments are by small- and medium-sized companies and not part of a large multinational network, typical outward investments from Taiwan only go to one location. Only the very few big firms have more than one subsidiary in Southeast Asia. Unlike Japanese investment, the formation of a regional production network is not important for Taiwanese investors.

Relatively few respondents (around 10 percent) identified good infrastructure, good supporting industries, attractive fiscal incentives and little government intervention as the reason they chose Indonesia. This reveals the inherent barriers in Indonesia to increasing investment and growth, namely the physical infrastructure bottlenecks and the lack of an intermediate and capital goods industry that can provide quality inputs in a timely way. Indonesia stopped providing tax holidays in 1984 and the only fiscal incentive the foreign investor gets is duty-free imports of machinery and equipment at the beginning of the investment, and duty-free imports of inputs used in export production. Other than that, there are no fiscal incentives and the government is unlikely to provide such incentives given the philosophy of a neutral tax system. However, recently the government has reduced the overall corporate tax rate by 5 percent in recognition of the lower corporate tax rates in countries that are competing for investments with Indonesia. Moreover, government bureaucracy and red tape is still considered a major obstacle to investing in Indonesia.

The final set of factors are those that were identified by none or very few respondents as being influential in their decision to invest in Indonesia, in other words, these factors are considered to be weak in Indonesia. They are sound legal framework and commercial practices, racial homogeneity, and a high level of education. The lack of a sound legal framework has been identified by many investors as a major problem, as is not being able to enforce contracts or seek compensation or judgment if one is wronged. This increases the cost of transactions and is a big contributor to the so-called high-cost economy. Racial homogeneity is a problem that Taiwanese investors in particular are sensitive about because in Indonesia there are periodic tensions between the local Chinese, who dominate in business although they are a minority in the population, and the indigenous people. In particular, Taiwanese investors are affected by one vestige left over from the days when Indonesia was overtly suspicious of anything Chinese. The use of Chinese language characters has been banned in Indonesia and this poses a practical problem for Taiwanese investors who get a lot of literature, market information, and other communications in Chinese characters.

6.4 Nature and Characteristics of Taiwan's FDI

6.4.1 Firm Characteristics

Substantial outward Taiwanese FDI really only began in 1986 when capital outflows were liberalized. Indonesia's foreign investment climate improved around the same time, as discussed above. Thus, unlike Japanese investments, which began in the early 1970s in the import substitution phase of Indonesia's import substitution industrialization, Taiwanese investment is a much more recent phenomenon and also tends to be much smaller than Japanese investments.[5]

Most (90 percent) of the firms in the survey were set up in the last six years, from 1986 onwards. There was also a difference in date of establishment between small and large firms, with a predominance of small firms (83 percent) being established since 1990 compared with a lower percentage for large firms (43 percent). This indicates that some small firms followed large firms in making FDI. The smaller firms followed the larger firms, either because of some relationship back in Taiwan or because of Taiwanese technicians-turned-entrepreneurs setting up their own companies when they saw the opportunities created by the FDI of large firms.

Another characteristic of Taiwanese firms is that 60 percent are majority-owned by Taiwanese, that is with half or more of the shares being Taiwanese, and the average amount of Taiwanese ownership being 71 percent. A larger percentage of the small firms are majority Taiwanese-owned (88 percent) compared with large firms (73 percent). In most of the interviewed cases, the main partners of Taiwanese-invested firms are local firms or individual persons that the owner had past business relations with.

The main industries in which the surveyed firms were involved were textiles (10 firms); electrical and electronic machinery (8 firms); clothing and accessories (5 firms); wood products, bamboo products and other non-metallic furniture (5 firms); paper and paper products (5 firms); and chemical materials (4 firms). There are also more small firms (26) than large firms (23) in the sample. There are more small firms than large firms in the paper and paper products, chemical materials, fabricated metal products, electrical and electronic machinery, and repair of transport equipment sectors.

Another interesting observation is that the export orientation of Taiwanese investment varies between sectors, with almost all or most of the firms surveyed in the clothing, wood and wood products (mainly furniture), and electronic and electrical machinery products (mainly electrical goods and appliances, not consumer or industrial electronics) industries being export-oriented. The rest, such as textiles, paper and paper products, chemicals and plastic products, tend to be oriented to the domestic market. Of course some are indirect exporters, since their products are processed or used to produce a final product that is exported, such as in the case of textiles and chemicals (many are chemicals related to the textile industry).

Most of the firms (79 percent) have a parent company in Taiwan. However, the insights obtained from the interview case studies reveal that except for the large companies, the parent company in Taiwan is usually a small office to ensure a continued presence in Taiwan which undertakes the market intelligence and sometimes the trading function. Normally there are very few production activities remaining in Taiwan. With the exception of the large firms, there is almost a total relocation of production activities.

About half of the firms investing in Indonesia invest less than US$3 million in terms of stored-up capital (that is, this does not include the borrowed component). Interestingly, there are eight which have a capital of less than US$1 million, indicating the response to Indonesia's relaxation of foreign investment policy made in 1989. There are only seven firms or 15 percent of firms with a registered capital of US$10 million or more. As for sales, 55 percent of firms have sales of less than US$5 million, while quite a high percentage, or 35 percent, have sales of more than US$10 million.

6.4.2 Decision-Making Process

The influence of the parent company on the decision-making process for the various decisions such as finance, marketing, production, personnel and R&D reveal the expected pattern. A significant proportion of important decisions related to finance (57.8 percent), marketing (42 percent) and R&D (50 percent) are made by the parent company or by expatriate managers with regular influence from the parent company. The remaining decisions are made by the expatriate managers independently; a small number or around one quarter of the decisions are made by the local managers independently. The pattern is expected to change in five years, with less parent company influence, but the continuing importance of expatriate managers with and without consultations with the parent company. The role of local managers making independent decisions is still limited to around one quarter, with only the share of decision making by expatriate managers expected to increase in the next five years.

There is much more independence from the parent company in decision making involving production and personnel, with most of the decision making being done by expatriate managers independently. Furthermore, independent decision making by local managers in these two areas is expected to increase significantly in the next five years.

Interestingly enough, there is a major difference between the pattern for small and large firms. For decision making in finance, marketing, and R&D, there appears to be more influence by the parent company directly or through expatriate managers for small firms than for large firms. But the role of expatriate managers in general is much higher in small firms than in large firms.

6.4.3 Marketing Channels

Most of the marketing of products is undertaken by the subsidiaries themselves (71.4 percent). Only 20 percent is done through the parent company. The same situation prevails between small and large firms. This indicates that the Taiwanese subsidiaries are independent from the parent company with regard to marketing, with the independence being slightly greater for small firms than for large firms. The observation that marketing is done through the local subsidiaries themselves can be contrasted to Japanese or even Korean investments from large companies whose marketing is often done through the parent company or related trading house. It appears that Taiwanese firms' specific advantage of marketing know-how and access to foreign markets is also relocated to the subsidiary and is often embodied in the owner or senior manager who relocates with the company.

6.5 Effects of Taiwanese Investment on the Local Economy

6.5.1 Exports

The contribution of Taiwanese investments to Indonesia's manufactured exports appears not to be strong. Out of the firms interviewed, slightly more than half (51 percent) sell to the local market and 39 percent export to third-country markets, with the rest (less than 10 percent) to the parent company and other firms in Taiwan. However, large firms are much more export-oriented, with close to 60 percent of their sales destined for third-country markets, compared with 21 percent for small firms. Small firms are much more oriented to selling in the domestic market, although their products may be indirectly exported.

As noted above, export orientation varies with industry, with export orientation being dominant in clothing, furniture, and electrical products. Other industries such as textiles and textile chemicals are indirect exporters, whereas investments in paper and paper products are targeted at the domestic market (partly for domestic use and partly to be used for packaging destined for export). Therefore, Taiwanese investments do play a role in providing intermediate goods and supporting inputs to be used for export of other finished goods.

The following analysis of other aspects of the contribution of Taiwanese investments to the Indonesian economy will also discuss the particular role of export- versus domestic-oriented firms.

6.5.2 Employment

Given that large firms are more export-oriented and the definition of large is employing 300 persons or more, then it can be expected that export-oriented firms create more employment. Of course, this division is in some sense artificial because the non-export-oriented firms are usually indirect exporters, and could very well also contribute to employment generation.

The number of employees of the firms surveyed ranges from 25 to 8600 for mid-1994. About 18 percent of the firms employed fewer than 100 persons, while another 18 percent employed more than 1000 persons. The bulk, or 40 percent, of the firms surveyed employed between 100 and 300 persons.

On average, Taiwanese subsidiaries employ 742 workers, 66 percent of whom are unskilled workers and 25 percent are skilled workers. The remaining employees are made up of the staff and R&D personnel, and the number of the latter is still very low at 1.2 percent of the average number of employees.

6.5.3 Linkages with the Local Economy

One of the main advantages of foreign investment as viewed from the host-country perspective is the extent to which the foreign investment creates spillovers in terms of linkages to the local economy through purchase of inputs and capital equipment. It is well known that often the foreign investor will provide technical assistance, quality control, training, and sometimes even credit, to develop their network of suppliers. This is to be seen as mutually beneficial both for the foreign investor and the local supplier. Having a reliable and high-quality network of suppliers is an important source of competitive advantage.

Sourcing of components and parts from local sources accounts for 40 percent of the purchases of small firms and 46 percent of the purchases of large firms. This is surprising because large firms tend to be more export-oriented and past studies find that export-oriented firms tend to source more from imports because of their need for international quality inputs and because they can get duty exemptions for their imported inputs. The explanation probably lies in the types of industries in which the large export-oriented firms are involved. If they are in paper and pulp, and furniture, then clearly most of the inputs come from domestic sources. Export-oriented firms may also be under more pressure to buy locally because they need to be cost-competitive.

Imports from third countries account for roughly 20 percent of components and parts, whereas around 40 percent is sourced from Taiwan through other suppliers in Taiwan and the parent company. The proportion of imports from Taiwan is slightly larger for small firms. This observation provides some support for the idea that there is increased economic integration between the East Asian countries, or in this case between Taiwan and Indonesia, whereby relocation has also spurred increased trade to the extent that these subsidiaries import their components and parts from Taiwan.

As for sourcing of machinery and equipment, a much higher percentage is imported. This is expected, given that the capital goods industry in Indonesia still suffers from many weaknesses, especially lack of technological capability.

On average, imports accounted for 92 percent of machinery and equipment with the largest source being suppliers in Taiwan. Small firms rely more on imports of machinery and equipment from Taiwan than large firms which tend to import more from third countries. A relatively small percentage, 16 percent, reported that their machinery and equipment consisted of old machinery being relocated from the parent company. This should allay some of the usual fears about the transfer of obsolete equipment and technology which are inappropriate and therefore not efficient and, worse still, use of which could be more environmentally damaging.

Insights from interviews suggest that for some industries where indigenous technological capability is high, such as in furniture making, a great deal of subcontracting goes on. The investors indicated that Indonesian workers were found to be skilled craftsmen, although they lacked design and quality control capability. However, with training and technical assistance, in some cases former employees could be set up as subcontractors, and firms in wood- and rattan-based furniture making could subcontract to these local suppliers. In these cases there is linkage to the local economy as well as some degree of technology transfer.

6.5.4 Technology Transfer

The question of the degree of technology transfer by Taiwanese subsidiaries is of course very subjective and not based on quantitative measures, so it must be interpreted with care. Nevertheless a rough idea can be obtained from the data. In general there is a high degree of technology transfer from the parent company to the subsidiary (70 to 80 percent) with regard to the standard functions such as operation technology, maintenance of machinery and equipment, quality and process control. The degree of transfer does not differ between large and small firms, or between export- and domestic-oriented firms.

However, a lower percentage of technology transfer from parent to subsidiary was reported for more complicated tasks such as technological improvements, adoption of new technology, product design, product innovation, development of molds and tools, and design of machinery and equipment. The percentage of transfer with respect to adoption of new technologies, design of molds and tools, and design of machinery and equipment was higher for large and export-oriented firms than for small and domestic-oriented firms. This is of course a reflection of the greater technological capability of large firms compared with small firms, and that technological capability is seen as a source of competitive advantage in exporting.

However, the source of technology for new product innovation is still mainly the parent company (69 percent of total respondents), especially for small firms (84 percent of small-firm respondents), and domestic-oriented firms (81 percent of domestic-oriented-firm respondents). Compared with survey results for other countries, small Taiwanese firms in Indonesia rely abnormally heavily on parent firms for introducing new products, probably because they have only been established in Indonesia for a brief time. Other important new technology comes from firms undertaking their own R&D. This is much more important for large and export-oriented firms, indicating once again their greater technological capability. Only about one quarter of total respondents reported imitating other firms to get new technology. There was little difference between small and large firms with regard to this source of new product innovation, but this source was much more important for domestic-oriented than export-oriented firms. This simply means that in the export market, competitive advantage is not obtained by imitating other companies, but by finding some niche by introducing product differentiation. Hayashida (1993) found that the Taiwanese firms that were interviewed utilized mass production to reduce costs as one source of competitive advantage, but that when facing increased competition they focussed on improving their marketing capabilities through such efforts as product differentiation and improving the quality of the product.

6.5.5 Profitability and Financing

Based on the survey, the average time for capital recovery is 5.4 years, with a slightly shorter period for large firms (4.9 years) than for small firms (5.7 years). This is the opposite of the results for other countries and indicates that small firms face a bigger problem in offsetting the high cost of doing business in Indonesia. It could also be because small firms are more geared to selling in the domestic market and it is often said that selling domestically is more risky because one has to know the local market, where there are fluctuations in demand and one has to know the appropriate marketing approach. There is more certainty in the export market once one has a network with buyers or direct access to it.

Another interesting finding is that most of the firms in the survey (72 percent) retain their profits for reinvestment in the company, with a higher percentage for large firms than for small firms. Only 21 percent of profits are remitted back to Taiwan, and this percentage is much higher for small firms. This is slightly inconsistent with the earlier observation that small firms' owners tended to relocate physically with the company, which should mean that a higher degree of profits is retained by small firms. It should be noted that since Indonesia does not have any capital controls, the reinvestment and remittance decision is purely based on the firm's decisions and is not influenced by regulations. The high percentage of reinvestment is positive from the perspective of the host country. Another possible explanation for the high amount of profits retained for reinvestment is that many of the investments are new and only established in the last few years.

As for sources of finance, the main source of financing is local financial institutions and capital from the parent company. The percentage of financing by local financial institutions is the same for small and large firms, whereas the degree of reliance on capital from the parent company is larger for small firms than for large firms. While funding from local partners and offshore borrowing is not important, accounting for only 14 percent of funding, these sources were much more important for large firms, indicating the greater advantage of large firms in accessing offshore borrowing. This is a type of firm-specific advantage that is related to size. The observation that large firms obtain more capital from local partners than small firms could just reflect the fact that there are more large firms with a higher share of domestic ownership. The small firms tend to be almost all wholly owned by Taiwanese owners.

6.5.6 Comparison of Business Operations

One question in the survey asked the respondents to compare different aspects of their operations with a similar domestic firm and with other subsidiaries in advanced countries (as a proxy for the international benchmark). The respondents were asked to evaluate their firm's performance by indicating whether they thought that its performance with regard to that particular aspect was higher, the same, lower, or could not be determined, when compared with domestic firms and other subsidiaries.

Foreign investors are often thought to be more productive and technologically capable than local firms. Dahlman (1993) refers to this as the best practices of firms in the local economy and the farther away local firms are from this technological level, the less there is national technological capability in the host country. The result is likely to vary by industry or subsector, however. When compared with local firms, the respondents thought that they were more productive, had a higher or better capacity for quality control, a higher level of production technology, better after-sales service, a higher capacity for new product development, a higher capacity for technological innovation and improvement of existing technology, better internal management, product flexibility and company image, had a larger scale of production, and a higher degree of automation. However, they ranked themselves lower than domestic firms with regard to local purchasing, reflecting that lack of familiarity with the local economy is a disadvantage when operating abroad.

When compared with similar subsidiaries in advanced countries, or the international benchmark, the Taiwanese subsidiary mostly considered itself lower with respect to technology transfer to local firms, degree of joint research and development with local firms, and capital intensity. In turn they rated themselves higher or the same with regard to the proportion of unskilled labor employed, ratio of local procurement, job training and education of local employees, and ratio of exports to domestic sales.

6.5.7 Regulatory Framework

In addition to the deregulation and macroeconomic policies already discussed above, the Indonesian government has adopted a pragmatic approach in the last few years with regard to foreign investment and has also taken specific steps to encourage investments from ANIEs, including Taiwan. This is in sharp contrast to the pre-1980s period when nationalist sentiments were still strong and tended to lead to restrictive policies on foreign investment. A clear example of such new pragmatism in the case of Taiwanese investment is the waiving of the ban on the establishment of a Chinese language school for the children of Taiwanese investors and technical experts attached to joint ventures. Chinese language materials for the school and companies are also allowed. This is a remarkable step, given the sensitivities demonstrated by the ban on Chinese character publications and after the closing-down of Chinese schools in the aftermath of the 1965 communist coup. However, interviews reveal that despite the more open attitude towards publications in the Chinese language, Taiwanese investors still faced difficulties in clearing technical publications and information in the Chinese language. This is because these still have to pass the security clearance.

6.6 Conclusions and Policy Recommendations

The crucial question that this study hopes to answer is whether Taiwanese investments are different from other investments in some way which can confer both positive and negative effects on the Indonesian economy. If so, then what are the policy implications?

If we go back to the original hypothesis, then the study indicates that Taiwanese firms, which tend to be smaller than other foreign investments, have certain firm-specific advantages and disadvantages. The firm- or individual-specific advantage lies in their technical know-how in production and process, especially mass production, which can reduce costs substantially. A second source of firm- or individual-specific advantage is access to export markets. This type of advantage is in fact easily relocated because it is embodied in the company, its people, including the owner, and its reputation or brand. On the other hand, firm-specific and individual-specific disadvantage lies in not knowing the domestic market, and in regulatory obstacles such as the ban on majority foreign ownership in place until recently. Another disadvantage is that they have a less developed network of suppliers, and a less developed distribution and marketing network compared with the large multinationals. Often the subsidiary is the only one in Southeast Asia, which precludes the setting up of a production network with subsidiaries exchanging parts and components. This reduces the possibility of forging strategic alliances and strengthens the case for having well-established supporting industries since small firms are less able to access inputs through a network of subsidiaries and suppliers than are the large multinationals. By the same token, there is less chance for one investment to lead to other investments as their suppliers and related companies follow.

It would appear that, with smaller firms, there is a development of local networks so presumably there are more linkages with the domestic economy and greater enhancement of domestic technological capability, and eventually the creation of viable supporting industries in the host country.

Another possible advantage arising out of Taiwanese investments is that to the extent that they maintain their firm-specific advantage by setting up a local network and given that the firms tend to be SMEs so that their capital is limited, there is less likelihood of such companies being footloose. The small size and the fact that the move to Indonesia is almost a full relocation appears to have also led to a high degree of retention of profits for reinvestment purposes. It is also possible that the export-oriented firms that bring and create their networks can be a catalyst for local exports. The demonstration effect could become important as buyers follow their suppliers and begin not only to buy the products from Taiwanese firms, but also to purchase from the local suppliers or influence other buyers to purchase from these local suppliers.

From a regulation perspective, it is clear that Taiwanese investments did not take off until after the liberalization of capital flows in Taiwan in 1986. As already noted, this coincided with improvements in Indonesia's investment climate and various deregulation and reform measures to encourage and facilitate exports, reduce protection and go toward a more open and market-oriented economic system. However, lack of physical infrastructure, red tape, lack of a reliable legal system, and lack of high-quality human resources still stand out as factors that are not favorable for Indonesia. The policy recommendation is clear: remove the infrastructure bottlenecks, focus on education and human resource development, and reduce government intervention.

The surge in foreign investments, including those from Taiwan, has been due to the improved investment policies and stable macroeconomic conditions. The most recent spate of deregulation of foreign investment in Indonesia should encourage a greater flow of foreign investments. Removal of the equity restrictions and phasing out of divestment requirements is a step in the right direction in terms of recognizing that the importance of foreign investment is to enhance the technological capability of local firms as well as to benefit the national economy. It is hoped that the more open regime will mean that Indonesia will gain more benefits from foreign investment.

One should also be aware of the potential dangers of foreign investment in general, not just Taiwanese investment, with regard to environmental degradation. Appropriate government policy is needed to ensure that the regulations on waste control and disposal, emission requirements, and so on are met.

As was noted above, one of the most important potential benefits of Taiwanese investment is that there is a greater probability of the creation of a local network of suppliers. To the extent that Taiwanese firms tend to be small and medium, this could also encourage the development of Indonesian SMEs.

Notes

1. Essentially the drawback amounted to a subsidy because of the way the drawback was calculated, that is, based on averages, which meant that the drawback obtained was higher than the duty paid.
2. The office bases its records on voluntary reporting and through its network of Taiwan business clubs. However, a large number of Taiwanese firms probably go undetected. It is also possible that some come in as domestic investments, using the local partner's name.
3 It is possible to obtain more disaggregated investment data from the Board of Investment by requesting directly. For instance an attempt was made to try to get data on Taiwanese foreign investment by sector and for each sector by export orientation, and also to compare these with other source countries.
4. The questionnaires were sent by the Taiwan business club associations based in Jakarta, Bandung and Surabaya. It is not known how many were actually sent, but the number of completed questionnaires amounted to 49, although for some questions the sample is less, due to incomplete questionnaires. Twenty interviews were conducted in Jakarta, Bandung and Surabaya in a number of sectors.
5. Of course it is known that there were some Taiwanese investments in earlier periods, but they might have been registered as domestic investments.

7. Taiwanese Investment in Malaysia

Mohamed Ariff and Sor Tho Ng

7.1 Background and Overview

7.1.1 Policy Environment

Without a doubt, Malaysia owes much of its economic progress during the last three decades to the constructive role played by foreign direct investment (FDI). FDI has brought in capital, technology, marketing outlets and managerial expertise, with considerable positive externalities from which even local firms have gained significantly. In particular, Malaysia's export-oriented industrialization would not have been possible had it not been for FDI. Needless to say, all this could not have taken place in the absence of liberal policies towards foreign investment. Malaysia has long been actively seeking FDI for a variety of reasons, not to mention its long-cherished and time-honored open-economy traditions. Initially, the accent was on employment creation, and diversification of the economy. Subsequently, the focus has shifted to technological upgrading, skill development and export-led growth. Malaysia is no longer a labor-surplus economy. There is already an acute shortage of labor. The country's comparative advantage in unskilled labor-intensive activities is being eroded by rising wages. Hence the current emphasis is on technology and skill-intensive manufacturing. Such structural changes hinge critically on continued inflow of FDI because they call for massive investments in human capital and R&D (research and development) as well as increased technology transfers. The 'Vision 2020' program, which aims at achieving developed country status by the year 2020, implies increased economic openness, with FDI playing an increasingly important role in the development process.

It is noteworthy that Malaysia has remained quite attractive to foreign investors. The attractiveness of Malaysia as an investment center is attributable only partly to specific fiscal incentives. Equally if not more important is the conducive 'business environment' prevailing in the country. Factors contributing to this healthy environment include political stability, sound macroeconomic management, a liberal trade regime, policy transparency, consistency and predictability, and a pro-business policy orientation. To all this one must add enlightened political leadership, an efficient bureaucracy, and good institutional and infrastructural support facilities.

Macroeconomic stability sets the tone for the economic environment. Accordingly, Malaysia has given much attention to monetary, fiscal, and exchange rate policies, especially since 1986, after the worst recession in Malaysia's history in 1985, when the economy registered negative growth. Since then Malaysia has been observing budgetary discipline, restraining government expenditures, and reducing taxes to stimulate private sector investments. Corporate tax rates have been reduced from 48 percent to 30 percent over a four-year period. This has been accompanied by a prudent monetary policy aimed at keeping the cost of funds at reasonably low levels. The country's exchange rate regime is liberal enough to allow market rates to be at realistic levels determined by demand and supply. Malaysia has learned from its bitter experience in the first half of the 1980s that overvaluation of the domestic currency (ringgit Malaysia) hurts its exports and misallocates resources.

A bold measure undertaken by the government was to deregulate the economy after the 1985 crash. The New Economic Policy (NEP) of 1970–90, with quantitative inter-ethnic redistributive targets, was downplayed in the face of the recession in the mid-1980s, and was eventually replaced by a more flexible National Development Policy (NDP) in 1991. Deregulation and decontrol, removal of unnecessary red tape and streamlining of government agencies (for instance, the creation of one-stop agencies) have led to enormous improvements in the efficiency of the government bureaucracy and substantial savings in transaction costs for the private sector.

Reference must also be made to the privatization of many public enterprises and public utilities. These include electricity, water, telecommunications, postal services, port facilities, airport management, railways and civil aviation. All this is consistent with the new paradigm which recognizes the superior efficiency of the private sector. The private sector is allowed to steer the economy with the public sector taking the back seat.

The country's liberal trade regime represents an important component of what constitutes the policy environment. By developing country standards, Malaysia's tariff rates are very low. Even in the heyday of import substitution in the 1960s, tariff protection was mild, with *nominal* tariff rates averaging 25 percent, although the average *effective* rates were much higher. In recent times, there have been significant unilateral and multilateral tariff reductions, in addition to preferential tariff cuts under the AFTA (ASEAN Free Trade Area) agreement. Between 1988 and 1994, tariffs on more than 3600 items were either abolished or drastically reduced through the annual budgets. Under the

Uruguay Round of the GATT negotiations, Malaysia has offered to reduce or eliminate tariffs on 7218 items which cover nearly 80 percent of the country's total imports. Consequently, the trade-weighted average tariff rate has fallen to just about 8 percent. At present, roughly 14 percent of the tariff lines are duty-free, while about one-third of the tariff lines are subject to low tariff rates of up to 5 percent. Mild tariff rates of 5–20 percent account for 28 percent of the tariff lines. High tariffs of 40 percent and above are applied only on 3 percent of tariff lines. It is also noteworthy that Malaysia's treasury does not rely heavily on tariff revenue, as import duties account for only one-tenth of total federal government revenue. Nor does Malaysia resort to quantitative restrictions (QRs) to protect its industries. QRs have been used very sparingly, and the number of QRs has declined from 135 in 1973 to 12 in 1982 without any subsequent additions.

Malaysia has also been liberal in its immigration policy, allowing foreign workers to take jobs in the construction sector, plantations and factories, in the face of acute labor shortage. It is estimated that there are about 2 million guest workers in the country. The resort to a foreign workforce, however, is seen as a stop-gap measure and efforts are underway to phase them out gradually through industrial restructuring which would shift the country's manufacturing base from labor-intensive to skill- and technology-intensive operations. The acute shortage of skilled workers also presents a serious problem which is being addressed through HRD (human resource development) programs.

Investments in R&D are being stepped up to facilitate industrial upgrading. However, R&D investments still account for a tiny proportion of GNP, that is, about 0.8 percent, which pales in comparison with Japan's 2.8 percent. There are only 1300 engineers for every one million people, which is low compared to 7300 in the United States. The current Malaysian emphasis on science and technology in the educational system is aimed at increasing these ratios significantly.

Infrastructural development is also receiving much attention. Good infrastructure has always been a selling point in luring foreign investments into Malaysia. However, infrastructure has not been keeping pace with the rapid growth of the economy in recent years. To maintain its competitive edge, the Malaysian government is investing heavily in infrastructural development, which includes the expansion and upgrading of port facilities, road and railroad transport, and telecommunication networks.

Malaysia's policy towards foreign investors has been fairly liberal. It offers a variety of investment incentives, including tax holidays, investment tax credits, accelerated depreciation, export incentives and locational incentives. The establishment of FTZs (Free Trade Zones) and LMWs (Licensed Manufacturing Warehouses) which serve as export processing areas has made Malaysia an attractive offshore base for foreign companies, especially MNCs (multinational corporations). Firms operating in these areas have access to duty-free imports of not only machinery and equipment but also intermediate inputs.

7.1.2 The Role of Foreign Direct Investment

Malaysia has experienced several FDI 'booms' over the years. The first wave occurred during 1970–74, when FDI inflows grew from US$94 million annually to US$571 million before declining to US$350 million in 1975. The second wave witnessed an increase of FDI inflows from US$381 million in 1976 to US$1.4 billion in 1982. From this peak, they subsequently declined rapidly to a trough of US$397 million in 1987 (Ariff 1991). Between 1987 and 1991, FDI inflows increased sharply by almost ten times (Athukorala and Menon 1994), constituting the third wave. Since the beginning of 1994 through 1996, it appears that Malaysia is currently enjoying the fourth wave, after experiencing a lull during 1992–93 in FDI inflows.

The character of FDI in Malaysia has been changing over the years. Historically, in the early 1960s, FDI was concentrated mainly in agriculture, mining and trade. FDI involvement in the manufacturing sector was initially confined to import substitution activities until the early 1970s. It was only in the later years that export-oriented FDI became prominent. The main focus of FDI in export manufacturing has been in labor-intensive sectors such as electrical and electronic assembly operations and textiles and garments. However, some industrial upgrading has occurred more recently, with technology- and skill-intensive operations gaining importance in FDI activities.

Source-country composition of FDI has also changed over time. The share of the United Kingdom in FDI stock has fallen from over 90 percent at the time of independence in 1957 to 2.1 percent in 1995. Singapore, Japan, and the United States emerged as the major sources of FDI for Malaysia in the 1970s and continued to dominate the investment scene through the 1980s. The share of Japan in total approved FDI projects increased from 26.4 percent in 1982 to 31.1 percent in 1989 before falling back to 22.9 percent in 1995, while that of the United States rose from 4.4 to 19.7 percent between 1982 and 1995 (Table 7.1). The East Asian NIEs (Newly Industrialized Economies) have made their presence felt since the late 1980s. The combined share of Taiwan, South Korea, and Hong Kong in FDI projects approved in 1988 stood at 24 percent, the bulk of which was accounted for by Taiwan. After ranking second only to Japan in 1988 and 1989, Taiwan became the number one investor in Malaysia in 1990, contributing 36 percent (Table 7.1). In terms of FDI stock (cumulative investment), however, Taiwan pales in comparison with the 'old timers' Singapore and Japan, accounting for only 15 percent of the total in 1995.

The Malaysian economy has become increasingly integrated with the Asia–Pacific region through FDI networks. The predominance of the

Asia–Pacific as a source of investment has increased significantly, with its share rising from 64.5 percent in 1982 to 81.3 percent in 1995. By contrast, the relative importance of the EC (European Community) as a source of new FDI for Malaysia has been declining from 21.8 percent in 1982 to 6.4 percent in 1995 (Table 7.1), although in terms of cumulative investment, the EC accounts for as much as one-fifth of the total. Of the EC countries, the United Kingdom, Germany, and the Netherlands are among the top ten in Malaysia.

Table 7.1 Malaysian Foreign Investment in Approved Projects by Source Country, 1982–95 (%)*

Country	1982	1988	1990	1992	1995
Australia	12.0	0.5	0.3	12.0	1.5
Canada	2.6	0.1	0.5	0.1	0.5
China	0.0	0.0	0.1	0.0	0.2
Hong Kong	0.9	6.1	2.1	0.4	1.9
Indonesia	5.4	0.5	6.1	2.7	1.0
Japan	26.4	25.1	23.9	15.1	22.9
Korea	0.1	0.9	3.7	0.6	6.6
New Zealand	0.2	0.1	0.1	0.0	0.0
Philippines	5.3	0.0	0.2	0.1	0.1
Singapore	1.8	8.6	5.1	2.5	11.0
Taiwan	0.3	17.0	36.0	8.4	15.8
Thailand	5.1	1.2	0.0	0.0	0.1
USA	4.4	11.0	3.2	18.6	19.7
Asia–Pacific	64.5	70.9	81.3	60.5	81.3
EC	21.8	18.4	6.3	31.6	6.4
Others	13.8	10.6	12.4	7.9	12.3
Total investment (billion ringgit)	0.52	4.88	17.63	17.77	9.14

Note: * Foreign investment comprises equity and loan components.

Source: Malaysian Industrial Development Authority.

The ratio of FDI to total investment in the Malaysian manufacturing sector amounted to 35.5 percent in terms of paid-up capital and 40.2 percent in terms of fixed assets as of end-1989 (Ariff 1992). However, there are considerable inter-industry variations in these ratios. In some industries FDI has a higher profile than in others. The electrical and electronics industry is by far the most important in terms of FDI presence. FDI also has high visibility in the manufacture of beverages and tobacco, textile and textile products, petroleum and coal, and rubber products.

The 'new' FDI differs from 'old' FDI in terms of sources of supply, scale of operation, market orientation, externalities, factor intensity, and geographical dispersion. An upshot of all this is the growing presence of SMEs (small- and medium-sized enterprises) in the FDI profile in Malaysia. Taiwanese investment in the country has contributed significantly to this changing pattern. This is not surprising, since Taiwan's own industrial structure is conspicuously devoid of conglomerates, quite unlike that of Japan or Korea. Even Japanese FDI in recent years has taken mostly the form of SMEs catering to the needs of Japanese multinational corporations (MNCs), and driven mainly by the *endaka* (high yen) phenomenon.

In the 1960s and early 1970s, most of the FDI projects in Malaysia were oriented toward the protected domestic market. Export-oriented FDI projects were then aimed at third-country markets, with the notable exception of US investments in the electronics sector. Almost all new FDI projects nowadays have an explicit export orientation towards not only third-country markets but also 'home'-(investing) country destinations. Thus, for example, Japanese MNCs – which have been exporting their Malaysia-made products to third-country markets in North America and Western Europe – have begun to export to their home country as well.

It is noteworthy that manufactured exports from Malaysia have been growing at an annual compound rate of 35 percent during 1980–92, and that manufactures accounted for 68 percent of total exports in 1992 (Athukorala and Menon 1994), with FDI being the main driving force behind it. The share of foreign affiliates in total manufactures was 51.2 percent in 1986 (UNCTC 1991).

Understandably, the import content of Malaysian manufactures is high, estimated at 75 percent (Fong 1990). Imported intermediate inputs were considered necessary to ensure high quality and low cost. However, the behavior of foreign firms in this regard is changing. There is now a tendency for these firms to source more and more inputs locally, now that many efficient ancillary industries have emerged in the country. For example, it is reported that the percentage share of local parts and materials in total output of Japanese firms in Malaysia has increased from 20 percent to 24 percent in 1989 (Aoki 1992). A survey of semiconductor firms in Malaysia's FTZs has produced concrete evidence of substantial integration of foreign firms into the domestic economy since the mid-1980s (Liebau and Wahnschaffe 1992). The establishment of small- and medium-scale FDI projects in recent years has reinforced this trend. Taiwanese investments, in particular, are making significant contributions to this integration process.

7.1.3 Taiwanese Investment

Taiwan has emerged as a major source of FDI for Malaysia since 1988. It ranks second among the top ten foreign investors in the country for the period 1988–95 in terms of capital in approved projects (Table 7.2). A distinguishing feature of Taiwanese investments in Malaysia, as noted earlier, is that they belong to the small- and medium-scale category. The average capital size in approved Taiwanese investment projects has been below US$10 million in all of these years except for the projects approved in 1994. Small investment projects (defined as capital investment of 5 million ringgit or less) have accounted for 52 percent of the Taiwanese FDI projects approved during the period 1988–96.

Table 7.2 Malaysia's Top Ten Sources of Foreign Investment in Approved Projects, 1988–95 (US$ million)

	Rank	1988	1990	1992	1995	1988–95
Japan	1	461	1584	1077	839	8097
Taiwan	2	313	2383	602	577	7991
USA	3	202	213	1324	721	4587
Singapore	4	158	337	178	403	2581
France	5	198	7	1632	39	1963
UK	6	74	326	523	76	1627
South Korea	7	16	245	40	242	1587
Indonesia	8	9	20	193	35	1305
Australia	9	10	141	857	56	1225
Hong Kong	10	113	141	32	70	1153

Source: Malaysian Industrial Development Authority.

During the period 1988–96, a total of 1482 Taiwanese projects received approvals, with a total employment potential of 290 259 workers, with an average of about 200 workers per project. Taiwanese FDI in Malaysia is concentrated in the manufacture of electronics, basic metals and metal products, chemicals, and textiles. In terms of capital investment, basic metals and metal products represents the largest category, whereas in terms of employment size, electrical and electronics is by far the largest (Table 7.3). While larger projects have a clear export orientation, the smaller ones are targeted mainly at the local market. Many small Taiwanese firms in Malaysia produce components and parts which are sold to the bigger assembly firms for further processing and eventual export.

Taiwanese FDI in Malaysia appears to be an extension of industrial operations back home in Taiwan, with a horizontal integration producing similar products, albeit slightly different in quality, with very little vertical linkage between the parent and the subsidiary. The Malaysian subsidiaries source about 40 percent of their intermediate inputs and raw materials from Taiwan, but there are signs that this ratio is declining, with more and more local procurement. However, some large firms have brought with them satellite firms from Taiwan.

Table 7.3 Approved Taiwanese FDI Projects in Malaysia by Industry, 1980–96

Industry	No. of firms	Share by employment (%)	Share by capital investment (%)
Food and beverages	30	6.2	2.3
Textile and textile products	116	7.6	16.4
Wood and wood products	139	15.4	6.2
Furniture and fixtures	82	5.1	1.6
Paper and printing	31	0.9	0.5
Leather products	13	0.9	0.2
Rubber and plastics	160	6.3	2.8
Chemicals	72	1.7	4.5
Petroleum refineries	4	0.6	7.7
Non-metal mineral products	53	2.4	1.6
Basic metal and metal products	62	3.7	22.8
Fabricated metal products	77	2.6	7.9
Machinery	60	2.0	1.3
Electrical and electronics	481	39.9	22.6
Transport equipment	34	1.4	0.5
Scientific and measuring equip.	9	0.5	0.2
Other manufactures	59	2.8	0.9
Total	1482	100.0	100.0

Source: Malaysian Industrial Development Authority.

7.1.4 Objectives and Methodology

An attempt is made in this study to systematically examine the role of Taiwanese investments in Malaysia in the wider context of the contribution of FDI to the growth and development of the host economy. The main objective is to take a close look at the development of linkages not only *among* the Taiwanese firms but also *between* Taiwanese firms and other firms in the country, both domestic and foreign. More specifically, the study probes into the motivations for investment, parent–subsidiary relationships, inter-firm and intra-firm linkages, technology transfers and R&D activities, among other things. Problems faced by Taiwanese firms in Malaysia are also examined, with a view to finding some solutions.

The study relies mainly on primary data collected through questionnaires, in addition to using secondary data. A total of 300 questionnaires were sent to the potential respondents, who are registered members of the Taipei Investors' Association in Malaysia. The questionnaires were designed to extract information on FDI relating to employment, trade, induced local investment, technology transfer, and so on (see Appendix). The survey was carried out during June–July 1994, yielding 126 responses from Taiwanese affiliates, of which two cases provided incomplete information. The analysis is therefore based on 124 completed questionnaires, although this number varies by question. The survey was followed by interviews with some selected firms to gain further insights.

The rest of this chapter is organized as follows. The next section deals with the determinants and motivations of Taiwanese investment activities in Malaysia. The nature and characteristics of Taiwanese operations in Malaysia are examined in the third section. The role of Taiwanese FDI in the local economy is the focus of the fourth section. Finally, an evaluation and some policy suggestions are made in the fifth section.

7.2 Motivations and Determinants of Taiwanese FDI

Since 1986, overseas investment by Taiwanese entrepreneurs has been increasing. The appreciation of the Taiwanese currency (NT), shortage of labor, increasing wages and environmental regulation in Taiwan have contributed to the increase in overseas investment, especially in Southeast Asian countries (Ku 1994, p. 1). The surveyed firms were asked to rank in order of importance possible reasons for overseas investment. 'To expand the sales in the local market or markets in other countries' is cited by 25 percent of the respondent firms as the most important reason for overseas investment. Other reasons considered important are 'the availability of low-cost local labor' (reported by 17 percent of the firms), 'following other firms' action' (reported by 16 percent of the firms), and 'appreciation of the new taipi (NT) which reduces export capability' (mentioned by 15 percent of the firms). Among the reasons considered not important for overseas investment are 'to collect market information', 'to avoid environmental regulations in Taiwan', and 'to take advantage of local (host) resources such as electricity and water'.

Small and large firms cited different reasons for overseas investment. For the large firms (with 300 or more employees), 'the appreciation of the new taipi' is the main reason for overseas investment. 'To take advantage of low cost of labor' is mentioned as the secondary reason. For the small firms, the main reason for investing in Malaysia is 'to expand sales in the local market or markets in other countries', while the secondary reason is simply 'following other firms'.

Only 9 percent of the firms have investments in other Southeast Asian countries. The top reasons cited by the firms for investing in Malaysia rather than in other Southeast Asian countries are political stability and good infrastructure. Reasons such as racial homogeneity and good potential for local market are considered important by a much smaller percentage of the firms. A few firms gave 'no language/communication problem' as a reason for choosing Malaysia over other Southeast Asian countries.

Between large and small firms, there are significant differences in the proportion of firms reporting 'good potential for local market', 'cheap labor', and 'have familiar entrepreneurs or people'. More small firms reported 'good potential for local market' and 'have familiar entrepreneurs or people' as their reasons for choosing to invest in Malaysia, while a higher percentage of large firms reported 'cheap labor' as their motivation for investment in Malaysia. This may be due to the fact that a majority of the large firms are mainly export-oriented (39 percent of them with an export ratio of 100 percent), whereas about 20 percent of the small firms sell all their products locally. Not surprisingly, therefore, more small firms than large firms cited 'good potential for local market' as one of the reasons to invest in Malaysia.

The in-depth interviews with some of these firms found that despite rising wages and the labor shortage, Malaysia is still an attractive base as there are many other positive things which more than compensate for the shortage of labor and rising wages, such as labor quality and infrastructural facilities. Some of them have plans to make Malaysia their regional center for company networks in the ASEAN region.

The responses from the parent companies in Taiwan are not much different from those of the subsidiaries. The main reasons for investment in Malaysia reported by the parent companies include 'to take advantage of the low cost of labor', 'to expand sales in the local market or markets in other countries', 'to take advantage of the low cost of land', and 'the appreciation of the new taipi'. The main motivation for parent companies to invest in Malaysia, in the case of small firms, is to expand sales in the local market or markets in other countries. For the large firms, the main determinant is the availability of low-cost labor in Malaysia (Ku 1994, p. 7).

7.3 Nature and Characteristics of Taiwanese FDI in Malaysia

7.3.1 Background Information

About 70 percent of the firms surveyed were established in Malaysia between 1989 and 1991. This is mainly due to the 1989 liberalization of the guidelines for foreign equity participation in the manufacturing sector of Malaysia. These firms have been in operation in Malaysia for about three to five years. However, three of the firms surveyed started operation about 27–30 years ago, in the mid-1960s.

About 72 percent of the Taiwanese firms have paid-up capital of US$3 million or less, while 11 percent of them have paid-up capital of US$10 million or more. The majority of the shareholders are Taiwanese. On average, 87 percent of the shareholders are Taiwanese, 8 percent are Malaysians, 5 percent are from other countries.

Some 53 and 27 percent of the firms felt that there are restrictions imposed by the Malaysian government on export ratio and local content, respectively. The time-lag from application for investment to operation of the factories in Malaysia ranges quite widely, from one month to 4 years and 10 months. The average time taken to commence operation from the time of application for investment is about 11 months for all firms surveyed. The majority of Taiwanese subsidiaries are newly established and wholly Taiwanese-owned, while 6 percent take the form of equity acquisition by Taiwanese investors of existing local companies, and 2 percent are newly established joint ventures.

7.3.2 Decision-Making Processes

Decision making in various departments of the subsidiary firms is influenced, to a certain extent, by the decisions of parent companies. Some decisions are solely made by the headquarters of the parent company or expatriates from the parent company. There are, however, instances where decisions are made solely by local staff or jointly with parent companies. It would appear that decision making will increasingly shift from the parent company to local staff in the future (see Table 7.4).

About 10 percent of the firms reported that decisions in the finance department are made by local staff; one firm reported joint decisions with the parent company; but for the bulk of the companies surveyed, decisions in the finance department come from the parent company. It is not surprising that parent companies control the financial operations of the subsidiaries.

In the marketing department, about 20 percent of the firms reported that decisions are made solely by local staff, and 6 percent reported joint decisions, with 74 percent reporting that all marketing decisions are made by the parent company. Within the next five years, 34 percent of the local firms expect to be making their own decisions in the marketing area, however.

Decision making in the production and personnel departments is the most localized among all departments. In the next five years, decison making by local staff in these areas is expected to reach 50 percent. In contrast, decisions on research and development (R&D) are mostly made by the parent companies. Only 13 percent of the firms said such decisions were made by local staff. In the not-too-distant future, however, 30 percent of the firms expect to make R&D decisions locally.

Table 7.4 Firms' Decision-Making Responsibilities by Department at Present and in the Future (%)

Decision maker	Department				
	Finance	Marketing	Production	Personnel	R&D
At present					
Parent company	89.2	74.3	62.0	61.4	83.8
Local staff	9.8	19.8	27.0	29.7	13.1
Joint decision*	1.0	5.9	11.0	8.9	3.0
Sample size	102	101	100	101	99
In the future (5 years)					
Parent company	82.7	60.6	39.6	42.3	67.0
Local staff	16.3	34.0	52.1	49.5	29.8
Joint decision*	1.0	5.3	8.3	8.2	3.2
Sample size	98	94	96	97	94

Note: * By parent company and local staff.

Source: This study.

7.3.3 Product Marketing

The products of Taiwanese subsidiaries in Malaysia are generally sold in the local market or exported to third-party countries. Very little is exported back to Taiwan. On average, about 49 percent of the goods are sold locally, 44 percent are exported to other countries, while 7 percent are exported back to Taiwan (including the share to parent companies). Large firms are more export-oriented than small firms. None of the large firms sell all their products locally and about 39 percent of them export all their products, whereas 20 percent of small firms sell all products locally and 13 percent of them export all products. Many large firms use Malaysia as an export platform while small firms sell part of their products to large firms for further processing into exports.

7.3.4 Marketing Channels

The products are mainly sold by the subsidiaries themselves; only 16 percent of the surveyed subsidiaries do not market any of the products. Small firms have a greater tendency to market their own products compared with large firms. On average, about 70 percent of the products are marketed by the local subsidiaries, 20 percent are sold through parent companies, 7 percent through trading companies in other countries (including Taiwan), and only 5 percent through local trading companies.

7.4 The Role of Taiwanese FDI in the Local Economy

7.4.1 Reinvestment

It is estimated that, on average, Taiwanese subsidiaries take about five years to recover their initial capital investment. Of the firms making profits, most of them retain the profits locally. On average, 72 percent of the profits have been retained in the company as capital for expansion, 11 percent are reinvested in other projects in the host country, and only 17 percent are remitted back to parent companies. The fact that a majority of profits are retained locally for reinvestment indicates the determination of Taiwanese subsidiaries to stay in Malaysia and to explore other opportunities there.

7.4.2 Technology Transfer

Training is provided locally by technicians from Taiwan, or done overseas by sending the senior staff members to Taiwan. On average, about ten staff members from each firm are sent to Taiwan for training every year; but only about one-third of them stay with the firms after training.

The number of expatriate workers in Taiwanese subsidiaries is relatively small. Of the firms which have a parent company in Taiwan, 4 percent of them do not employ any expatriate workers from their parent companies; about 51 percent of them employ one to two expatriate workers from parent companies and only 7 percent employ more than ten expatriate workers. Large subsidiaries have an average of seven expatriate workers, which is double the number of small subsidiaries. The majority of expatriates from parent companies serve in Malaysian subsidiaries as president or vice president, or are in charge of production, finance, marketing, or research and development.

The degree of technology transfer from parent companies varies in different fields of technology: more than 50 percent of technology transfer is reported for plant operation, service and maintenance, quality control, production management, and technological improvement. In contrast, the acquisition of new technology is primarily by parent companies and only transferred to the subsidiaries occasionally. About a third of the firms reported not being provided with any technology for new or improved product designs from their parents; even fewer reported being involved in an independent development of new products.

Also rarely transferred are technologies for molding and equipment designs. About 33 percent of the firms reported that the technology for development of molds for manufacturing in Malaysia is not transferred at all from the parent companies. The rest reported sparse transfer of such technology. With respect to the technology for design of the manufacturing equipment, about 36 percent of the Taiwanese subsidiaries reported that this information is not shared with them by the parent companies. The rest reported limited involvement of subsidiaries in the design of manufacturing equipment.

Cross-tabulation of the degree of technology transfer with respect to ownership, size and export ratio of the firms finds that there is no significant difference made by these variables, except in the case of export ratio. The more export-oriented the firms, the higher the level of technology transfer in the area of technological improvements. On the other hand, the more export-oriented the firms, the less likely it is that the technology for product design will be transferred. This implies that export-oriented subsidiaries, which serve as export platforms for the parents, are keen on improving their production efficiency to stay competitive but are insensitive to product design for which the parent firms are largely responsible.

The majority of the Taiwanese firms acquire product designs or production technology from their parent companies, but some of them also carry out their own research and development projects locally. Large firms are more likely to acquire product designs or production technology from parent companies compared to small firms. A larger proportion of small firms carry out their own research and development locally, or emulate products and technologies from other companies.

7.4.3 Employment Creation

The number of employees in the Taiwanese subsidiaries ranges from four persons to 5871 persons. About 44 percent of the firms employ fewer than 100 workers while 7 percent have 1000 or more employees. Of these employees, about 11 percent are in the administrative and managerial category, 2 percent are in research and development, and the rest of the workforce are categorized as unskilled labor (58 percent) and skilled labor (30 percent). Some of the firms have experienced labor shortages and some of the workers are foreign nationals from Sri Lanka, Bangladesh, Pakistan and Indonesia.

Statistics show that the more export-oriented the firms, the larger the number of employees. Some 48 percent of the fully export-oriented firms employ 300 workers or more, compared to only 11 percent of the firms with an export ratio less than 50 percent. This means that the export-oriented firms create more jobs for the people in the host country.

7.4.4 Sourcing and Financial Leverage

The components and parts for local production are partly procured from local suppliers and partly imported (see Table 7.5). There is not much difference between large and small firms in this respect. On average, about 42 percent of the components and parts used by Taiwanese firms are local, with another 26 percent being imported from other suppliers in Taiwan, 17 percent from third-party countries, and 15 percent from their parent companies.

Table 7.5 Firms by Share of Local (Malaysian) Components and Parts, Machinery and Equipment (%)

Percentage of local share	Small firms	Large firms	Total
Components and parts			
0	18.4	7.1	15.4
1–24	24.1	14.3	21.4
25–49	11.5	25.0	15.4
50–74	24.1	39.3	27.4
75–99	17.2	10.7	16.2
100	4.6	3.6	4.3
Total	100.0	100.0	100.0
Sample size	89	28	117
Machinery and equipment			
0	61.8	50.0	59.0
1–24	25.8	39.3	29.1
25–49	4.5	7.1	5.1
50–74	4.5	3.6	4.3
75–99	2.2	0.0	1.7
100	1.1	0.0	0.8
Total	100.0	100.0	100.0
Sample size	89	28	117

Source: This study.

Further cross-tabulation with export ratios in relation to sourcing strategies reveals that the more export-oriented the firms, the higher the percentage share of local components and parts used in local production. That is, about 39 percent of the local-market-oriented (with export ratio less than 50 percent) firms utilize half or more local components and parts compared to 57 percent of the export-oriented (with export ratio equal to 50 percent and more) firms.

Machinery and equipment, on the other hand, are mainly imported from Taiwan. About 94 percent of the surveyed firms use some imported Taiwanese machinery and equipment, and 20 percent of the firms used Taiwanese machinery only. Dependency on Taiwan-made machinery is necessitated by the need to duplicate production methods of the Taiwanese parent firms in the Malaysian operations. Identical machinery is the best way to ensure conformity.

About half of the firms surveyed indicate that they are provided with some loans by the parent companies. Meanwhile, more than 80 percent of firms receive loan financing from local financial institutions. On average, about 59 percent of the loan financing of Taiwanese firms is from local financial institutions, 28 percent from their parent companies, 3 percent each from third-party countries and the informal credit market, and 2 percent from local shareholders. Large firms are more capable of tapping into the local financial markets than small firms. About 43 percent of the large firms obtain their loans solely from local financial institutions, compared to only 29 percent of the small firms (see Table 7.6).

Table 7.6 Firms by Share of Loans from Local Financial Institutions (%)

Loans from local financial institutions (%)	Small firms	Large firms	Total
0	20.7	7.1	17.5
1–24	4.3	0.0	3.3
25–49	17.4	7.1	15.0
50–74	19.6	35.7	23.3
75–99	8.7	7.1	8.3
100	29.4	42.9	32.5
Total	100.0	100.0	100.0
Sample size	92	28	120

Source: This study.

7.4.5 Comparison with Local and Other Multinationals

The firms surveyed were given two lists of business activities to compare themselves with other firms: one to compare with nearby local firms and one to compare with multinational firms from other countries.

In comparison with local firms, the majority of the Taiwanese subsidiaries felt that their business activities are at a higher level in the areas of production technology, product flexibility, quality control, company image, export ratio, capacity for technological innovation and process improvement, marketing ability, scale of production, capacity for new product development, quality of after-sales services, and degree of automated production. On the other hand, about one-third of the Taiwanese subsidiaries reported that the ratios of materials procured locally are lower than those of local firms.

In comparison with multinational firms from advanced countries, about 30 percent of the Taiwanese subsidiaries felt that they are at a higher level in a number of business activities such as the ratio of exports to total sales, proportion of unskilled labor in total employment, and technology transfer to local firms. About a quarter of the Taiwanese subsidiaries claimed that their local procurement ratios are higher than those of MNCs from advanced countries. Taiwanese firms felt that they are less capable of conducting joint R&D with local firms when compared with their counterparts from advanced countries. In the other areas they felt that they are comparable with other MNCs: these include technology transfer to local firms, the willingness to build a plant in a remote area, export ratio, capital intensity, and job training and education for local employees.

7.4.6 Contributions to the Host Country

When the Taiwanese subsidiaries were asked to assess their contributions to the host country, most of them (90 percent) claimed that Taiwanese firms fully utilize local labor, and make a great contribution to job creation and expansion. A smaller percentage, but still a majority (60 percent) of them agreed that 'Taiwanese firms get along with local people well', 'regularly offer technical services to local suppliers', 'maintain a good relationship with local government', 'regularly transfer technology to local firms through joint ventures or technical assistance arrangements', 'make a great contribution to the host country's economic growth', 'contribute to export expansion significantly', and 'use local materials adequately'.

7.5 Evaluation and Recommendations

To be sure, FDI is not a zero-sum game. The investors are rewarded by the profits they make, while the host country gains through increased employment, technology transfers, industrial restructuring, the demonstration effect and other positive externalities emanating from FDI activities. Taiwanese investments in Malaysia conform to the above pattern. In SMEs, the factor intensity of the Taiwanese operations seems compatible with the factor endowments of Malaysia. The stage of development in Malaysia seems particularly suited to Taiwanese investors, who experienced a similar phase in their home country not too long ago. The fact that Malaysia is not too far behind Taiwan in terms of economic development thus provides a tremendous advantage for Malaysia over other host countries in the region.

The question of Taiwanese firms 'crowding out' local firms does not seem very pertinent, since they are not in direct competition with local firms. On the contrary, they have created opportunities for local investors. Nearly all of the Taiwanese companies are export-oriented, directly or indirectly. The growing linkages between Taiwanese manufacturers and local companies which act as sources of intermediate inputs have drawn the latter into export activities. There is much that local firms can learn through their commercial relationships with the Taiwanese firms operating in Malaysia, for ideas are no less important to business than physical inputs. However, as the Taiwanese FDI firms increase local borrowing over time, they tend to compete with local firms for credit facilities.

Although tax incentives are not amongst the most important reasons for Taiwanese investments in Malaysia, it would be folly to remove them abruptly, as fiscal incentives do make up for what is lacking. Of course, it would be better to remove the disincentives in the system gradually than to continue compensating for them all the time. Clearly, Malaysia's attractiveness lies not in fiscal incentives but in its political stability and policy consistency, continuity and transparency, not to mention its bureaucratic efficiency, good infrastructure, and trainable labor force. Malaysia must continue its liberal policies. Specific fiscal incentives also can still play a useful role. For example, tax rebates on training and R&D expenditures could stimulate industrial upgrading. This would make considerable economic sense, since the social benefits of such activities vastly exceed private benefits. It is not difficult to understand why firms are reluctant to undertake such investments, since costs, but not benefits, are internalized. Tax incentives can persuade the firms to pay more attention to these important aspects.

Industrialization in Malaysia has arrived at a crossroads. Malaysia is no longer a labor surplus economy. The country has been oversold as a base for labor-intensive manufacturing. The current shortage of labor and the need to employ guest workers from other countries are clear indications of the fact that Malaysia's comparative advantage in labor-intensive products is being eroded. Malaysia needs to shift gear and change direction by moving into technology-intensive and skill-intensive manufacturing. The dilemma, however, is that there is also a shortage of skilled manpower in the country. It is not possible to increase the domestic supply of skilled workers in the short term. This observation underscores the need for the continued presence of immigrant workers until such time as the country is really ready to take on skill-intensive manufacturing in a big way. Although foreign workers do play a useful role, this option is not without serious constraints. For one thing, companies are unwilling to invest in skill development for foreign contract workers. For another, the availability of such workers would remove the pressure on companies to adopt technology-intensive methods of production. Thus, there is a need to strike a balance: the dependence on guest workers needs to be phased out gradually without disrupting industrial activities. At the same time, Malaysia needs to beef up vocational education and increase the supply of technicians. At the university level, the emphasis has to be on science and technology.

There is a need for a closer rapport between Taiwanese companies and the government machinery. It is important that the bureaucracy be sensitive to the problems faced by foreign investors. Taiwanese investors are not familiar with local laws and business practices. It will take time before these companies can develop 'mutual trust' - the basis of their commercial relations back home in Taiwan - in Malaysia. There are areas of dispute between Taiwanese firms and local counterparts which need to be amicably settled. A dispute settlement mechanism has to be put in place. It is important that the Malaysian government agencies have regular consultations with the Taipei Investors' Association of Malaysia.

Taiwanese investors, on their part, need to take a long-term view of their role in the Malaysian economy. They can contribute much to and also profit a lot from structural changes in the economy by responding positively to problems encountered. For instance, the labor shortage problem can be resolved by adopting technology-intensive methods and the shortage of skilled manpower can be overcome by training. Recourse to immigrant labor needs to be seen as no more than a stop-gap measure during the transition.

It is commendable that Taiwanese investors in Malaysia have extensive local linkages not only with local Chinese firms but also with Bumiputra companies. To ensure quality inputs at competitive prices, some technical assistance to local suppliers from Taiwanese companies is necessary. It appears that the present local linkages of Taiwanese firms are largely confined to commercial dealings. Taiwanese firms can play a useful role by interacting with local institutions of higher learning. This need not be viewed merely as a social obligation. Indeed, it can bring much benefit to Taiwanese enterprises. For example, internship arrangements with local universities and colleges can be a mutually rewarding exercise, as this constitutes an avenue for recruiting personnel, in addition to providing industrial experience for the interns. Another area of profitable cooperation is R&D. Collaboration with local universities can have a stimulating effect on R&D activities.

A thorny problem faced by Taiwanese investors in Malaysia has to do with the treatment of Taiwan as a province of China rather than as a political entity on its own. This has given rise to problems of passports and visas. A simplification of the immigration procedures and relaxation of immigration rules by the Malaysian authorities would go a long way toward solving this problem.

8. Taiwanese Investment in Thailand

Bunluasak Pussarungsri

8.1 Background and Overview

In spite of significant improvements in domestic saving mobilization, there still exists a substantial savings–investment gap in Thailand, necessitating foreign capital to finance public and private investment. Foreign direct investment (FDI) has become increasingly important in the domestic capital formation of Thailand. The share of FDI in domestic private investment increased from only 3 percent in 1980 to about 10 percent in 1990. It has also become an increasingly important form of capital flow to Thailand. Its share in total foreign capital inflows increased from only 10 percent in the early 1980s to about 30 percent in 1990 (Pongpisanupichit and Pussarungsri 1992). Among investor countries, Taiwan has ranked second or third since the end of the 1980s. Thus it has the potential to contribute significantly to the Thai economy.

The objective of this chapter is to examine the characteristics, motives, and impacts of Taiwanese investment in Thailand, and to investigate problems associated with the operations of Taiwanese firms in Thailand. To examine various aspects of Taiwanese investment, we use both primary and secondary data. The primary data are from our survey of Taiwanese firms. The survey includes both Taiwanese firms in Thailand and their parent firms in Taiwan. The secondary data are from various government sources, including the Bank of Thailand, the Thai Board of Investment (BOI), and others.

8.1.1 The Role of Foreign Direct Investment

In the first half of the 1980s, FDI in Thailand was rather low and fluctuated dramatically due to the instability of both the domestic and world economies. FDI in Thailand started to expand rapidly after 1987, as the rising costs of production, especially labor costs and the appreciation of the currencies of Japan and Asian Newly Industrialized Economies (NIEs), led to the relocation

Table 8.1 *Net Flow of FDI into Thailand by Country (million baht)*

	1980	1985	1986	1987	1988	1989	1990	1991	1992	1993	1994	1995	1996(Q1–Q3)
US	730.3	2 387.4	1 293.7	1 815.7	3 184.9	5 220.6	5 844.7	5 918.6	11 788.3	7 235.9	3 908.8	6 471.2	14 698.3
Japan	902.9	1 534.0	3 049.0	3 268.7	14 605.0	18 761.6	27 821.6	19 611.9	8 571.8	7 733.0	3 091.2	13 855.8	7 967.9
NIEs	1 123.7	816.2	1 092.9	1 505.8	6 235.5	11 032.2	14 174.7	14 614.9	17 032.2	6 503.8	10 401.0	9 661.4	7 100.7
Taiwan	1.9	170.6	132.6	687.3	3 136.4	5 062.3	7 138.0	2 753.5	2 220.8	1 236.6	2 073.8	2 405.0	1 480.2
Korea	9.7	(3.4)	4.6	22.3	304.6	254.2	487.5	295.9	262.4	368.8	323.0	308.2	558.4
ASEAN	431.0	(1 082.0)	359.9	535.4	1 646.8	2 809.6	6 439.6	6 576.2	7 170.0	1 521.7	4 918.6	3 988.7	3 516.0
Singapore	277.3	(1 121.9)	401.3	535.5	1 571.9	2 746.1	5 909.6	6 469.3	6 722.0	1 545.1	4 629.6	3 393.5	2 421.5
Others	153.7	39.9	(41.4)	(0.1)	74.9	63.5	530.0	106.9	448.0	(23.4)	289.0	595.2	1 094.5
Other countries	690.3	786.2	1 112.6	1 918.1	2 291.3	7 873.6	10 414.4	4 667.5	9 202.0	20 817.6	10 921.4	15 909.9	7 844.6
Total	3 878.2	4 441.8	6 908.1	9 043.7	27 963.5	45 697.6	64 695.0	51 389.1	53 764.3	43 812.0	33 241.0	49 887.0	41 127.5

Note: Parentheses indicate a negative value.

Source: Bank of Thailand.

of their production bases to Thailand and other developing countries. The flow of FDI into the country increased threefold from about 9000 million baht (Thai currency) in 1987 to about 28 000 million baht in 1988, reached a peak in 1990 at about 65 000 million baht before it started to decline at the beginning of the 1990s. The decline in FDI was probably due to the completion of the shifting of production bases from Japan and the NIEs, the emergence of infrastructure and human resource bottlenecks in Thailand, and domestic political instability in Thailand. But the declining trend was reversed again in 1995 as the flow of FDI increased from 33 241 million baht in 1994 to 49 887 million baht in 1995 and 41 124 million baht in the first three quarters of 1996.

FDI from the Asian NIEs (excluding Singapore) and ASEAN (including Singapore) has surged since 1988 (Table 8.1). The Asian NIEs' share in total FDI rose successively and accounted for a highest proportion of 31 percent in 1992. FDI from ASEAN also reached a peak in 1992, accounting for 13.3 percent in that year. FDI from Japan and the United States also peaked in 1991–92 and surged again in 1995–96.

FDI in Thailand has been predominantly in the manufacturing sector, which accounted for more than 50 percent of total FDI in 1987 and 1988 (Table 8.2). The proportion of FDI in the manufacturing sector decreased sharply after 1988, from about 47 percent in 1989 to only about 32 percent in 1992. Nevertheless, the share of FDI in the manufacturing sector remained the highest among all sectors at about 35 percent in 1996. With a declining investment in the manufacturing sector, the share of FDI to the construction and financial sectors has increased significantly since 1989.

Within the manufacturing sector, FDI is concentrated in the subsector of electrical appliances, which accounted for almost one-third of total FDI in the manufacturing sector (Table 8.2). Other important subsectors are chemicals, machinery and transport equipment, metal and non-metallic products, and textiles. FDI in these subsectors, except for textiles, has decreased rather sharply since 1990, however.

8.2 Taiwanese Investment

In this section, we present various aspects of Taiwanese investment in Thailand. We start with a presentation of the profile of Taiwanese investment in Thailand, followed by an overview of the characteristics of Taiwanese firms in the country. The characteristics include firm size, year of establishment, ownership and legal restrictions, mode of investment, sources of inputs, decision-making processes, and performance of Taiwanese firms in Thailand.

8.2.1 Profile of Taiwanese Investment in Thailand

Taiwanese investment was rather low at the beginning of the 1980s, amounting

Table 8.2 Share of Net Flow of FDI to Thailand by Sector (%)

	1980	1985	1986	1987	1988	1989	1990	1991	1992	1993	1994	1995	1996(Q1–Q3)
Financial institutions	-4.46	-27.91	7.39	4.90	9.22	6.23	6.13	13.26	12.19	3.7	0.5	1.3	8.3
Trade	19.35	24.35	25.82	9.43	13.87	14.90	20.81	14.86	13.20	12.7	25.8	22.3	23.7
Construction	20.18	35.69	17.88	14.92	6.58	8.60	5.27	6.52	27.03	8.8	5.3	1.8	2.5
Mining and quarrying	15.39	11.61	3.48	2.12	1.69	1.26	1.82	4.02	5.81	7.2	3.9	2.8	2.3
Agriculture	5.41	1.73	2.93	3.16	1.13	1.32	1.22	1.16	-0.28	0.8	-0.5	0.5	-0.1
Manufacturing	26.09	30.58	30.74	52.51	57.79	47.86	46.49	45.44	32.49	26.1	16.0	28.3	35.8
Food	2.35	8.89	4.15	4.83	3.81	4.30	3.10	3.28	2.31	2.2	3.5	2.0	2.2
Textiles	-0.04	1.35	1.24	11.01	3.97	1.50	2.82	2.19	2.72	-0.5	2.6	1.9	3.0
Metal and non-metallic products	1.23	-2.83	-0.33	4.04	7.56	6.05	4.54	4.27	3.15	5.5	3.4	4.6	4.1
Electrical appliances	11.56	6.30	8.93	12.57	22.59	19.39	17.32	17.38	10.99	8.2	4.5	11.7	12.3
Machinery and transport equipment	2.37	0.72	-0.22	1.77	2.26	2.42	3.88	4.25	2.02	3.6	0.9	7.2	7.1
Chemicals	5.50	11.00	7.01	9.60	7.00	7.62	7.39	7.46	3.02	11.7	2.5	4.7	7.5
Petroleum products	0.06	0.00	0.12	-0.17	2.75	-2.60	1.44	-0.73	2.38	-9.4	-8.6	-8.1	-11.4
Construction materials	0.03	0.86	0.08	0.07	0.09	0.19	0.02	0.28	0.70	0.3	0.4	1.3	0.1
Others	3.02	4.29	9.76	8.81	7.77	9.01	5.99	7.05	5.20	4.6	6.8	3.1	10.9
Services	18.04	23.94	11.77	12.95	9.05	19.05	17.50	10.53	6.90	1.1	4.2	4.4	2.0
Others	0.00	0.00	0.00	0.00	0.67	0.79	0.76	4.21	2.65	39.6	44.7	38.6	25.5
Total	100.00	100.00	100.00	100.00	100.00	100.00	100.00	100.00	100.00	100.0	100.0	100.0	100.0

Source : Bank of Thailand.

to about 2 million baht a year (Table 8.1). It increased slightly in the second half of the 1980s to 690 million baht in 1987, and then surged sharply to 3 billion baht in 1988. Taiwanese investment reached its peak in 1990, totaling more than 7 billion baht. It started to level off in the following years. In 1995, FDI from Taiwan was 2.4 billion baht.

Among investing countries in Thailand, FDI from Taiwan ranked either third or fourth in the second half of the 1980s, following Japan, the US, and sometimes Hong Kong. In 1990, the share of FDI from Taiwan was as high as 11 percent of total FDI to Thailand, second only to that of Japanese investment. In 1996, however, Taiwan's share decreased to only 3.6 percent.

FDI from Taiwan has been concentrated in the manufacturing sector, followed by the trade and real estate sectors (Table 8.3). FDI in the manufacturing sector accounted for more than one half of the total FDI from Taiwan. Within the manufacturing sector, the electrical appliance, textiles and chemical industries were the most active investment areas.

8.2.2 Characteristics of Taiwanese Investment

Firm size

The data from the Thai Board of Investment reveal that Taiwanese subsidiaries on average are smaller than other foreign firms. However, the average size of Taiwanese firms has tended to increase since 1989 along with that of other foreign-invested projects.

Our survey of Taiwanese subsidiaries on their capital size confirms the data from BOI. Taiwanese companies in Thailand are rather small compared to other foreign companies. About 28 percent of the firms in the survey indicate that their capital is less than US$1 million. The proportion of firms having capital between US$1 and US$3 million is about 41 percent, while companies having capital of more than US$10 million make up only about 12 percent of the total sample.

The distribution of company size according to their sales shows a similar pattern. About 7 percent of companies in the survey indicate that their sales are less than US$1 million per year. About 50 percent of companies in the sample indicate that their annual sales are less than US$5 million.

Ownership and legal restrictions

According to the survey, only about 71 percent of 'Taiwanese' companies in Thailand have parent companies in Taiwan. Many small firms do not have parent companies because the parent companies were shut down after new firms were established abroad or because they were established by Taiwanese nationals who do not own a business in Taiwan.

The ownership distribution of Taiwanese firms is rather surprising. A large proportion of Taiwanese firms in Thailand are 100 percent Taiwanese-owned.

Table 8.3 Net Flow of FDI from Taiwan by Sector (million baht)

	1980	1981	1982	1983	1984	1985	1986	1987	1988	1989	1990	1991	1992
Financial institutions	0.0	0.0	0.0	0.0	0.0	53.2	0.0	0.0	172.0	20.6	20.2	-0.9	25.0
Trade	1.2	1.4	0.0	4.3	0.0	0.3	5.4	143.1	580.7	717.2	2 709.1	865.5	233.1
Construction	0.0	0.0	0.7	4.8	12.3	84.7	104.6	184.1	151.1	206.7	50.4	133.2	23.0
Mining and quarrying	0.0	0.0	0.0	0.0	0.0	0.0	0.0	0.0	0.0	127.5	-1.3	0.0	0.0
Oil exploration	0.0	0.0	0.0	0.0	0.0	0.0	0.0	0.0	0.0	127.2	0.0	0.0	0.0
Other	0.0	0.0	0.0	0.0	0.0	0.0	0.0	0.0	43.3	0.3	0.0	0.0	0.0
Agriculture	0.0	0.0	0.3	0.0	0.5	0.4	0.0	14.5	0.0	280.4	354.2	32.2	26.2
Industry	0.7	7.5	0.7	19.1	32.2	32.0	22.6	317.3	1 928.1	3318.9	3 328.5	1 354.5	1 376.1
Food	0.0	4.6	0.0	2.2	0.0	0.0	1.5	47.1	73.3	168.5	183.1	144.6	155.3
Textiles	0.0	0.0	0.4	0.0	0.6	0.0	0.0	4.1	357.7	212.1	710.1	179.0	329.2
Metal-based and non-metallic	0.0	0.0	0.0	0.0	0.0	0.0	0.5	10.4	247.3	216.8	157.4	84.6	101.9
Electrical appliances	0.0	2.7	0.0	0.1	0.0	0.0	2.1	64.3	151.4	649.3	599.0	375.4	260.6
Machinery and transport equipment	0.0	0.0	0.0	0.0	2.6	0.0	0.0	0.6	49.0	167.9	38.9	11.9	24.6
Chemicals	0.0	0.2	0.0	16.1	28.4	32.0	0.3	111.0	389.0	451.7	260.1	108.4	179.4
Petroleum products	0.0	0.0	0.0	0.0	0.0	0.0	0.0	1.0	0.0	0.0	105.5	0.0	0.0
Construction materials	0.0	0.0	0.4	0.8	0.0	0.0	0.0	0.0	0.0	51.4	8.4	90.5	39.0
Other	0.0	0.0	0.0	0.0	0.7	0.0	18.2	78.6	0.0	1 401.3	1 266.1	360.1	286.1
Services	0.0	3.0	0.0	0.0	0.0	0.0	0.0	28.2	8.0	373.7	672.8	311.1	185.5
Transportation	0.0	0.0	0.0	0.0	0.0	0.0	0.0	0.0	261.2	15.4	11.7	2.5	47.2
Housing and real estate	0.0	3.0	0.0	0.0	0.0	0.0	0.0	23.3	2.5	277.0	584.4	272.5	145.1
Hotel and restaurant	0.0	0.0	0.0	0.0	0.0	0.0	0.0	0.0	159.0	64.8	62.1	4.4	0.0
Others	0.0	0.0	0.0	0.0	0.0	0.0	0.0	5.0	91.7	16.5	14.7	31.7	-6.8
Others	0.0	0.0	0.0	0.0	0.0	0.0	0.0	0.0	8.0	18.3	4.0	57.9	361.9
Total	1.9	11.9	1.7	28.2	45.0	170.2	132.6	687.2	2 847.9	5 063.3	7 137.9	2 753.5	2 230.8

Source: Bank of Thailand.

The study also shows that small Taiwanese firms tend to form joint ventures more often than do large firms. About 33 percent of small firms are minority-owned by Taiwanese, as compared to only 8 percent of large firms. According to this study, large Taiwanese companies in Thailand on average have more control over their overseas operations and are less dependent on local partners than are small firms. This pattern is in sharp contrast with the ownership structure in other Southeast Asian host countries where small firms are found to be more reluctant to hold minority ownership. The contrast reflects Taiwanese investors' exceptionally congenial relationship with Thai partners. In other countries, small firms opt for joint venture only when they are local-market-oriented.

The results of the survey show quite clearly that most operations of Taiwanese firms in Thailand are not subject to export or local content restrictions. About 64 percent of the surveyed firms respond that they are not subject to any export restrictions. As high as 87 percent of companies in the survey reveal that they do not encounter any restriction on local content.

Mode of investment

Most Taiwanese investments in Thailand start with new companies. About 86 percent of companies indicate that they started as a green-field project. Very few of them invest through acquiring, merging or joining with other companies. There is no significant difference between large and small firms in this respect.

To gauge the profitability of Taiwanese companies in Thailand, the study examines average time of capital recovery and disposition of profits by Taiwanese companies. The average time for capital recovery is about 5.2 years. Small firms recover their capital slightly faster than large firms. The average time for large firms is about 5.7 years while that of small firms is about 4.8 years. It shows that Taiwanese companies in Thailand make considerable profits.

According to the study, most companies in Thailand retain profits made in Thailand for future operations there. The result of the survey reveals that on average Taiwanese companies retain 67 percent of their profits in Thailand for internal financing. Other projects in Thailand consume another 11 percent; only about 20 percent is remitted back to Taiwan. The study finds that large and small firms are similar in this respect. This suggests that once a Taiwanese firm succeeds in Thailand, it expands like any indigenous firm.

The average time required for approval of an application for investment is rather long in Thailand. The survey shows that about 17 months are needed for an application for investment to be approved. This suggests that improvements can be made on the rules and regulations governing foreign investment, as well as on the efficiency of Thai government officials in charge of investment approvals.

Sources of inputs

Although not required to do so by law, Taiwanese firms still use considerable amounts of local parts and components. About 39 percent of parts and components are purchased from local sources. Small firms use a slightly higher proportion of local parts and components than large firms. Aside from local sources, about 22 percent of parts and components are sourced from third-party countries, approximately 21 percent are from their parent companies, and 17 percent from other suppliers in Taiwan. Although imported materials still dominate the procurement, local content tends to increase rapidly over time.

In contrast, however, the survey shows that local suppliers play minimal roles in providing machinery and equipment to Taiwanese subsidiaries. On average, about 49 percent of the machinery and equipment is provided by Taiwanese suppliers. About 19 percent of machinery and equipment are imports from third-party countries and 17 percent are old machines relocated from parent companies in Taiwan. Only about 15 percent of machinery and equipment is purchased from local suppliers. Thus local suppliers are only marginal sources of machinery and equipment for Taiwanese firms in Thailand, especially for large firms, which indicate that only 7 percent of machinery and equipment is bought from local suppliers. Furthermore, large firms tend to relocate old machinery from parent companies in Taiwan more often than do small firms. This suggests that FDI by large firms is essentially a transplantation of the export platform from Taiwan to Thailand.

In sharp contrast to the case of machinery and equipment, a large proportion of Taiwanese firms, especially large firms, rely on local financial institutions for financing. Taiwanese firms in the survey indicate that they receive 54 percent of their funds from local financial institutions. Large firms in the survey indicate that local financial institutions provide up to 61 percent of funds for them, while the ratio is only 49 percent for small firms. The next most important source of funds is parent companies, which provide about 27 percent of funds. Other sources of finance include local partners and even informal financial markets.

Decision making

One particularly interesting aspect of Taiwanese investment is the decision-making processes of foreign subsidiaries. According to the survey, a few expatriate managers from Taiwan take high-ranking positions in the subsidiaries, like president or vice president. About 82 percent of firms in the survey indicate that Taiwanese expatriates hold these positions. Expatriates are also commonly involved in production management. About 69 percent of the sample indicates that there are Taiwanese expatriates present in the production department, suggesting the importance they assign to fine-tuning production. About 43 and 37 percent of firms in the sample reveal the presence of

Taiwanese expatriates in the finance and marketing departments, respectively. It is interesting to note that the proportion of expatriates in the top executive positions, and in the finance and marketing departments of large firms, is larger than that of small firms. This indicates that large firms are keen on exercising control through expatriate managers.

A rather small proportion of firms in the survey responded that their expatriates are in the planning, R&D, or personnel departments. It is apparent that most planning, as well as R&D, is done by parent companies. There is no need for parent companies to send a large number of expatriates to work in these departments. For the personnel department, it is obvious that Thai managers are more effective in dealing with Thai staff and workers. Therefore, there is also no reason for parent companies to send a large number of expatriates to work in this department.

With regard to the decision making of Taiwanese subsidiaries, the study suggests that parent companies still make major decisions with respect to finance, R&D, and marketing. On the other hand, local managers and expatriate managers in Thailand can make decisions involving production and personnel management with a considerable degree of freedom. More and more decision making in finance and marketing is also expected to be delegated to local managers in the future.

According to our survey, there is not much difference between large and small firms in terms of the decision-making processes, except for marketing. About 54 percent of the large firms in the survey indicate that parent companies make decisions on marketing compared to only about 33 percent of small firms. This indicates that large subsidiaries adhere to the parent companies' global marketing plans while small subsidiaries have more discretion over their own marketing strategies.

One observation can be made from this survey regarding the decision making of Taiwanese subsidiaries in Thailand. That is, local managers make decisions on matters involving day-to-day operations and they usually have more freedom than Taiwanese expatriate managers. The latter make decisions involving higher-level and more general issues. Sometimes those issues may relate to common policies of subsidiaries and parent companies. The study indicates that although subsidiaries may make more independent decisions in the future, for important issues parent companies will still retain influence through their expatriate managers.

Performance of Taiwanese firms in Thailand

To assess the performance of Taiwanese firms in Thailand, the study surveyed the opinions of Taiwanese firms both in Thailand and in Taiwan. Two questions in the survey are related to this issue. The first question asks the respondent to compare Taiwanese firms with locally owned firms. The second question asks him or her to compare Taiwanese firms with other foreign firms in Thailand.

According to the opinions reflected by the respondents in the survey, Taiwanese firms consider themselves to be better than locally owned firms in most respects. Taiwanese firms believe they are superior in the areas of production, technological capability, management, marketing, training of local workers, and exporting. Superiority in production includes average production value per employee, production flexibility, quality control, and scale of production. Superiority in technological capabilities includes degree of automation, level of technology adopted, new product development, technology innovation, and process improvement. A large proportion of Taiwanese firms also think that they are better than locally owned firms in the areas of after-sales service and company image. The respondents believe that Taiwanese firms also have a higher rate of return on investment and higher unit price of output. About 50 percent of Taiwanese firms in the survey believe that they purchase less local materials than locally owned firms, however.

Despite the favorable assessment Taiwanese firms give themselves in comparison with locally owned firms, comparison with multinational firms from advanced countries, such as the US and Japan, shows an opposite pattern. Taiwanese firms think that they compare less favorably to advanced countries' subsidiaries in all areas, except that of exports. A considerable proportion of firms in the survey express the impression that Taiwanese firms fall behind multinational firms from advanced countries in the areas of technology transfer to local firms, local procurement, joint research and development with local firms, employment of unskilled workers, job training, capital intensity, and the willingness to build plants in remote areas.

8.3 New Developments Affecting FDI in Thailand

Some recent developments in the Asian region may have a significant impact on FDI in Thailand, including that from Taiwan. They are the rising Japanese yen, the emergence of Indochinese countries and the People's Republic of China (PRC), the formation of the ASEAN Free Trade Area (AFTA), the reform of the tariff system in Thailand, and the Looking South policy of Taiwan. It is obvious that the rising yen will significantly increase the price of Japanese exports. It will force Japan to relocate its production bases to developing countries, including Thailand. However, unlike the last wave of FDI erupting in the second half of the 1980s, this time it is likely that Japanese FDI in Thailand will be concentrated more on automobile assembly, and manufacture of automobile and machinery parts and components, rather than electronics and electrical appliances. The reason is that, compared to other countries in ASEAN, Thailand has many capable suppliers in the auto industries. Meanwhile, Malaysia may be the most attractive production base for electronics and electrical appliances among the countries in ASEAN.

The emergence of Indochina and the People's Republic of China unquestionably will have an impact on FDI in Thailand at present and in the future. Indochina consists of Laos, Cambodia and Vietnam. These countries have abundant natural and human resources. Vietnam, in particular, also has a well-educated workforce. Although they still lack infrastructure and a suitable legal framework for foreign investment, the development is under way. Vietnam, for example, may replace Thailand in some labor-intensive industries in which Thailand is losing its comparative advantage (Pupphavesa and Grewe 1994).

Meanwhile, the People's Republic of China may be the most attractive country for foreign investment now. It has the largest population in the world and, therefore, one of the largest markets in the world. The country is well endowed with natural resources and a competent labor force. It comes as no surprise that in 1994, PRC received FDI second only to the US. However, due to inflation, income disparity has persisted between developed regions and underdeveloped regions within the PRC. There are also problems facing foreign business operations, like corruption, infrastructure bottlenecks, and the inefficiency of government agencies. Besides PRC, India has also received much attention from foreign investors recently. Nevertheless, from our interviews with Indian economists, it seems foreign investors there are mainly interested in producing to serve the local market and not for export. Hence, competition with Thailand is not imminent.

The next development is the formation of the ASEAN Free Trade Area (AFTA). The formation of AFTA aims to increase trade and competitiveness by reducing tariffs and other trade barriers among member countries. Such reductions, if effective, would undoubtedly increase trade among member countries and reduce the costs of production, especially for some industries like electronics and electrical appliances. A study by Thailand Development Research Institute (TDRI 1994) shows that the reduction in cost of production would be greater in Thailand than in most other countries, except the Philippines. The reason is that the tariff rate of Thailand has been the highest among ASEAN members, next to the Philippines. For industries like electrical appliances and electronics, the reductions of production costs in Thailand would be rather large because more than 15 percent of the imported parts and components used by the Thai industry are from other members of AFTA, principally Singapore. As we will see in the next section, FDI in Thailand has shifted from a focus on local markets to cost reduction and productivity orientation. Thus the reduction in the costs of production through the formation of AFTA should have some positive impact on FDI in Thailand, especially in the electronics and electrical appliances sector.

Unfortunately, under the AFTA liberalization scheme currently implemented, the increase in trade and the reduction in costs of production are not likely to be significant. The study by TDRI finds that most member countries reduce tariffs only on items in which they have a comparative advantage. For items where they do not have a comparative advantage, tariffs remain high. Furthermore, under the current tariff structure, preferential tariff rates implemented under AFTA may not create as much multilateral trade as expected.

At the end of 1994, Thailand drastically reformed its tariff system as part of AFTA initiatives. The tariff rates of most items were reduced, especially that of raw materials, intermediate products, and machinery, which were reduced to the 5 to 10 percent range. This measure was expected to significantly reduce costs of production for many industries such as electronics and electrical appliances, textiles and garments, and machinery. This reduction of tariff rates is likely to induce more FDI into Thailand.

8.4 Determinants of Foreign Direct Investment

In this section, we present a study of factors affecting FDI in Thailand, including that from Taiwan. Before the study, we review previous studies investigating motives and factors affecting a company's decision to invest in foreign countries, specifically in Thailand. The study investigates the motives of Taiwanese investment in Thailand and asks why Taiwanese investors chose Thailand over other ASEAN countries.

8.4.1 Review of Studies on Factors Affecting FDI

A study by Allen (1973) found that the most important factor affecting Japanese investors' selection of host countries was the economic and political stability of the host country, followed by the quality of the labor force, sufficiency of local funds, the availability of good joint-venture partners, tax incentives, sufficiency of foreign exchange reserves, stability of the currency of the host country, exemption from import duties, objectives of economic planning, and the attitude of the people and the government of a host country, in that order. He also found that the most important motive of Japanese investors was the protection of an export market, followed by the exploitation of natural resources and raw materials.

There are numerous studies investigating the factors affecting FDI in Thailand conducted in the 1970s. The findings of these studies almost reach a consensus that the most important factor affecting FDI is the domestic market potential (Attakorn 1975; Tambunleartchai 1980; Sibunruang 1984).

Other important factors are trade protection, including tariff barriers (Tambunleartchai 1980), abundance of low-cost materials (Attakorn 1975; Tambunleartchai 1980; Sibunruang 1984), low labor cost (Attakorn 1975; Tambunleartchai 1980), good environment for investment (Attakorn 1975), and incentives provided by the host country (Tambunleartchai 1980; Sibunruang 1984).

A study by Karnjanapunka (1978) found that FDI in different industries may have different motives. For example, foreign investors in resource-based industries such as food, mining, agriculture and paper were concerned about the exploitation of domestic resources more than other factors. Foreign investors in market-oriented industries such as the chemical and textile industries were concerned about the availability of low-cost labor, and access to the local market.

8.4.2 Motives of Taiwanese Investment in Thailand

In this study, we conduct our own survey on the motives of Taiwanese investment in Thailand. About 60 percent of the Taiwanese investors indicate that they invest in Thailand because of the appreciation of the Taiwanese currency, NT. Large firms appear to be more concerned about the appreciation of the NT than are small firms.

However, the most important motive for Taiwanese investment in Thailand is to take advantage of the low labor cost in Thailand. About 89 percent of firms in the survey indicate that low labor cost is an important motive for investing in Thailand. Similar to the case of the appreciation of the NT, large firms appear to be more concerned about low labor cost than are small firms. Low cost of land also appears to be an important factor motivating FDI in Thailand. In this case, however, small firms are more concerned.

Besides the cost-related motives, the other important motive is to expand sales in the local market or third-country markets. Small firms appear to pay more attention to the expansion of sales than do large firms. In addition, avoiding trade restrictions and environmental regulations in Taiwan also motivates FDI. Again, small firms appear to be motivated by these two factors more often than large firms. Other factors, such as securing a supply of raw materials, joint actions with other firms, and collecting market information, appear to be insignificant.

Our survey also indicates that Taiwanese investors choose Thailand over the other ASEAN countries because of its racial homogeneity and political stability. Large firms appear to be more concerned about political stability than small firms, while small firms are more concerned about racial harmony than large firms. The other factors that affect investors' selection of Thailand over other ASEAN countries are low-cost labor and fiscal incentives. These two factors appear to be more important to large firms than to small firms.

8.5 Impact of FDI on the Thai Economy

8.5.1 Previous Findings

Studies on the impact of FDI on the Thai economy are summarized by Sibunruang-Brimble (1992). Her study classifies the impact of FDI into several categories including export generation, employment creation, backward linkages, and technology transfer, and concludes that the most noticeable impact of FDI is on Thai exports. Sibunruang (1986) examined the impact of FDI on Thai exports in the 1970s and found that foreign-owned and foreign joint-venture firms on the Thai government promotion list contributed about 25 percent of total manufactured exports from Thailand. Foreign firms accounted for very large shares of total exports in some industries such as electronics and machinery.

A recent study by Pupphavesa and Pussarungsri (1995) used the causality test technique to identify the causal effect of FDI on Thai exports. The study did not find any evidence of causal effect of FDI on manufactured exports from Thailand. On the contrary, FDI appeared to be induced by the export expansion of the country. Only FDI in the electrical appliances industry was found to generate exports from Thailand. Since Taiwanese investment concentrates on this industry, it is also likely to generate exports for the country.

The effect of FDI on manufacturing employment was found to be much less significant. Using BOI survey data on 600 manufacturing firms, Sibunruang and Brimble (1988) showed that, in 1985, foreign firms accounted for only 8.8 percent of manufacturing employment. The reason may be that foreign-invested firms have higher capital-to-labor ratios, compared to Thai firms (Khanthachai et al. 1987).

According to Lipsey (1991), transfer of technology by multinational firms can occur in three channels. First, technology may be transferred through the training of local personnel who, in turn, train other local personnel or establish their own firms. Second, foreign technicians train local parts and components suppliers to improve the quality of their products. Third, competition introduced by foreign firms forces local firms to become more efficient, and induces them to acquire new technology.

In relation to the first channel of transferring technology, a recent study by Kaosa-ard (1992) illustrated that foreign firms invest much more in training for high-level staff than they do for low-level staff. Foreign firms generally conduct on-the-job training for unskilled and semi-skilled workers. There is only a limited degree of technology transfer through the training of local suppliers, however (Sibunruang and Brimble 1988). The transfer of technology through subcontracting arrangements is also found to be minimal (Dahlman et al. 1991). The study of Pupphavesa and Pussarungsri (1995) followed the concept of Wong (1991) by taking into account the indirect transfer of technology by multinational firms. They found that indirect transfer is, in fact, more important than direct transfer. However, suppliers in Thailand can absorb only the basic level of technology. The study also found that technology transfer in industries with a long process of production which requires a considerable number of parts and components, such as the machinery industry, is much more difficult than that in industries with a shorter process of production, such as the electronics industry. It is also found that technology diffusion through job mobility is minimal because workers rarely move from foreign firms to Thai firms.

FDI may also have a negative impact on the local economy by creating pollution and foreign exchange reserve leakages due to dependence on imported parts and components, or by remittance of royalty payments and profits. Studies by Pongpisanupichit (1985) and TDRI (1989) indicated that the loss of foreign exchange reserves caused by foreign firms has not been substantial, however. In the case of foreign-invested firms in Thailand, capital inflows to Thailand far exceeded remittances from Thailand. As for pollution, the study of Pupphavesa and Pussarungsri (1995) found that FDI is not systematically biased towards activities creating massive air and water pollution, although the proportion of foreign firms operating in industries producing modest pollutants is higher than that of the local firms.

8.5.2 Employment Created by Taiwanese Investment

We turn now to an investigation of employment generation within Thailand by Taiwanese FDI. To do this, we use our survey data and secondary data from BOI and the Bank of Thailand.

The employment-to-capital ratios of Taiwanese investment are substantially higher than those of other multinational firms. This indicates that Taiwanese investment is more labor-intensive than the rest of FDI in Thailand. The same amount of investment from Taiwan generates more employment opportunities. The labor intensity of Taiwanese FDI has declined over time, however. The decline is attributable to several factors. First, since the end of the 1980s Taiwanese investment has gradually shifted from labor-intensive industries such as textiles toward more technology-intensive industries such as electronics and electrical appliances. This shift caused Taiwanese investors to hire fewer workers for the same amount of investment. Second, there was a downward adjustment in labor-to-capital ratio throughout Thai industries due to a rising cost of labor in Thailand. Third, labor shortages, particularly that of skilled labor, have undermined labor-intensive operations as skilled and unskilled labor are often complements in large-scale assembly operations (Chen and Tang 1987).

The amount of employment generated by FDI in Thailand was quite substantial. In 1988, total employment generated by promoted[1] new foreign investment projects was as high as 210 140 workers, or 34 percent of the increase in non-farm employment in that year (Table 8.4). However, after this peak, employment generated by promoted new foreign investment projects started to decline. In 1995, only 60 637 jobs were generated, accounting for 7.7 percent of new job creations in the non-farm sector.

The employment generated by Taiwanese investment was also quite substantial in 1988. About 37 000 people were hired by newly established Taiwanese subsidiaries promoted by BOI, or 6 percent of the total increase in non-farm employment in that year. Similar to the overall pattern, employment generated by Taiwanese subsidiaries also declined after 1988. In 1995, jobs created by Taiwanese subsidiaries totaled only 8353 or 1 percent of the increase in non-farm employment in that year. The decline in employment generation is a combination of falling FDI amount and falling labor intensity in each investment project.

Table 8.4 Employment Generated by Promoted New Foreign Investment Projects

Year	Total	All projects		Taiwanese projects		
	Increase in non-farm employment (persons)	Employment (persons)	% of total employment	Employment (persons)	% of total foreign firms	% of total employment
1988	620 000	210 140	34.0	37 110	17.6	6.0
1989	510 000	197 160	38.6	32 900	16.7	6.4
1990	460 000	189 263	41.1	26 034	13.7	5.6
1991	460 000	130 494	28.3	13 234	10.0	2.9
1992	470 000	80 289	17.1	4 812	6.0	1.0
1993	610 000	59 866	9.8	13 134	21.9	2.2
1994	620 000	49 464	8.0	8 792	17.8	1.4
1995	790 000	60 637	7.7	8 353	13.8	1.1
1996*	670 000	99 780	14.9	7 764*	7.8	1.2

Note: *1996 data are January to September.

Sources: Bank of Thailand and Board of Investment (BOI), Thailand.

8.5.3 Technology Transfer

For Taiwanese subsidiaries in Thailand, parent firms are the most important source of technology. About 64 percent of firms in the survey indicated that parent firms supply new technology to the subsidiaries. Large firms seem to depend on parent firms more than small firms for new technology. Nonetheless, there were about 47 percent of firms in the survey which responded that the subsidiaries also acquire new technology through their own research and development efforts.

Most technology transferred to Thai subsidiaries is to support existing production activities, including technology for operation, maintenance of machinery and equipment, quality control, and process control. In comparison, the transfer of technology related to innovation and product design is much less common. The latter technology can be supported by the parent firms from a distance since it is only needed intermittently.

In most cases, the Taiwanese subsidiaries in Thailand produce goods requiring similar or lower technology levels than the goods produced by their parent companies. About 48 percent of firms in the survey reported that they produce essentially the same products as those produced by their parent firms. In this case, parent firms usually transferred their production technology to the subsidiaries without modifications. Large firms are particularly keen on transferring technology to overseas subsidiaries intact because the subsidiaries simply duplicate the products made at home.

About 42 percent of firms in the survey revealed that their subsidiaries in Thailand manufacture products with a lower unit price and somewhat higher labor intensity than those produced at home. In this case, Thai subsidiaries usually adopt simpler technology compared to their parent firms. Surprisingly, only a very small proportion of Taiwanese firms (9 percent) in the survey indicated that their subsidiaries manufacture something vertically related to products of their parent firms. Lack of vertical integration indicates that Taiwanese multinational firms are unable to pursue international division of labor along value-added chains. Division of labor among Taiwanese multinationals is mostly horizontal in nature.

Our survey indicates that large firms are more sluggish in making technical adaptations to the local environment. Large firms often engage in mass production, so they are subject to higher risks from technical failures. When technical adaptations do take place adjustments in production method are often made to take advantage of low-cost labor in Thailand. Adjustment is more extensive among small firms than large firms, indicating small firms' strong incentive to localize.

Several implications may be drawn from the results of our survey. First, production technology adopted by a considerable proportion of Taiwanese subsidiaries in Thailand is identical to that used by parent companies. Large subsidiaries seem to have greater capability to absorb technology than small ones. In most cases, technology adopted by subsidiaries in Thailand is also the most advanced technology available to their respective parent firms.

The survey indicates that more than half of Taiwanese parent companies train workers on behalf of their subsidiaries in Thailand. There are more parent companies training blue-collar workers than training white-collar workers. The training is mostly aimed at transferring production-related technologies, including those for operations, maintenance of machinery and equipment, quality control, and process control. Training in other fields such as marketing and financial management is much less common. In general, more training opportunities are provided by large parent firms than by small parent firms.

The average training period provided by Taiwanese parent firms is quite long: 39 days for white-collar workers and 63 days for blue-collar workers. Small parent firms provide a much longer training period than do large parent firms. The number of workers trained by parent firms is rather small, however: on average, 4.3 white-collar and 11.8 blue-collar workers are trained by each firm.

The transfer of technology from Taiwanese parent firms to their subsidiaries in Thailand and training of local workers are found to be quite successful. Such success may be due to the simplicity of technology to be transferred. Apparently, technology transferred from Taiwanese parent firms to Thailand is mostly confined to Taiwanese subsidiaries. The diffusion of technology from Taiwanese subsidiaries to Thai producers through subcontracting arrangements or labor mobility is limited. Our interviews revealed that Taiwanese firms usually do not invest in their local suppliers in terms of providing technology support.

8.5.4 Taiwanese FDI and Exports from Thailand

Based on the typical Heckscher–Ohlin theory, capital flow is a substitute for commodity trade (Mundell 1957; Naya and Imada 1988) as FDI brings about factor-price equalization and commodity trade is not needed any more. In this case, FDI would reduce the volume of trade. Nevertheless, when imperfect competition, market distortions, and differences in technology and consumer preference are allowed for, the above conclusion may be reversed; FDI may lead to a greater volume of trade (Markusen 1983).

In a dynamic perspective, FDI may also lead to an expansion of international trade. The product-cycle literature explains the flow of FDI from developed countries to developing countries as driven by the evolution of the country's comparative advantage (Vernon 1966; Akamatsu 1961; 1962). According to this theory, when a product becomes mature and standardized, the technological know-how becomes readily available in most countries; it is then more efficient to relocate production bases from high-wage to low-wage countries. Low-wage countries, which are recipients of FDI, play catch-up with leading countries which are sources of FDI. Despite the trade-oriented nature of FDI emanating from the product life cycle, there are some concerns that the process of FDI and the product-cycle evolution itself may bring about slower economic growth to the host country (Naya and Imada 1988).

In relation to product-cycle theory, Kojima (1978) observed that Japanese FDI created exports for host countries. Kojima classified motives of FDI from Japan into four types: to exploit natural resources, to take advantage of cheap labor, to exploit the local market, and a strategic motive in the oligopoly industries. Labor-seeking FDI will stimulate trade between the host country on the one hand, and the investing country (Japan) and the third parties on the other. The investing country exports capital goods and parts and components to the host country. The host country, in turn, exports finished products to the investing country and the third-party countries, like the US and Europe. Market-seeking FDI will also create trade but largely between investing and host countries. Only the strategically motivated FDI may reduce trade by substituting local production for exports from the investing country.

The relationship between FDI and exports in Thailand has been studied by Pupphavesa and Pussarungsri (1995) and TDRI (1994). Both studies employ the causality test method to examine the linkage between FDI and exports. They find that FDI in export-oriented industries, such as electronics and electrical appliances, has a strong causal effect on the exports from those industries. This causal effect is particularly evident for FDI from Japan and the NIEs.

Our survey indicates that more than half of the products made by Taiwanese subsidiaries are exported, mostly to third-party countries. The other 9 percent are exported back to their parent firms, and 3 percent to other firms in Taiwan. Large firms have a particularly strong export orientation as they export 83 percent of their products. Small firms, in comparison, export just above 50 percent. Large subsidiaries in Thailand are apparently designated as offshore export platforms to serve international markets which have previously been served by exports from Taiwan.

8.6 Problems Faced by Taiwanese Investors in Thailand

This section provides information about problems encountered by Taiwanese investors in their business operations in Thailand. Some of these problems could have been avoided by making good preparations. Others could not. The information presented in this section was obtained from on-site interviews and interviews by phone. Surprisingly, most of the Taiwanese firms had similar problems.

The first common problem faced by Taiwanese investors is with the legal and fiscal incentive scheme of Thailand. There is no official English or other foreign language version of laws and regulations governing foreign business operations. Sometimes even Thai officials do not really know the laws and regulations well enough to give advice to foreign investors. The Thai fiscal incentive scheme is complicated and perplexing. Some conditions set by the

BOI for foreign investment projects to be eligible for fiscal incentives are discretionary and changing over time. Some Taiwanese investors had their tax privileges revoked because they could not reach the target sales agreed upon with the BOI. Most of them underestimated the severity of the punishment for failing the targets. Problems are made worse by Taiwanese investors who usually do not use the services of qualified lawyers (Pussarungsri and Thongpakdee 1992).

The second common problem faced by Taiwanese investors is the bureaucracy in Thailand. The most troublesome area seems to be the customs and duties. The problem arises from a lengthy procedure for customs clearing and a duty assessment system that depends heavily on the subjective judgment of officers. Classification of customs items, which makes a big difference in the tariff burden, depends mostly on the discretion of customs officers.

The third problem that concerns most Taiwanese investors is the lack of schools to offer the Chinese-language-based education to the children of expatriate workers. The problem comes from the high costs of operating such a school and a lack of qualified teachers. Currently, there is a new Taiwanese school established in suburban Bangkok, partly sponsored by the Taiwanese Business Association in Thailand. Many believe that it is still not sufficient, however.

The fourth problem is the communication barrier between Thai workers and Taiwanese managers. Taiwanese investors speak Chinese, and sometimes English. Most Thai workers speak only Thai. Thus, communication is rather difficult. The language barrier, among other things, slows the training of Thai workers and reduces the efficiency of local operations.

The fifth problem is a shortage of skilled labor. Most Taiwanese investors complain that skilled workers at all levels are difficult to find in Thailand. Indeed, Thailand has been experiencing a shortage of labor at all skill levels (Poorpongskorn 1992). The experience of Taiwanese investors is not unique among manufacturers in Thailand. Fortunately, the turnover rate of skilled workers is relatively low for most Taiwanese firms compared to other multinationals and even local producers.

The sixth problem is related to parts suppliers in Thailand. For Taiwanese investors, finding qualified suppliers is difficult. Some Taiwanese firms complained about delayed delivery and substandard products of local suppliers. Compared to Japanese and American subsidiaries, which are mostly larger than Taiwanese firms, the problem with suppliers seems to be more acute for Taiwanese firms since they are less capable of cultivating local suppliers of their own.

The final problem is unique to Taiwanese investors. Because of the peculiar political and international status of Taiwan, Thailand does not accept applications for either permanent residency or citizenship from Taiwanese citizens. Lengthy procedures in the application and extension of work permits reduce the mobility of Taiwanese expatriates.

There are also problems with the protection of minority shareholders and restrictions on land ownership by foreigners. This study as well as other studies, such as Pussarungsri and Thongpakdee (1992), have found that there is always a way to circumvent these restrictions, however.

8.7 Conclusion

The amount of Taiwanese investment in Thailand was rather small in the first half of the 1980s. It then accelerated rapidly from 1985, reached a peak in 1990, and started to decline. In recent years, Taiwanese investment ranked third or fourth in importance following Japan, the United States and Hong Kong. It was concentrated mostly in the manufacturing sector, and construction and trade to a lesser extent. Within the manufacturing sector, Taiwanese investment was concentrated in the electrical appliances and textile industries, which were also the top two exporting sectors of Thailand.

There are several interesting characteristics of Taiwanese investment in Thailand. Most Taiwanese firms in Thailand are small in terms of capital and sales. A large proportion of Taiwanese firms are 100 percent owned by Taiwanese. On average, they earn considerable profits in Thailand; the average time for capital recovery is about five years. A large proportion of profits are retained in Thailand and used mostly for internal expansion purposes.

Taiwanese firms are shown to use a sizable proportion of local parts and components, but a majority of them still import machinery and equipment from Taiwan and third-party countries. An interesting characteristic of Taiwanese firms is that they tend to assimilate rapidly with the local economy, as decision making in Taiwanese subsidiaries is done increasingly by expatriates and local managers, and procurement of locally made parts and components increases rapidly over time.

Taiwanese investment is shown to have contributed significantly to the Thai economy in terms of trade expansion and employment generation. The transfer of technology to indigenous workers is still limited, however, because of communication problems between Taiwanese managers and local workers. Although training is extensive, the technology tends to stay within the perimeters of Taiwanese subsidiaries, because of the low labor turnover and inability of Taiwanese firms to invest in local suppliers.

Despite the considerable length of time that Taiwanese investors have been operating in Thailand, most of them still face significant problems. The most common problem faced by Taiwanese investors is the legal framework and regulations set by the BOI. Sometimes promotion privileges were withdrawn from Taiwanese firms because they did not meet the conditions agreed upon with the BOI. Many partnerships have been broken up because of misunderstandings of some legal aspects in Thai regulations. Other problems include shortages of labor, inadequate government service, insufficient Chinese-language schools for the children of Taiwanese expatriates, communication problems between Taiwanese managers and Thai workers, difficulty in locating and dealing with local suppliers, and restrictions against Taiwanese applications for permanent residency and citizenship in Thailand.

Observing Taiwanese investment in Thailand reveals that, in most cases, FDI is beneficial to both parties, Thailand and Taiwan. Both parties could gain still more from the investment if some of the problems could be alleviated. On the Taiwanese side, Taiwanese investors should learn more about the rules and regulations governing operation of a foreign company in Thailand. On the Thai side, the Thai government needs to lessen unnecessary restrictions on Taiwanese investors. Improvement of Thailand's infrastructure and human resources is also needed. Moreover, better policies are needed to facilitate technology transfer from Taiwanese investors to Thai workers and suppliers.

Note

1. In Thailand the term 'promoted' is used to refer to companies that receive special privileges or incentives such as tax holidays, or exemption from customs duties, from the Thai government.

9. Taiwanese Investment in the Philippines

Thomas G. Aquino

9.1 Background and Overview

9.1.1 Policy Environment

In general, the government of the Philippines takes a favorable stance towards foreign investment, although the investment regime has evolved over time in line with the Philippines' economic conditions and development strategies. Right after World War II, the central focus of the economic policy was to promote import-substituting industries. Tax concessions, preferential allocation of credits and foreign exchange were given to 'new' industries in which FDI was expected to take place. The incentives were counterbalanced by controls on the remittance of profits by foreign investors. The growth of import-substituting industries, including those invested by foreign nationals, was once promising but soon became sluggish at the end of the 1950s because such an industrialization strategy was constrained by the limited size of the domestic market.

From 1962 to 1986, a series of actions was taken to liberalize the foreign investment regime and to encourage export-oriented FDI. First, in 1962, foreign exchange control was removed, resulting in a devaluation of the Philippines currency, the peso. The devaluation made the investment climate more favorable to export industries.

Second, in 1967, a new law (R.A. 5186), known as the Investment Incentives Act, was passed to create institutions and provide policy instruments to promote investment, including foreign direct investment. The Act established a Board of Investments (BOI), under the Office of the President, to take charge of the promotion and review of investment projects. BOI defined the 'pioneer' industries that were eligible for fiscal incentives. Foreign investment was allowed in pioneer industries with 100 percent ownership, while foreign ownership was capped at 40 percent in non-pioneer industries unless the foreign-invested company exported 70 percent of its products or more.

Then, in 1970, a new law (R.A. 6135), known as the Export Incentives Act, was promulgated to specifically promote the manufacturing of non-traditional export products. Tax incentives and other benefits were awarded to producers and traders of these products. FDI in these product categories was encouraged.

In the 1980s, a series of new laws and amendments was enacted to consolidate existing incentives and provide new initiatives for investment. For example, new incentives were awarded to exporters based on their performances in terms of local content and net value added. With the advent of the Aquino Administration in 1986, a series of reforms was proposed to further liberalize the trade and investment regimes, including removing import restrictions, foreign exchange decontrol, and tariff reductions. But the strong lobbies mounted by powerful interest groups prevented the government from fully implementing the liberalization plans. Despite the reform efforts, foreign investors did not seem to be impressed. The annual gross inflow of FDI had been erratic and had never gone beyond US$255 million before 1987. A significant rise of FDI in the Philippines occurred between 1987 and 1990, but that was attributed largely to debt-to-equity conversions. Moreover, the outflow of capital, partly consisting of capital withdrawn by foreign investors from the Philippines, increased in the 1980s, reflecting investors' dissatisfaction with the investment climate (Aquino and Bolaños 1995).

From 1990, a more comprehensive program for economic liberalization has been implemented and sustained with pressure from the International Monetary Fund (IMF), which provided a stand-by credit facility to the Philippines, and with commitment from President Ramos who succeeded Aquino in 1992. At the heart of the current policy reform are liberalization, deregulation, and privatization, improvement of the business operating conditions, infrastructure development, and improvement of financial markets. Full foreign ownership is allowed in all industries except those stipulated in the 'negative list'. Some traditionally 'sensitive' industries, such as downstream oil products, shipping, domestic and international aviation, telecommunications, mining, to name just a few, are opened to private participation, including foreign investors. To improve the business operating conditions, initiatives are taken to liberalize the banking sector, lift foreign exchange controls, provide foreign investment with insurance against political risks, and offer assistance and services to foreign investors. As for infrastructure development, the measure of the Build–Operate–Transfer (BOT) scheme has been actively promoted. Efforts are also geared towards the development of export processing zones, special economic zones, industrial estates, and investment-ready regional growth centers.

Historically, the American and Chinese were the major foreign investors in the Philippines. In recent years, influx of foreign capital has come from other countries, like Japan, Great Britain, Hong Kong and Taiwan. Foreign equity investment has increased sharply in recent years, with almost two-thirds of the total foreign investment accumulated since 1968 coming during the 1990s (APEC 1998).

9.1.2 Taiwanese FDI in the Philippines

Taiwanese investment in the Philippines declined considerably in the period 1989–1993, from a peak level of 2.2 billion pesos in 1989. During this period, the average annual growth rate was minus 49 percent. In 1994, a remarkable turnaround in Taiwanese investment occurred. From its lowest level in 1993, Taiwanese investment shot up to 7.1 billion pesos in 1994. This was not sustained, however, as investment fell to 349.4 million pesos in 1995 and went down further to 194.7 million pesos in 1996.

In 1997, for the period of January to April, total foreign investment in the Philippines amounted to 17 billion pesos, with Europe and the Caribbean region emerging as the top foreign investors, pouring in some 7.5 billion pesos and 4.4 billion pesos, respectively. During this period, the top Asian investors in the Philippines were Malaysia, Japan, and Hong Kong (Table 9.1). For the same period, Taiwanese investment constituted only 0.39 percent of total foreign investment.

The decline in the Taiwanese interest in the Philippines as a prospective overseas investment site from 1989 to 1993 can be mainly attributed to the perceived political, social and economic instability in the country. Foreign investment, being sensitive to political risk, was driven away for three years after the failed coup d'état in December 1989. Also, a major ruling by the Supreme Court in 1991 to deny a prospective Taiwanese investor (USI Far East) its choice of plant location and raw material source affected considerably the investment decision of many Taiwanese firms to make the Philippines their destination. Moreover, frequent power shortages, the inadequacy of vital infrastructure, and the lack of law and order during the period contributed to the increasing level of uncertainty in the country. Given the unstable environment, most foreign investors were forced to hold back their decision to invest in the Philippines.

This high-risk perception continued for three years (1990–93), until changes in the political and economic spheres of the Philippines slowly reduced that perception. The first change was the election of President Fidel V. Ramos in May 1992, which signaled the successful democratic reorientation of the government. Three months after assuming office, President Ramos launched a volley of political and economic policy reforms, which continues until today. His reforms were aimed at restoring the peace and order situation and

Table 9.1 Total Foreign Investments in the Philippines, by Area, 1989–97 (million pesos)

	1989	1990	1991	1992	1993	1994	1995	1996	1997 Jan–Apr
Australia and Oceania	521.4	302.8	127.7	14.9	11.6	263.1	436.4	142.9	48.7
Asia	11 568.5	15 668.6	6 652.9	3 750.6	6 032.7	26 935.2	14 046.4	11 971.3	3 762.5
Taiwan	3 232.7	1 229.8	286.9	232.0	145.1	7 075.6	349.4	194.7	65.2
North America	3 095.8	2 641.9	2 053.7	1 623.0	2 405.1	18 015.3	16 421.7	868.8	977.2
Central America	21.2	45.6	133.7	0.0	0.0	4.1	0.0	0.0	0.0
South America	1.6	4.5	0.6	87.7	0.0	0.7	0.0	0.7	0.0
Caribbean	37.0	228.8	324.9	101.3	1 574.0	8 713.3	3.8	645.6	4 361.3
Europe	1 594.7	1 243.9	7 084.7	1 222.9	3 417.6	2 997.1	3 427.9	4 433.1	7 537.0
Africa	11.9	162.4	3.4	17.0	0.0	21.7	594.2	0.0	0.0
Middle East	24.2	3.1	1.5	2.0	0.0	1.4	7 579.4	23.0	0.0
Others (not specified)	604.2	685.7	726.2	430.9	973.6	5 773.2	5 602.8	7 295.9	2.5
Total	17 480.5	20 987.3	17 109.3	7 250.3	14 414.9	62 725.1	48 112.6	25 381.4	16 689.2

Source: Board of Investments, the Philippines.

promoting an economic environment conducive to trade and investment. After two years, the reforms have resulted in the restoration of investor confidence as evidenced by the strong growth in foreign investment as indicated.

9.1.3 Small- and Medium-Sized Firms

Based on the amount of total project cost registered at the Board of Investment (BOI), the bulk of Taiwanese investment in the Philippines is composed of small- and medium-sized firms. As shown in Table 9.2, the capital investment of about 88 percent (231 out of 262 firms) of the total number of Taiwanese firms in the country is below US$2 million each. Twenty-four firms have an investment of more than US$2 million but below US$18 million. Only seven firms posted a capitalization of more than US$18 million.

Table 9.2 Investments of Taiwanese Firms, by Size, 1989–96*

Level of capital	Number of projects	Share (%)	Total investment (US$ million)	Share (%)
Below US$1.1 million	209	79.8	67.0	4.8
US$1.2–1.9 million	22	8.4	34.2	2.4
US$2.0–3.7 million	12	4.6	31.6	2.2
US$3.8–18.0 million	12	4.6	95.3	6.8
Above US$18.0 million	7	2.7	1181.3	83.8
Total	262	100.0	1409.4	100.0

Note: * Fifteen Taiwanese firms did not report their total project costs to the BOI.

Source: Board of Investments, the Philippines.

On average, the project cost of a small-scale Taiwanese firm ranges from US$13 000 to US$1 800 000, while that of a medium-sized firm is not more than US$8.3 million. The average capitalization of the seven large-scale investments which poured into the country in the period 1989–96 was US$210 million.

As for the sectoral distribution of Taiwanese investment in the Philippines, the electrical and electronics industry, followed by clothing, attracted the largest number of Taiwanese investors (Table 9.3). This may be attributed to the abundance of low-cost but highly trainable labor in the Philippines, which can greatly contribute to the viability of export-oriented industries. Taiwan's FDI had high visibility, too, in other labor-intensive industries, such as the manufacturing of toys and novelties, plastic products, and ceramics.

Table 9.3 Investments of Taiwanese Firms in the Manufacturing Sector, 1989–96

Major manufacturing industry	Number of projects	Share (%)	Total investment (US$ million)	Share (%)
A. Consumer goods	97	35.0	37.5	2.7
1. Food and beverages	15	5.4	9.5	0.7
2. Clothing	46	16.6	14.5	1.0
3. Leather products	12	4.3	7.8	0.5
4. Toys and novelties	24	8.7	5.7	0.4
B. Intermediate goods	92	33.2	1117.5	79.3
1. Textiles	21	7.6	186.4	13.2
2. Basic chemicals	3	1.1	3.8	0.3
3. Plastics	14	5.1	6.1	0.4
4. Paper products	11	4.0	19.8	1.4
5. Wood and fiber products	12	4.3	6.4	0.5
6. Glass products	3	1.1	1.3	0.1
7. Rubber products	8	2.9	3.9	0.3
8. Ceramics	14	5.1	12.2	0.9
9. Marble	2	0.7	3.8	0.3
10. Minerals	2	0.7	4.9	0.3
11. Cement	2	0.7	868.9	61.7
C. Capital goods	88	31.8	254.4	18.1
1. Electrical and electronics	57	20.6	69.4	4.9
2. Iron and steel products	7	2.5	40.0	2.8
3. Fabricated metal products	9	3.2	7.3	0.5
4. Professional, scientific and controlling instruments	7	2.5	7.6	0.5
5. Vehicles and parts	8	2.9	130.1	9.2
Total	277	100.0	1409.4	100.0

Source: Board of Investments, the Philippines.

Large-scale investments from Taiwan, on the other hand, were directed into the manufacturing of cement. Due to the increased demand for cement during the property boom in the Philippines in 1994, Taiwanese investments in the cement industry also shot up in 1994, amounting to US$868.9 million, and comprising nearly 61.7 percent of Taiwan's FDI in the Philippines in the same year.

9.1.4 Objective and Methodology

The main purpose of this chapter is to contribute to a better understanding of the economic and social impact of Taiwanese outward direct investment in the Philippines. The approach consisted initially of an analysis of recent macroeconomic and industry-level data that served as a background for understanding Taiwanese firms' interactions with the Philippine economy and society. In-depth interviews were later conducted on a sample of 28 Taiwanese subsidiaries in the Philippines from a larger sample of 70 firms that were surveyed by questionnaires.

The findings from the interviews and surveys comprise the substance of this chapter. The companies invited to participate in the study were selected by considering their level of investment and the type of product. The names of Taiwanese firms in the Philippines were obtained from a list of projects approved by the Board of Investments of the Philippines government from 1989 to 1994.

The listed firms were classified according to major manufacturing industries, such as the consumer goods (clothing and leather goods), the intermediate goods (textiles and ceramics), and the capital goods (electrical, electronic and fabricated metal products), for sampling. Our interviewees included eight firms in the consumer goods industry, twelve in the intermediate goods industry, and eight in the capital goods industry.

The survey questionnaire is provided in the Appendix. It served as a guide for the in-depth assessment of the local Taiwanese firms' motives of investment, and of the characteristics of their business operations. A copy of the questionnaire and a cover letter explaining the background, objectives and importance of the study were sent to sampled Taiwanese firms. Actual interview appointments were arranged by telephone. Given the kind of viewpoints that had to be solicited, interviewees were generally the president, the chief operating officer, or the plant manager of the firm. The survey was conducted in Metro Manila and nearby provinces such as Rizal, Cavite and Laguna.

The information gathered and the implications and generalizations drawn in this report came solely from the firms surveyed and interviewed. There was no intention of arriving at representative responses although an attempt at getting a comprehensive coverage of views and issues was made. Due to the limited number of respondents in the study, the findings should be viewed as exploratory rather than conclusive. Also, the listing of companies used did not include those which might be foreign direct investments but did not avail themselves of incentives from the Philippine government as BOI only kept the record of foreign companies that were awarded fiscal incentives.

9.2 Determinants and Motivations of Taiwan's FDI

9.2.1 Reasons for Investing Overseas

For most Taiwanese investors, gaining access to a relatively lower cost of manpower appears to be the most important reason behind investment in the Philippines. Most of the participating firms in the study consider the high cost of labor in Taiwan a disadvantage to the international competitiveness of their products and a threat to their business viability.

Market expansion is another principal reason for embarking on business operations in foreign countries. Most Taiwanese firms seek to strengthen their parent companies' hold in the export market by establishing a market presence in a number of countries. Some firms also invest overseas to avoid the harsh effects of the appreciation of the NT (Taiwanese currency) and of trade restrictions imposed in major export markets, which dampen export capability. For some of the companies we interviewed, the low cost of land and the opportunity to form a joint venture with local firms in the host country are among the main reasons for overseas investment.

In the survey of parent companies in Taiwan,[1] the primary motives for parent companies to make foreign direct investment are almost exactly the same as the main reasons cited by the surveyed Taiwanese subsidiaries in the Philippines. The availability of low-cost labor and the potential of the local and export markets are likewise considered by parent companies as the most important motivations for overseas investment.

Most Taiwanese firms' direct investment overseas was self-motivated. Based on interviews with parent companies in Taiwan, about 50 percent of the firms established businesses abroad on their own initiatives. Some investors were convinced by ethnic Chinese businessmen in the host countries, while a few were attracted to invest via their connections with local sales agents. The potential market of the downstream industries in the host countries also motivated a few Taiwanese firms to set up manufacturing facilities abroad.

Because of the provisions of the one-China policy, which governs the relations that most host countries in Southeast Asia have with the People's Republic of China, it appears that most Taiwanese direct investment overseas was done via independent firm-level negotiations and without much third-party or government participation. Consequently, none of the direct investment overseas was induced by the host-country governments nor urged by the Taiwanese government. No local firm or supplier in the host country, nor group actions by firms in the same industry in Taiwan seem to have mobilized any foreign direct investment from Taiwan to the Philippines.

9.2.2 Reasons for Investing in the Philippines

The abundance of highly trainable and low-cost labor appears to be the main attraction for Taiwanese firms to select the Philippines over other Southeast Asian countries in locating their overseas productions. Most Taiwanese firms consider the Filipino workers' ability to effectively communicate in English and their open attitude towards job training and continuous education as highly contributory to the improvement of the company's productivity.

Generally, local Taiwanese investments are export-oriented. Hence, the export quota of the Philippines in countries like the US and Canada offers a good opportunity for Taiwanese firms to expand the sales (mainly of textiles) of their parent companies in these big foreign markets. About 50 percent of local Taiwanese firms consider the Philippines to have a more favorable status for exports than other Southeast Asian countries.

Some Taiwanese firms choose the Philippines for FDI because of its racial homogeneity, and to take advantage of the growth of the domestic market. Other reasons considered important by a smaller percentage of investors in the study are their good personal connections (mainly with local Chinese) in the Philippines and the attractive fiscal incentives offered by the Philippine government.

9.3 Nature and Characteristics of Taiwanese FDI

The characteristics of investment from Taiwan may be examined from the standpoints of investment mode, sources of financing, market orientation, marketing channels, average annual sales, capital recovery period, and disposition of profits.

9.3.1 Nature, Size and Origin of Investments

Almost all Taiwanese investments in the Philippines take the form of green-field projects. This can be mainly attributed to the liberalization of foreign equity participation in the export-oriented manufacturing industries in recent years. Fiscal incentives, such as a five-year income tax holiday and duty-free importation of all equipment and machinery, are only available to newly established manufacturing firms. Mergers with and acquisition of existing firms do not qualify for incentives.

To gauge the bureaucratic efficiency of the Philippines, we asked Taiwanese subsidiaries to estimate the waiting time and the length of the preparatory period before a commercial operation could be officially started in the country. The result shows that the average pre-operating period for small- and medium-scale projects is about six months. Larger investments of more than US$5 million, however, need 12 to 18 months before they can start commercial operations. All firms considered, the average time-lag between the application for investment and the start of business operations is about seven months.

Regardless of the size of the project, the majority of the Taiwanese investments are controlled by Taiwanese owners. Equity participation from third-party countries like Japan and Hong Kong is limited. Local participation is also limited; the ownership share of local Filipino investors ranges from 10 to 45 percent in the case of joint ventures. Wholly owned Taiwanese subsidiaries are most pervasive in labor-intensive industries, such as textiles, clothing, toys and novelties, rubber products and fabricated metal products. These firms are also export-oriented.

About two-thirds of the firms that we interviewed operate customs-bonded warehouses, thereby exporting all their products by definition. The remaining firms, which may sell to the domestic market, still face export performance requirements to export up to 70 percent of their production to protect Filipino manufacturers. Likewise, about half of the Taiwanese firms that we interviewed face restrictions on local content which in most cases require a minimum of 30 percent of materials to be purchased locally.

9.3.2 Sources of Financing

The sources of finance of local Taiwanese firms generally come from parent companies and from financial institutions in the Philippines and Taiwan. Parent companies appear to be the main financial source, providing an average of 48.1 percent of the capital requirements of the Philippine subsidiaries. Taiwanese investors also avail themselves (for instance by offering a guarantee) of the lending facilities of financial institutions in Taiwan, which supply about 14.1 percent of the subsidiaries' finance. Local financial institutions, on the other hand, provide 20.9 percent of the capital requirement and local partners contribute another 15.4 percent. The proportion of local financing tends to increase over time, however, as Taiwanese subsidiaries gradually establish their credibility in the Philippines.

Among Taiwanese subsidiaries, the manufacturers of clothing, toys, rubber shoes, and fabricated metal products appear to be the most dependent on parent-firm financing. These are relatively small firms, apparently lacking the means to provide security interests to obtain loans from regular local financial institutions. Other manufacturing industries, such as the electrical and electronics, chemicals, and ceramics industries show relatively low exposure to financial resources from Taiwan. These firms also have more local equity participation.

9.3.3 Market Orientation

The export market is the main destination of locally made products. Among 28 Taiwanese firms that we interviewed, an average of 75.2 percent of their output is exported to third-party countries, and only about 15.6 percent of the output is sold locally. A few firms are sending back a small fraction of their output to Taiwan.

Export orientation seems to be the norm in all industries where Taiwanese FDI is present. Taiwanese firms earmark at least 90 percent of their sales for export to countries like the US, Canada, Italy, and Japan. Only two conspicuous exceptions stand out in our sample: one clothing firm is sending back all its output to its parent company in Taiwan while a producer of adhesive resins for rubber and leather shoes is marketing all its products locally.

9.3.4 Marketing Channels

Most Taiwanese firms in the Philippines are able to access the world market through their own contacts and place the products through their own marketing efforts. Parent companies only play a secondary role in marketing. Only about 36 percent of local products in the Philippines are marketed by parent firms. To penetrate non-traditional markets and to maintain a satisfactory level of profitability, the marketing efforts are further enhanced through alliances with local and foreign trading firms. However, no more than 10 percent of the products of Taiwanese subsidiaries are sold through local and foreign trading companies.

9.3.5 Annual Sales

The average annual sales of Taiwanese subsidiaries ranged from US$2.4 million to US$9.1 million. Firms which were small in terms of capital also reported small annual sales. Most firms reported high growth rates in the 1991–93 period. This is attributable to the Philippines' economic recovery in this period. Most small-scale firms reported higher growth rates than large firms. Small firms with capital less than US$1 million posted an annual growth rate exceeding 30 percent in 1991–93, whereas firms with capital of US$5 million or more posted an annual growth rate of 18 percent.

9.3.6 Capital Recovery Period

Based on the growth experience in sales, Taiwanese firms estimate the time needed to recover the initial investment to be three to seven years. Small-scale businesses in terms of capital (less than US$1 million) take 3.8 years, medium-scale businesses (with capital US$1–5 million) take 4.2 years, while large-scale firms (with capital US$5 million or more) take 6.8 years.

9.3.7 Disposition of Profits

Taiwanese firms retain an average of 82 percent of their profits in the local company for future plant expansion and modernization. The other 6 percent are reinvested in some other local projects distinctive of the original businesses. Only 11 percent of profits are remitted to their parent firms in Taiwan.

In the survey of parent companies in Taiwan, Taiwanese firms rarely consider the possibility of an investment venture in the supporting industries in the Philippines. The inter-industry linkages among local Taiwanese subsidiaries appear to be weak. When Taiwanese subsidiaries reinvest in other local businesses, they are mostly horizontally integrated with the original businesses, for example, making related but differentiated products.

9.4 The Role of Taiwanese FDI in the Local Economy

In addition to the infusion of much-needed foreign capital into the Philippine economy and foreign exchange generation through exports, the contributions of Taiwanese direct investment stand out in the areas of:

(a) job creation and training of local employees,
(b) technology transfer through joint ventures and technical assistance or services, and
(c) introduction of new products and stimulation of local investment.

These major contributions greatly boost the productivity and hence the growth of the Philippine economy.

The contribution of Taiwanese investments in the Philippines is highly visible in the creation of job opportunities. The 28 firms that we interviewed employ a total of 7431 workers, among which 5290 are skilled or semi-skilled workers. Unskilled labor is limited to about 13 percent of each firm's total labor force, ranging from 12 to 56 workers per firm. Jobs created for office personnel, on the other hand, account for nearly 7 percent of employment, ranging from 14 to 22 employees per firm.

The size of employment generated by each firm, however, appears not to be very elastic to an increase in capital investment. On average the employment of small-scale businesses is about 210 workers, while each medium- and large-scale firm employs about 270 workers. Small differences in employment are attributable to automation and modernization of production processes by large-scale investment projects. Taiwanese firms involved in the manufacturing of leather products, rubber shoes, and toys and novelties employ the largest number of workers since the production operations of these firms are very labor-intensive.

9.4.1 Job Opportunities

The employment of Taiwanese firms seems to be biased towards skilled labor. This limits the job opportunities for local unskilled labor. Only firms in the textile and fabricated metal industries employ a larger proportion of unskilled labor. Meanwhile, top positions in management, marketing, technology, and supervision are often occupied by Taiwanese expatriates. Local personnel only take the secondary positions.

A typical management structure of a Taiwanese subsidiary is that expatriate managers occupy the positions of president or vice president and of production manager; an additional expatriate is employed to handle either the marketing, financial or planning department. Similar observations were obtained from the survey of parent companies in Taiwan. The overall supervisory functions and production operations of subsidiaries in the Philippines are managed by expatriates from the parent firms, indicating parent firms' concern with production efficiency and product quality in the subsidiaries.

9.4.2 Decision Making

Under the current organizational structure, most decisions in the major fields of subsidiary operations are made by expatriate managers. Decisions concerning financial, production, and marketing operations of most Taiwanese subsidiaries are made by expatriate managers with regular consultation with the top management of the parent companies. Personnel management is the only area where most of the decisions are made independently by either local managers or the expatriates. R&D programs, like other major decisions, are under the control of the parent companies. Local research activities are limited.

In the next five years, however, the scope of decision making by local staff is expected to increase in all fields of operation, except in financial management. One Taiwanese firm said it would probably relinquish all marketing decisions to the local managers, while four other companies indicated that production management might be transferred to local staff. Another three firms appeared ready to allow local managers to play a more active role in making R&D decisions in their forthcoming expansion and modernization of local production. No firm was ready to relinquish its control over the top management positions (presidency or vice presidency) in the subsidiaries, however. Financial management is also likely to remain in the realm of the parent firm.

9.4.3 Technology Transfer

Almost all Taiwanese subsidiaries reported some technology transfer from their parent companies in Taiwan. More technology was transferred to the areas of production operations, maintenance and inspection, and quality and process control. On-the-job training was among the most widely used methods to transfer technology. A few firms were sending local workers to their parent companies or joint-venture partners in Taiwan for a deeper and wider immersion in manufacturing processes and operations. Taiwanese technical experts supervised production through middle management composed of Filipino supervisors. In-house training of workers in the fields of production operation and quality control was continuously done to ensure the availability of skills on the production floor as the firm matured in the Philippines.

In the fields of new technology, product design, and product innovation, the degree of technology transfer was limited, with five to seven firms reporting zero transfer. Most local Taiwanese firms acquired new product and production technologies from parent firms and sources in advanced countries. In fact, about 71 percent of the firms that we interviewed obtained new product design and process technologies from developed countries like the US, Germany, and Japan. These firms were marketing their products on a consignment or job-order basis to patrons in the developed countries who furnished product designs and process technologies to them.

Independent R&D activities of Taiwanese subsidiaries were very limited. Hence, the products of Taiwanese subsidiaries in the Philippines were generally similar to the products of the parent firms, although slight modifications might be made to make the production method more labor-intensive, and requiring a lower technology level to suit the local environment. Because of lower labor costs, products made in the Philippines were cheaper than those produced in Taiwan and hence were used to supplant the parent-firm production in servicing the low-end markets.

Similarly, the degree of technology transfer in the development of equipment and machinery and metal molds and machine tools was low. This was mainly brought about by the sourcing of equipment and machinery components by most local Taiwanese firms from suppliers in Taiwan and other foreign countries. Almost all firms that we interviewed obtained some machines from Taiwan. Altogether, an average of 69 percent of their machinery requirements were purchased from Taiwan. It is quite evident that production operations in the Philippines were concentrated in the assembly of products and not much effort was made by Taiwanese firms to develop locally made machinery and equipment parts.

9.4.4 Comparison with Local and Other Multinational Firms

Because of the edge created by technology transfer, the overall business operations of Taiwanese firms in the Philippines seem slightly superior to those of local firms. In particular, the productivity of Filipino workers employed by Taiwanese firms appears to be higher than that of those employed in local businesses. The accumulation of knowledge and skills and the efficient management of Taiwanese firms seem to be the main catalysts for the better performance of Filipino workers in Taiwanese subsidiaries.

Production operations of Taiwanese firms are also more technically sophisticated and cost-efficient than their local counterparts. The closer interaction between technical experts from the parent companies and local workers, and continued investment in equipment modernization by Taiwanese subsidiaries, gear up the productivity of local labor.

Local Taiwanese firms also appear to have better access to the world market than the indigenous Filipino firms as local subsidiaries or affiliates of Taiwanese firms benefit from the strong market linkages of the parent companies. The transfer of technology from the parent companies also makes their products more quality- and price-competitive. Consequently, though the wages paid by Taiwanese firms for local workers may be higher than those paid by the indigenous firms, the ex-factory prices of their products are still lower than those of local producers.

On the other hand, local material procurement by Taiwanese firms in the Philippines is generally lower than that by Filipino firms. This observation is also noted by most parent companies interviewed. Taiwanese subsidiaries are heavily dependent on imported raw materials for production. On average, over half of the materials needed are supplied by the parent companies and other Taiwanese suppliers, while about a quarter are sourced from other countries. Only about 16 percent of the raw materials required are sourced from local suppliers. The parent company in Taiwan is generally used as a direct channel to secure the supply of materials. Some local Taiwanese subsidiaries work with traders from third-party countries to procure materials while a few of them source from satellite firms of their parent companies in Taiwan or the subsidiaries of these satellite firms in the Philippines.

All participating firms in the study knew very little about the business activities of the local subsidiaries of multinational firms based in advanced countries like the US and Europe, probably because they were in different fields of business. Hence, the operations of local Taiwanese firms in the Philippines were compared to those of subsidiaries from other countries in Asia, such as Japan, South Korea, and Thailand. The comparison shows that subsidiaries from other Asian countries are as export-oriented as local Taiwanese firms. These subsidiaries also give a similar degree of training and education to their employees. The composition of employment of skilled and unskilled labor was also similar among Asian subsidiaries.

However, in some areas of business operations, local Taiwanese firms in the Philippines are rated as lower than the subsidiaries from other Asian countries. For example, joint research and development between the local subsidiaries and parent companies in Japan, South Korea and Thailand seems more prevalent. Taiwanese firms in the Philippines are also shown to be less capital-intensive than subsidiaries from other Asian countries whose parent firms are likewise larger and more capital-intensive than Taiwanese parents. The operations of subsidiaries from other Asian countries are generally more integrated, covering the manufacturing of raw materials and equipment to the production of finished products. In contrast, Taiwanese subsidiaries are more likely to be specialized.

9.5 Summary and Recommendations

9.5.1 Summary

Taiwanese investments in the Philippines amounted to about US$1409.4 million from 1989 to 1996, most of which were small- and medium-scale projects. The electrical and electronics industries attracted the greatest number of projects, while the cement industry posted the highest level of investment value at US$868.9 million or 62 percent of all Taiwanese investments. Based on interviews with Taiwanese subsidiaries, it is clear that the capital share of most Taiwanese investors ranges from 55 to 80 percent while local Filipino investors control about 10 to 45 percent. Investment by partners from a third-party country, like Japan, is very limited.

All Taiwanese firms started their business operations in the Philippines by setting up a new company. A majority of the firms participating in the study experienced no restrictions on their export ratio in the Philippines; however, a minimum requirement of local content in their production was generally imposed on them. Parent companies appeared to be the main financial resource of local subsidiaries, providing nearly 48 percent of the operating capital; local partners provided nearly 15 percent of the remaining capital.

The majority of Taiwanese subsidiaries export 100 percent of their products to third-party countries like the US, Canada, Italy and Japan. Generally, Taiwanese subsidiaries in the Philippines market their products through their own channels. Only relatively large Taiwanese parent firms control the marketing channel of their subsidiaries in the Philippines.

The estimated time for capital recovery of Taiwanese investments in the Philippines is about four years for small- and medium-scale investments and six years for large-scale investments. About 82 percent of the profits earned are retained in the local subsidiary for future expansion and plant modernization while the remaining are remitted to the parent company in Taiwan as dividends.

Based on interview results, we know that the business operations of local Taiwanese firms contribute to the Philippines' economic growth through technology transfer, the introduction of new products, stimulation of local investment in related industries, job creation, and foreign exchange generation, in addition to simple infusion of capital.

At present, most decisions in the major fields of production operations are being made by expatriate managers with regular consultation with their parent companies. Personnel management is the only aspect wherein decisions are being made independently by either the expatriate or local managers. Decision making is expected to be increasingly localized in the future, however.

Taiwanese firms reported widespread technology transfer in almost all fields of technology. Technology transfer is most evident in the fields pertinent to daily production, such as operation technology, quality control, and maintenance of machinery and equipment. Intense pre-employment and on-the-job training programs are among the most widely used methods of transferring technology.

Based on interviews, Taiwanese firms in the Philippines are generally perceived to maintain good relationships, not only with the host government and its local people, but also with local enterprises. Taiwanese firms operating in the Philippines also appear to have an efficient management system. They generally care about workers' safety and comfort; hence labor disputes are rare. They are, however, generally perceived to be not active in R&D and not ardent in public affairs.

9.5.2 Policy Recommendations

The attraction of the Philippines' low-cost and highly trainable labor for Taiwanese firms seems evident. A large pool of Filipino workers remains underutilized or even untapped for deployment in the industry. To facilitate the entry of more labor into the workforce, efforts by public and private institutions should be made to provide and accelerate technical training. If this is done, more workers can be employed in plants put up by new foreign investors. Prospective foreign investors will benefit from having readily available manpower and hence will be more inclined to invest.

The expansion of export markets for the Philippines will be greatly aided by the entry of more foreign direct investments. In that way, learning opportunities across the whole spectrum of exporting industries will increase. The knowledge gained in this undertaking will have a multiplier effect as more local people are exposed to the export business. As the disciplines required in exports are learned and efficiency needed to compete in the world market is obtained, productivity gain will trickle down to supporting industries and pressure will be exerted on government agencies to likewise improve their performance. Political systems and policy-making procedures will be subjected to constant surveillance of market forces aimed towards attaining greater efficiency and effectiveness.

While the case for exporting to Taiwan from the Philippines appears isolated among the respondents (only one firm is doing this), it could serve as a clue to agencies involved in promoting investment in the Philippines as a new type of foreign direct investment to be encouraged. Companies serving the Taiwanese market could be enticed to manufacture their products in the Philippines, thereby increasing the degree of market integration between Taiwan and the Philippines.

Note

1. A survey was conducted on the parent companies of Taiwanese firms in the Philippines to compare and confirm our Philippine survey results. A total of eight parent companies responded to the survey, which are incorporated in the report in Chapter 3.

10. Taiwanese Investment in Vietnam

Da-Nien Liu and James Riedel

10.1 Background and Overview

10.1.1 The Environment for FDI in Vietnam

Vietnam is one of the world's few remaining communist states, yet it attracts enormous attention, though still relatively modest amounts of money, from foreign investors in both developed and developing countries. Potentially, Vietnam has much to offer foreign investors. With about 70 million inhabitants, it ranks as the twelfth most populous country in the world and is, therefore, a market of enormous potential. The market is, however, at this time still only a potential one, since Vietnam's 70 million people currently have an average income of only about US$250, which means that in terms of total purchasing power (gross national product), it ranks only about seventieth in the world. Vietnam's poverty is, however, both a deterrent and an attraction to foreign investors, since low per capita income also means low wages, which potentially makes Vietnam an attractive place to produce for export.

It is mainly the attraction of low wages which has stimulated the interest of foreign investors in recent years. As Table 10.1 shows, the average hourly wage in Vietnam is only about one-eighteenth that of Taiwan and the other East Asian Newly Industrializing Countries (NICs), and is well below that of other Southeast Asian countries. Only China competes closely with Vietnam in terms of wages.

Of course, low wages alone are not enough to make a country attractive to foreign investors. If it were, the flow of foreign direct investment to Vietnam would have begun long before it did, in 1988. A comparative advantage in low-wage labor requires not only low wages, but also some minimal standard of human resource development and a policy environment conducive to private economic activity.

With regard to human resource development, Vietnam is well beyond the minimal standard necessary for implementation of a strategy of export-oriented industrialization. As shown in Table 10.2, health and education levels in Vietnam are at levels comparable to those of Taiwan, Thailand, and China when each of those countries launched its export-oriented industrialization strategy.

Table 10.1 Labor Costs in Vietnam and Selected Other Countries in 1991

Country	Labor costs (US$/hour)	Population (millions)
Taiwan	4.42	20.4
Singapore	4.38	2.8
South Korea	4.32	43.3
Hong Kong	3.58	5.8
Malaysia	1.19	18.2
Philippines	0.42	62.9
Indonesia	0.40	177.6
China	0.24	1150.8
Vietnam	0.24	67.7

Source: Bandaralage and Nguyen (1994), p. 14.

With regard to the policy environment for private economic activity generally, and foreign direct investment specifically, enormous improvements have been made in a very short period of time. However, very much remains to be done to create an environment conducive to private sector development.

Economic reform, under the heading *doi moi* (renovation), was initiated in 1986, but it was not until economic stabilization was achieved in 1989 that the reforms made any headway. Since then, inflation has been brought down from about 400 percent in 1988 to around 10 percent in 1993 and 1994. During the same period, from 1989 to 1994, Vietnam has recorded real GDP growth at an annual average rate of about 8 percent. These remarkable achievements have generated euphoria about Vietnam's prospects. It has become routine to talk of Vietnam as a transition success and as another example, along with China, of the superiority of the gradual approach to the transition to a market economy.

It is, however, a mistake to describe Vietnam's reforms as gradual. In the late 1970s and early 1980s, Vietnam took some faltering steps to *improve* the system, but nothing was done to *change* the system until the late 1980s when Vietnam was pushed and pulled into that position – pushed by the collapse of its patron, the Soviet Union, and pulled by the successes of its ideological

Table 10.2 Health and Education Indicators in Vietnam and Selected Other Countries when Launching Export-Oriented Industrialization

Indicator	Taiwan 25–30 years ago	Thailand 15–20 years ago	China 10–15 years ago	Vietnam most recent years
Infant mortality per 1000	–	55	46	42
Life expectancy (years)	63	60	65	67
Calories per capita (daily)	2390	2285	2070	2233
School enrollment rate[a]				
Primary	97	83	135	102
Secondary	30	26	47	42
Tertiary	3	12	–	–
Illiteracy rate[b]	30	7	27	16

Notes: [a] Percentage of school-aged children.
[b] Percentage of population over 15 years of age.

Source: Riedel (1993), p. 404.

soulmate, the People's Republic of China. When Vietnam finally got down to reforming the system, the reforms it took were sweeping.

- Recognizing the importance of the private sector, the government has taken steps to promote the private economy. In particular, agriculture, the leading sector of the economy which provides the livelihood of over 80 percent of the population, was effectively privatized.
- The industrial sector is still largely state-owned, but since 1988 most direct government controls over it have been removed and state-owned enterprises no longer have free access to the government budget.
- Price controls were eliminated on all but a few sensitive sectors (for example, energy) in 1989. From 1991, the government further reduced its remaining control over prices: only the price of electricity is fixed. As a result the domestic prices have converged to world price levels which facilitated Vietnam's transition from a central planning economy to a market-oriented one.
- In 1988 and 1989, measures were taken to allow and even encourage foreign direct investment, and the state monopoly on external trade was loosened. Administered prices for exports and imports were replaced with tariffs and a few quotas. Perhaps as significant as any trade liberalization

measure was the government's willingness to turn a blind eye to smuggling, which made many imported consumer goods available for the first time at world market prices.

- Finally, along with economic restructuring, the government has initiated steps to stabilize Vietnam's economy. The stabilization program Vietnam adopted was extremely strong and indeed would qualify as shock therapy in any other country. The government budget deficit was reduced from 9 percent of GDP in 1989 to 1.5 percent in 1991. The rate of money growth was lowered from 440 percent per year in 1987/88 to 35 percent in 1989/90. These measures not only dramatically reduced the rate of inflation, but also worked by 1990 to eliminate the black market premium on foreign exchange, which only two years before was running at about 500 percent.

Vietnam's achievements are indeed impressive. However, it is premature to label Vietnam a transition success, as many observers in fact do. The transition to a market economy is only a means to a greater end – transition from a poor, stagnant economy to a prosperous, dynamic one. In order for Vietnam to achieve that goal, given the low base from which it starts, it must grow at the current rate of about 8 percent per annum for three decades or more just to begin to catch up with its neighbors in Southeast Asia. Thus, a key question is whether the recent high growth rates are sustainable. There are reasons to doubt that they are. The principal source of the recent growth is the agricultural and mineral resource (oil) sectors, which not only have provided the largest increments to the GDP but also have accounted for the bulk of the increase in foreign exchange earnings. Unfortunately, however, neither sector has sufficient resources to sustain growth in the long run. The agricultural sector is already close to the limit of its capacity to feed Vietnam's rapidly growing population, and the oil reserves of Vietnam, while greatly beneficial for financing infrastructure and industrial development, are far from sufficient to make Vietnam a rentier country or even to boost income as they have done in Indonesia.

The only way Vietnam can grow rapidly over the long term is by following the same path its successful neighbors took, that is, through private sector, labor-intensive, export-oriented industrialization. Unfortunately, however, this sector has not yet gotten off the ground. In 1993 there were only about 1200 private enterprises operating in the manufacturing sector. State-owned enterprises still played an important role in Vietnam's economy. Moreover, labor-intensive manufactured goods, in which Vietnam should find a strong comparative advantage in world markets, accounted for only a small proportion of Vietnam's total exports in recent years.

10.1.2 Foreign Direct Investment in Vietnam

Foreign direct investment (FDI) has the potential to make a significant contribution to Vietnam's long-term development goals. FDI constitutes an inflow of capital which allows a higher rate of investment and hence a higher rate of growth than would otherwise be obtainable. FDI is also a source of foreign exchange, which allows more imported intermediate inputs and capital goods than would otherwise be possible. In addition, FDI brings with it foreign technology, managerial know-how and experience of operating in world markets, which are critical ingredients currently in short supply in Vietnam.

Recognizing the potential importance of FDI to its transition to a market economy, the Vietnamese government pursued a policy of industrializing the economy and attracting foreign capital. One of the first steps taken under the *doi moi* program in 1987 was the promulgation of the Law on Foreign Investment. This statute offered a comprehensive incentive program to foreign investors. It allowed foreigners to establish wholly owned businesses and to form joint ventures with state-owned enterprises and, subsequently, with domestic private enterprises. In addition, FDI was given positive encouragement with various tax incentives, including preferential income tax rates on investments in priority sectors and tax refunds on profits reinvested for a period of more than three years (Bundaralage and Nguyen 1994, p. 11). In addition, foreign investors were given protection from nationalization and allowed to repatriate profits as well as approved payments for technology and other services, in foreign currency (ibid., p. 11). The statute was further modified in 1990 and 1992 to provide more incentives and some restrictions on foreign capital were lifted.

Moreover, FDI was given further encouragement with the establishment of export processing zones. Up to 1995, six export processing zones had been set up. Within the export processing zones, investors could establish and operate factories, undertaking the manufacture, processing, and assembly of goods for exports. The export processing zones not only offer all the privileges granted by the Law on Foreign Investment, but they also establish a unique 'one-stop service' which can provide administrative services to foreign enterprises. Unfortunately the infrastructures within and around most export processing zones have not been completed, and only Tan Thuan, the largest export processing zone, which is in the vicinity of Ho Chi Minh City, has come into operation.

The response of foreign investors to Vietnam's economic reforms and to the specific incentives provided for investment is shown in Table 10.3, which presents the annual figures for approved foreign direct investment in Vietnam and selected other Southeast Asian countries. As the table shows, the flow of investment to Vietnam has increased at a rate of almost 50 percent per year. Nevertheless, the amount invested in Vietnam over the past five years is still a small fraction (about 6 percent) of the total amount invested in neighboring countries, all of which, with the exception of the Philippines, experienced a foreign investment boom similar to Vietnam's in the late 1980s and early 1990s.

Table 10.3 Approved Foreign Direct Investment in Vietnam and Other Selected Asian Countries (US$ millions)

Country	1988	1989	1990	1991	1992	1993	Total
Indonesia	4 412	4 714	8 751	8 778	10 323	8 144	45 122
Malaysia	1 863	3 193	6 517	6 204	6 977	2 444	27 198
Philippines	452	804	961	778	284	532	3 811
Thailand	6 250	7 995	14 127	4 988	10 029	4 293	47 682
Vietnam	366	539	596	1 288	1 939	2 728	7 456
Total	13 343	17 245	30 952	22 036	29 552	18 141	131 269

Sources: *Vietnam Investment Review*, 1994; Nomura Research Institute, *Nomura Asia Focus*, Dec. 1994.

Table 10.4 Sectoral Distribution of Registered Foreign Investments as of July 1994

	Registered capital (US$ millions)	As % of total
Agriculture and forestry	457	4.8
Fisheries	225	2.4
Oil and gas	1 400	14.7
Industry	3 500	36.8
Communications	633	6.7
Hotels	1 900	20.0
Services	788	8.3
Banking and finance	156	1.7
Export processing zones	349	3.7
Other	60	0.9
Total	9 505	100.0

Source: Bundaralage and Nguyen (1994), p. 25.

The sectoral distribution of FDI is shown in Table 10.4. As of July 1994, about half of all approved investment was in the various branches of the service sector, with hotels receiving the largest proportion. The industrial sector, where Vietnam's future lies, had obtained approved investment amounts of only US$3.5 billion, or about 37 percent of the total. Foreign investment so far accounts for only a small share of gross domestic investment in industry, and its contribution to non-oil exports is insignificant. There is, therefore, the potential for a much larger role for FDI in Vietnam in the future.

The geographical sources of FDI in Vietnam are shown in Table 10.5. The most remarkable fact about FDI in Vietnam is the predominant role played by the four 'Asian tigers', which together account for about 43 percent of all foreign investment in Vietnam, with Taiwan being the single largest investor.

Table 10.5 Registered Foreign Investment in Vietnam by Country of Origin, 1980–95

	US$ million	As % of total
Taiwan	3 578	17.8
Hong Kong	2 155	10.7
Japan	2 082	10.3
Singapore	1 524	7.6
Korea	1 507	7.5
United States	1 138	5.7
Malaysia	855	4.2
Australia	703	3.5
France	639	3.2
Switzerland	585	2.9
Other countries	5 381	26.7
Total	20 147	100.0

Source: State Committee for Cooperation and Investment (SCCI), Vietnam.

The relative importance of these countries as foreign investors in Vietnam is, of course, grossly out of proportion to their relative importance in the world economy. Their disproportionate role as foreign investors suggests, therefore, that they possess some advantage over potential investors from the developed countries, which dominate FDI flows outside of the region, that is particularly decisive in Southeast Asia, and in Vietnam in particular. No doubt that advantage is based in large part on the experience the Asian tigers have gained over the past 30 years in exploiting a comparative advantage that is very similar to that which Vietnam and the other low-wage countries of East Asia currently possess.

As of 1994, the enterprises with foreign invested capital contributed more than US$1 billion of gross products and services (Le and Nguyen 1994, p. 4). The export products of these enterprises consist mostly of consumer goods. Furthermore, by 1994 the enterprises with foreign invested capital created nearly 70 000 jobs directly and a considerably larger number of jobs at the construction sites, and raw material production and other services to serve foreign investments. Altogether these enterprises contributed almost US$300 million in revenue to the State. In Ho Chi Minh City alone, the taxes contributed by the enterprises with foreign invested capital reached more than US$50 million (ibid., p. 4).

10.1.3 Taiwan's Foreign Direct Investment in Vietnam

Taiwan is Vietnam's largest foreign investor, but Vietnam is one of Taiwan's least important destinations for FDI. As can be seen from Chapter 1 (Tables 1.1 and 1.2), Vietnam accounts for only 12.4 percent of Taiwan's cumulative investment in China and Southeast Asia during the period from 1989 to 1996. A very important destination for Taiwanese investment in this period is China, which accounts for over one-fifth of the eight-year cumulative total. Since Vietnam has many of the same advantages as China - low wages and reasonably good human resource development – there is reason to expect a significant increase in Taiwanese FDI in Vietnam in the future. The magnitude of Taiwanese investment in recent years in Indonesia, Malaysia and Thailand, on the other hand, illustrates a point made earlier, namely, that low wages alone are not decisive; they must be accompanied by a policy environment that is conducive to private economic activity. In each of those countries, major trade and other economic policy reforms were undertaken in the mid-1980s which made these economies attractive to investors from Taiwan and the other East Asian NICs, even though (as shown in Table 10.1) their wage levels are substantially above those in China or Vietnam.

In general we can recognize the following characteristics of Taiwanese FDI in Vietnam. First of all, as for the geographic distribution of Taiwanese FDI in Vietnam, most investment projects of Taiwan were located in Ho Chi Minh City and southern provinces before 1992, but since 1992 Taiwan's investment has been expanding to other provinces of the northern and central parts of Vietnam. Second, most investment projects from Taiwan are not large ones. Up to 1994, the number of projects with investment capital under US$5 million accounted for about 80 percent of total projects from Taiwan. This more or less reflects the fact that most of the Taiwanese firms which invested in Vietnam are small- and medium-sized ones. Taiwan's investment, however, has increased both in quantity and in scale recently, with a few projects capitalized over US$500 million. In addition, joint venture has been the preferable form of investment. In recent years, due to further investment liberalization, the proportion of projects with 100 percent Taiwan capital has rapidly increased.

Finally, the sectoral distribution of Taiwanese FDI in Vietnam is shown in Table 10.6. It seems that the sectoral distribution does not accord very well with what one might expect based on Vietnam's comparative advantage, that is, in the kinds of manufactured products that Taiwan exported so successfully in the early period of its export-oriented industrialization strategy. Instead of textiles, garments, footwear and other miscellaneous light manufactured products, which together account for only 18 percent of registered investment, Taiwanese investors so far have invested more heavily in chemicals (fertilizers), construction materials (cement) and various service sector activities (hotels and tourism). We would expect that this distribution will change in the future, however, provided that Vietnam improves its infrastructure facilities and provides a more hospitable environment for small- to medium-sized private enterprises in the manufacturing sector.

Table 10.6 Sectoral Distribution of Taiwanese FDI in Vietnam as of July 1994

	Registered capital (US$ millions)	Projects (number)
Textiles	21.2	8
Garments	34.0	10
Leather products	8.8	6
Food products	58.9	14
Chemical products	193.2	11
Construction materials	226.9	7
Machinery and equipment	60.3	3
Metal products	4.5	4
Electric products	21.7	9
Paper and printing	27.5	8
Wood products	31.1	15
Agriculture and fishing	63.7	11
Services	260.7	26
Total	1 012.5	132

Source: Le and Nguyen (1994).

Of all the countries in the world, none provides a better model for economic development in a country like Vietnam than does Taiwan. Vietnam's relative resource endowment (land scarce, labor abundant) and comparative advantage are very similar to Taiwan's 35 years ago (Riedel 1993). If the experience of Taiwan over the past three decades is an appropriate lesson book for Vietnam, then Taiwanese investors are the appropriate teachers of those lessons. The best way they can teach their Vietnamese counterparts is by doing what they do best, which is doing business.

10.1.4 Method and Overview

Understanding how Taiwanese firms do business in Vietnam is the main objective of this research. In what follows, we present the results of a survey of some 30 Taiwanese firms operating in Vietnam. For the most part we rely on responses to our questionnaire by subsidiaries located in Vietnam, though we also make use of a few (four) responses from parent companies in Taiwan when their subsidiaries were unable or unwilling to respond. We make no claim to have obtained a statistically representative sample of Taiwanese firms in Vietnam. Indeed, we feel fortunate to have obtained any responses, given the difficulties of carrying out this kind of research in Vietnam. To highlight the uniqueness of small and medium enterprises in cross-country operations, we sometimes separate the sample into two groups: small-firm group and large-firm group. The small-firm group consists of subsidiaries with employment fewer than 300. The large-firm group consists of the rest.

As for the sectoral distribution of the sample, nearly half of the surveyed firms belong to the textile and clothing industries. Other surveyed firms are concentrated in industries such as chemical products, food manufacturing and wood products. Our sample is a fair representation of manufacturing investment in Vietnam. We present below the main results and findings from our questionnaire, organized into three separate sections. We begin, in Section 10.2, with an analysis of the determinants and motivations of Taiwanese investment in Vietnam. The nature and characteristics of Taiwanese firms operating in Vietnam are examined in Section 10.3. In Section 10.4, we analyze the role of Taiwanese firms in the local Vietnamese economy. The chapter concludes with a summary of our findings in Section 10.5.

10.2 Determinants and Motivations of Taiwanese FDI

The surveyed firms were asked about the reasons they chose to invest in Vietnam. Table 10.7 reveals that the predominant reason for both small and larger firms was to take advantage of low-cost labor in Vietnam. It reflects the fact that the average monthly wage in Vietnam is equivalent to about US$40, much lower than in other Southeast Asian countries. In addition to utilizing local cheap labor, taking advantage of low-cost land and energy and water resources are also two substantial motivations for Taiwanese investors.

Moreover, Table 10.7 shows that the deteriorating investment environment in Taiwan, such as the appreciation of the NT (Taiwanese currency) and tightening of environmental regulation, also prompted firms to invest in Vietnam. Among the factors considered unimportant for overseas investment are 'collecting information' and 'joint actions with other firms'.

Table 10.7 Motives for Overseas Investment in Vietnam (%)

	Total	Small firms	Large firms
Appreciation of NT	45.5	33.3	60.0
To take advantage of low-cost labor	86.4	75.0	100.0
To secure supply of raw materials	18.2	8.3	30.0
To take advantage of low-cost energy and water resources	22.7	25.0	20.0
To take advantage of low-cost land	40.9	41.7	40.0
To expand sales in the local market or third-party countries	40.9	58.3	20.0
To avoid trade restrictions	22.7	25.0	20.0
To collect market information	4.5	0.0	10.0
To avoid environmental regulations in Taiwan	36.4	33.3	40.0
Joint actions with other firms	9.1	8.3	10.0
Others	9.1	0.0	20.0
Sample size	22	12	10

Source: This study.

Small and large firms demonstrate significantly different motivations for investing in Vietnam only in two respects. For small firms, 58.3 percent reported that their desire to expand sales in Vietnam or third-country markets motivated investment, compared to only 20 percent of large firms reporting similar motivations. On the other hand, 30 percent of the large firms reported that securing a supply of raw materials was their major concern, compared to only 8.3 percent of small firms reporting a similar concern.

Firms were further asked to report their reasons for investing in Vietnam over other Southeast Asian countries. Out of our sample, only one firm has investments in other Southeast Asian countries. The important reasons quoted by surveyed firms for selecting Vietnam for their FDI are its cheap labor, racial homogeneity, good potential for local market, political stability and favorable status for exporting to third-party countries.

The above-mentioned important reasons differ significantly between small and large firms. More small firms reported 'good potential for local market' as their motivation for choosing to invest in Vietnam. On the other hand, a higher proportion of large firms reported 'political stability' and 'racial homogeneity' as their main reasons for investment in Vietnam. This may reflect the fact that small firms are far more local-market-oriented than large firms (small firms sell 40.4 percent of their FDI products locally, while large firms sell only 0.6 percent to the local market). As a result, more small firms than large ones cited 'good potential for local market' as a consequential reason to invest in Vietnam. Additionally, due to the larger scale of their investments, and hence a larger exit cost, a stable domestic political environment and racial homogeneity may be more appreciated by large firms than small firms.

10.3 Nature and Characteristics of Taiwanese Firms in Vietnam

All the firms in our survey except one were established after 1990. This is due to the fact that the liberalization of investment policy by the Vietnamese government occurred in 1988. It is noteworthy that two surveyed firms had invested in Vietnam before 1975, the year of the liberation (unification) of Vietnam, but since the new government nationalized all industries, these two Taiwanese firms had to stop operating in 1975. They set up facilities again after the implementation of more open investment policies in Vietnam in 1988. Consequently, from 1975 to 1988 the only sources of foreign direct investment in Vietnam were communist countries, mainly the former USSR.

Indigenous Vietnamese capital has played only a limited role in drawing Taiwanese investment as nearly half of the surveyed firms are wholly Taiwanese-owned. In particular, the Taiwanese share is generally higher in small firms than in large firms. All the small firms (with employment fewer than 300) have Taiwanese ownership of over 50 percent, and half of them are backed entirely by Taiwanese capital. Furthermore, nearly half of Taiwanese firms have paid-up capital of US$3 million or less, while only about one-fifth of them have paid-up capital of US$10 million or more. This suggests most Taiwanese operations in Vietnam are intrinsically labor-intensive.

We also surveyed the decision-making processes in the Taiwanese firms. It is observed that Taiwanese parent companies substantially influence the decision making of Vietnamese subsidiaries. Specifically, the authority of the parent company over decision making is more significant and is expected to be preserved longer in the finance and R&D areas of Vietnamese subsidiaries. In other areas such as marketing, production, and personnel, it appears that the decision-making authority begins to shift from the parent company to local staff quite swiftly.

On average, Taiwanese subsidiaries in Vietnam employ 391 persons, with large firms employing 713 persons and small firms 122 persons. Unskilled labor accounts for just about half of the employment. Staff members and R&D personnel only take up a small fraction of the employment. Out of the average employment of 391 persons, there are only 23 staff members and five R&D personnel. This reflects the nature of production-oriented FDI, with very limited other functions performed in the subsidiaries.

10.4 The Role of Taiwanese Firms in the Vietnamese Economy

Surveyed firms were asked to report the input sources of their Vietnamese operations. The result shows that Taiwanese firms in Vietnam mainly rely on parent companies to provide components and parts. On average, about half of the components and parts are furnished by the parent firms; only about one-fifth of them are procured from local suppliers. The rest are from suppliers in Taiwan or other countries. Large firms procure a slightly higher proportion of their components and parts locally than small firms. The difference is probably attributed to scale economies in local procurement by large firms.

It seems that the linkage between Taiwanese firms and Vietnamese suppliers is not strong, and Taiwanese firms rely mainly on imported input materials for operation. The weak linkage between Taiwanese companies and Vietnamese suppliers is also confirmed by the answers given in response to a question regarding the sources of machinery for Vietnamese investments. Taiwanese firms in Vietnam depend upon their parent companies or other suppliers in Taiwan for the supply of machinery and equipment, while indigenous suppliers provide only a negligible fraction of machinery and equipment needed. About 90 percent of machinery and equipment needed in Vietnam is provided from Taiwan, among which about a quarter is a transplantation of old facilities from the parent firms. Import from other countries constitutes less than 10 percent of the machinery and equipment needed in Vietnam, indicating that there is little demand for sophisticated machinery made in more advanced countries. Among all ASEAN host countries, Vietnam has the lowest percentage of machinery and equipment sourced from third-party countries. Many Vietnamese subsidiaries serve as subcontractors of their home operations in Taiwan; Taiwan-made machinery and equipment is a mechanism to ensure the compatibility of the products made at home and overseas.

The response to the question regarding the sources of financing shows that local partners or financial institutions do not contribute much to finance investments of Taiwanese subsidiaries. The main source of financing for Taiwanese subsidiaries is their parent companies, which on average provide 60.8 percent of the financial needs of the subsidiaries. Small firms in Vietnam depend relatively more upon local financial institutions and the local curb market than do large firms. Small firms draw almost one-fifth of their financing from the local curb market. They borrow from their customers, suppliers, or fellow Taiwanese investors. The financial market in Vietnam is underdeveloped and lending institutions are plagued by high interest rates. Large Taiwanese firms seek financing from financial institutions in Taiwan and third-party countries, whereas small Taiwanese firms may be forced to take some high-cost local financing because they lack alternatives.

The close relationship between subsidiaries and parent companies is also reflected in the marketing channels of subsidiaries. Nearly half of the firms have their products marketed by their parent firms, and this phenomenon is more prevalent in large firms, because large firms concentrate on export markets where sales are coordinated by parent firms in Taiwan and local subsidiaries acting as subcontractors. The dominance of parent firms in marketing products made at overseas subsidiaries is also a distinctive feature of Taiwanese FDI in Vietnam, which comes closest to being a Taiwanese offshore assembly base than any other of the ASEAN countries. Local trading companies play a rather limited role in this respect; less than 10 percent of products are marketed through this channel.

The products of Taiwanese firms operating in Vietnam are primarily sold to a third-country market. On average, about 59 percent of the goods are sold to a third country and about 18 percent are sold back to parent companies or other firms in Taiwan. Only 23 percent of the products are destined for the local market. In particular, large firms sell almost nothing locally and can be characterized as wholly export-oriented. It is evident that Vietnam serves mainly as an export platform for Taiwan's large exporters. On the other hand, the distribution of the final products of small firms is more dispersed than that of large firms.

As for technology transfer by Taiwanese subsidiaries operating in Vietnam, the survey results show that technology transfer made by Taiwanese subsidiaries in Vietnam is of a type similar to that of other investors in Southeast Asia: technology transfer is greater in areas of old technologies than in new technology. More technology transfer occurred in the fields directly related to production processes, such as operating technology, maintenance, and quality control, and less technology transfer took place in such areas as design of products and molds.

The pattern of disposition of profits is also similar to that in Taiwanese subsidiaries in other Southeast Asian countries but differs to some extent between small and large firms. Small firms remit about one-third of their profits to Taiwan, retain about 40 percent in the Vietnamese companies for internal operations, and reinvest about one-fourth of their profits in other projects locally. In comparison, large firms retain over half of the profits within the subsidiary for their own operations while they invest only about 5 percent for local diversification. In other words, large firms are keen on strengthening and expanding their main business in Vietnam whereas small firms look for opportunities to branch out. Small firms are more likely to make diversification investments to take advantage of the local assets they accumulate in overseas operations.

The survey also asked firms to compare their various business operations to those of nearby locally owned firms and subsidiaries from advanced countries. It is apparent that the majority of the Taiwanese firms believe that their business operations are superior to those of local firms in many ways including production technology, output per employee, capacity for product innovation, product line flexibility, provision of labor training. They are also more export-oriented than local firms. The only exception is that Taiwanese subsidiaries purchase a lower ratio of local materials than their local counterparts.

When asked to compare their business operations with those of local subsidiaries from advanced countries, far fewer of the Taiwanese firms indicated that their business operations in Vietnam are superior. Particularly in terms of R&D, Taiwanese firms felt that they are far behind the firms from advanced countries. Taiwanese firms felt, however, that they make greater contributions to the local economy in terms of creating jobs and generating exports because their operations are labor-intensive and geared for export. They also felt that they make a useful contribution to Vietnam in terms of capital formation because their capital is mainly sourced abroad.

10.5 Conclusion

In summary, Taiwanese investment in Vietnam has promoted trade relationships between Vietnam and the rest of the world including Taiwan. The Taiwanese firms in Vietnam employ essentially the same technologies used in Taiwan, which are not very advanced, and sometimes a modification in technology is required to conform to local conditions in Vietnam. Such technologies and adjustments are quite suitable because they generate more employment opportunities in Vietnam.

In general, the motivation for Taiwan's investment in Vietnam is a defensive one. The main impetus for firms to undertake such investment was rising labor costs at home. Getting access to cheap and abundant labor abroad to protect the export market position was their major concern. There are, nonetheless, investments aimed at exploiting the domestic market of Vietnam, which suffers from shortages of basic consumer goods and industrial raw materials. Interestingly, small firms are more active than large firms in pursuing the local markets.

In Taiwan's case, defensive outward investment also exhibited a 'nomadic' feature, in the sense that rising labor costs and other conditions in the neighboring Southeast Asian countries played a vital role in the shift of Taiwan's overseas investment from those countries to mainland China and Vietnam after 1990. It is worth mentioning that the lifting of the US embargo against Vietnam will invariably draw more foreign capital to Vietnam in the future. According to the results of our field interviews with some Taiwanese firms in Vietnam, the liberalization of the US market will induce them to expand their capacities and to diversify their export destinations to include the US market. Latecoming Taiwanese investors who are concerned about rising wages in Malaysia and Thailand will likely find Vietnam an attractive site for their first investments.

11. Conclusions

Tain-Jy Chen

11.1 Taiwanese Type of Small Transnationals

Foreign investment has two components: first, globalization to take advantage of the international division of labor and, second, transfer of production activities from the home base to a foreign location. For Taiwan's small investors, relocation carries a much greater weight than globalization. International division of labor within firms is limited. Their cross-border operations are usually limited to two countries and hence cannot be termed 'multinational'. They mainly rely on domestic and host-country resources to run their binational operations, lacking the capability to tap into global resources.

Constraining the scope of small firms' globalization are their limited managerial resources and capital, particularly the former. Limited managerial resources make coordination and communication across national borders and across different policy regimes very difficult. The proprietary assets of these small firms are usually personalized and embodied in the owners themselves. To exploit these proprietary assets overseas often requires migration of the owners with the plants. This reduces the small firms' capability of retaining their original scale of operations at home after a foreign investment is undertaken. The limited number of technical experts also constrains small firms' ability to dispatch expatriate experts abroad on a sustained basis if home operations are to be kept at the original scale. All these point to the likelihood of hollowing-out of domestic operations occurring after FDI.

The comparative advantage of small firms lies in their ability to engage in small-scale and flexible production. For Taiwan's small firms, it is a strong production network that underscores this ability. This network is composed of a large number of small and loosely connected specialty producers. Division of labor within the network forms the basis of its efficiency; and variations in the format of division of labor provide flexibility.

Without the aid of this network, Taiwan's small firms lose their competitiveness. Therefore, when these firms venture abroad, they maintain close links to this network at home. This dependence prohibits Taiwan's small firms from investing in a distant location. However, even at a close overseas location, small affiliates find it costly to rely heavily on Taiwan's networks. To wean themselves from this overseas network, Taiwanese affiliates are keen on localization.

11.1.1 Sourcing

Localization comprises many dimensions. The most common dimension of localization is local sourcing, that is, subcontracting to local firms and procurement of local materials. Searching for local subcontractors and suppliers takes time, and uncertainty about the quality of their products increases the risk of operation, which includes the likelihood of a production breakdown or substandard quality. For large firms which usually engage in large-volume production of brand-name products, the costs of a production breakdown or product failure are too high to be worth the risk. Furthermore, the market power associated with their brand-name products enables them to bear the costs of trans-border procurement for high-priced components and parts. If there is a need to localize, say, to satisfy a local content regulation, large firms normally prefer in-house production over subcontracting. This, of course, limits the scope of local linkage. Some host countries have to introduce regulations which explicitly require that some specified components be manufactured by unaffiliated local firms to bring about local linkages. In contrast, for small firms, which usually produce niche products with a short production run, risk of product failure is not as great as that of large firms engaging in mass production. Particularly for Taiwan's small firms which are export-oriented and exposed to acute competitive pressure, there is little room for excessive costs if alternative suppliers can be found or made available locally.

Taiwan's small firms operating overseas also undertake in-house production of key components and parts which they normally contract out in Taiwan because of the lack of competent local subcontractors. This makes their capital investment in overseas operations larger than the normal level of comparable operations in Taiwan. Therefore, only the relatively large SMEs can afford to invest abroad.

Some small firms opt to establish joint-venture subsidiaries to serve as their subcontractors. They may choose local entrepreneurs, their subcontractors in Taiwan or even their local employees to serve as joint-venture partners. Due to their small volume of demand, Taiwanese small affiliates usually lack the capacity to nurture a subcontractor with their own support, to say nothing of replicating a subcontracting network overseas. Nonetheless, because they usually manufacture niche products with essential firm-specific know-how, a close working relationship with subcontractors is indispensable. This forces them to seek out local subcontractors. More often, they take advantage of existing networks and train subcontractors within the networks to produce things suited to their needs or adapt themselves to what is available locally.

Unlike Japanese small firms which often belong to a *keiretsu* network that internalizes the proprietary asset and which trade only with other *keiretsu* members, Taiwanese small firms work with an open-ended network, members and functions of which evolve over time. When operating abroad, Taiwanese small affiliates establish working relations with local firms from different backgrounds: indigenous firms, other Taiwanese subsidiaries, Japanese subsidiaries, and the like, with little discrimination. Although they normally prefer Taiwanese subsidiaries, this is due to the low transaction costs of such relationships rather than because they belong to the same business group in Taiwan. Since agglomeration is a recognizable effect in foreign direct investment, small Taiwanese investors tend to cluster by industries. The presence of such a cluster of Taiwanese small firms can also initiate formation of a production network which expands by attracting new members from Taiwan as well as local sources. In essence, their pressing need for subcontractors provides an impetus for the formation of a subcontracting network, although the composition of the network and the interplay of network members can be very different from the one in Taiwan.

11.1.2 Technology Adaptation and Technology Transfer

The second dimension of localization is technology adaptation and technology transfer. Multinational firms are often criticized for employing 'inappropriate' technology in local economies and being unwilling to transfer their technology. They tend to adhere to the technologies that they employ at home to avoid the risk of production failure and the costs of adaptation. Since factor markets in the host economies are generally different from those of the home country, these technologies may be 'inappropriate' in the sense that the underlying factor proportion does not reflect the cost-minimization condition. Adherence to home-country technology also enables multinational firms to conduct intra-firm trade and reduces the possibility of local linkage. Multinational firms can indulge in suboptimal methods of production, probably to satisfy the manager's ego of being an 'engineering man' (Wells 1973), only if they operate in a permissive environment (Morley and Smith 1977). This implies that 'inappropriate' technologies are more often found in multinational firms operating behind the protection wall of the host countries. Taiwan's small firms generally export their products directly or indirectly (producing components and parts to be incorporated in final products for export); they have little of the kind of prestige it usually takes to receive trade protection from host countries although some fiscal incentives in the form of tax breaks are possible. We generally found export-oriented firms to be more adaptive than domestic-market-oriented firms, and small firms to be more adaptive than large firms.

Adaptation takes various forms. The most frequently observed adaptation is to deskill the production technology. For example, the original production process is broken up and reconfigured such that each step of the operation is simplified to require a minimum input of skills. Deskilling is designed to overcome the shortage of skilled labor in the host economy and to take advantage of the abundance of unskilled labor there. When substituting skilled labor with unskilled labor is infeasible, Taiwanese affiliates even introduce automated production procedures to reduce human error. In view of this, the criticism that multinational firms are overly capital-intensive may be a result of conscious adaptation rather than an unwillingness to adapt. Deskilling in production processes usually increases the complexity of job division and requires more managerial input to monitor and coordinate the work. The result is an increased demand for white-collar workers who are, unfortunately, also in short supply. To overcome this problem, affiliates either demand more expatriate managers be sent from the parent firms or engage in intensive training of local workers to assume the additional managerial responsibilities. For small transnationals, training local workers is preferred to hiring expatriate workers because the latter are too expensive to justify a small-scale operation.

Another form of adaptation is to modify the technology to increase the allowance for imprecision. This is again a reaction to the lack of experienced workers for high-precision jobs. This type of adaptation is often accomplished through introduction of less-than-modern machinery. Many Taiwanese affiliates find that second-hand machines are more 'appropriate' than the modern machinery made in Japan and the US because local workers may achieve a higher productive efficiency when using the less exacting type of machinery.

The third form of adaptation is what economists generally expect but find lacking in multinationals, namely, increasing labor intensity of production technology to reflect lower wages in the host countries. For example, each machine is attended by more workers than it would be in the parent firms; manual work is introduced to substitute for machines. This can be observed especially in the non-essential segments of the production process, for example, packing and labeling. It takes time for this type of adaptation to take place, however. The priority of Taiwanese transnationals, small or large, when they first engage in overseas production, is to ensure that the quality of the overseas product meets the international standard so that they may continue to serve the export market from this offshore platform. Only after the production runs smoothly will they start contemplating reducing costs by adjusting input combinations to suit local conditions.

Multinational firms are often criticized for being unwilling to transfer technology. In fact, whether to transfer technology to affiliates is an economic decision. Technology transfer incurs resources costs (Teece 1977). Technology transfer will be undertaken if it is needed for the smooth operation of the affiliates and if the cost of transfer is justifiable by economic returns. The degree of technology transfer thus depends on the nature of overseas operations. Our study, among others, found that Taiwanese parent firms are normally unreserved in transferring technologies related to manual operations, maintenance of machinery and equipment, quality control, and the like. Our survey indicates that more than 70 percent of these technologies have been transferred to the subsidiaries, with large affiliates holding a slight edge over small affiliates in the extent of technology transfer. These technologies are indispensable for successful overseas production. Taiwanese transnational firms usually conduct on-the-job training to facilitate the transfer of these technologies. They also send local workers, usually those who are to assume leadership roles on the shop floor, to parent firms for more thorough training. Meanwhile, like other multinational firms, Taiwanese firms are less enthusiastic in the transfer of technologies related to product innovation, process control and improvement, and design of machinery and equipment. The transfer of these technologies is more costly while support from the parent firm is feasible because these technologies are not needed on a daily basis.

Among Western multinationals, the internalized technology market is an important venue through which parent firms extract economic rents from their overseas affiliates. Taiwan's small transnationals do not seem to be capable of maintaining this type of internal market for technology because localization drives the technology used by overseas affiliates further and further apart from that of the parent firms, making technological support from the parent firms increasingly difficult. Taiwan's small affiliates have shown a strong tendency to engage in product innovation through their own R&D, through imitating the products of their peers, or through acquiring technologies from international sources. In essence, they strive to achieve technological independence from the parent firms because the latter lack the capability to support them. In fact, the essential know-how of small firms is often personalized and embodied in the owners. Since, in most cases, owners of Taiwanese small firms migrate with their factories to overseas, overseas affiliates actually possess the key technology for the entire operation of transnationals. Parent firms sometimes degenerate into a mere information-collecting agency, serving as an outpost in Taiwan to retain linkage to Taiwanese networks.

Small Taiwanese affiliates also undertake employee training, both on-the-job training and overseas training at the parent-firm headquarters. Although large affiliates, on average, train more overseas workers than small affiliates, small affiliates provide longer training hours for each trainee, presumably because managerial staff and technicians in small affiliates perform multiple functions which require more extensive and intensive training. They even arrange for technicians to be trained by their machinery suppliers in Taiwan or Japan, taking advantage of resources within the international networks.

Nonetheless, the most important element affecting technology transfer is probably the local capacity to absorb technology, and the key to this capacity is the availability of properly educated skilled workers amenable to training. Taiwanese affiliates often complain about the negligence of vocational training in host countries, making middle-level technicians hard to come by. Without them, technology transfer can hardly be accomplished.

11.1.3 Marketing

Another dimension of localization is marketing. Market access is an important asset for multinational operations, and especially so for Taiwanese transnationals, which are primarily export-oriented. Controlling marketing channels is seen by Taiwanese firms as protecting their lifelines. For large Western multinational firms, marketing channels of export-oriented affiliates are often under the control of parent firms. Parent firms dictate what to produce and where to sell as the decision is an integral part of the global strategy. For Taiwan's small firms, unification of production and marketing responsibilities is crucial to the flexibility and responsiveness of their marketing strategies. Production arrangements in terms of shipping schedules and product modification are often used as a part of marketing tactics.

Owners who possess the best knowledge of their products are also the best salespersons. Being able to make decisions on the spot also provides an advantage in marketing. Therefore, Taiwanese small subsidiaries assume more of their own marketing responsibilities than do Western multinationals. They are also reluctant to delegate marketing responsibilities to local sales agencies when their products are geared toward the local market. Direct contact with customers enables them to benefit from customer feedback and to forestall the interlopers trying to disrupt their customer relationship. In addition, most export-oriented small firms produce OEM products under the license of brand-name holders. Direct marketing by the subsidiaries lowers the costs of coordinating with the patrons in terms of certification of production capacity, supervision of production process, or inspection of semi-finished and finished products.

11.1.4 Local Sales

The fourth dimension of localization is to increase the proportion of local sales. Although most Taiwanese affiliates, large or small, are export-oriented in the beginning, they tend to increase their proportion of local sales over time. Due to trade protection in host economies, local markets often command above-normal profits. To penetrate the local market, however, modifications of products may be necessary to accommodate local consumer tastes or local industrial practices. Since modifications incur extra costs and risks, multinational firms will not undertake modifications unless they foresee a reasonable local demand. Small firms are more likely to find a 'sizable' local market than large firms. Taiwanese SMEs normally produce niche products or components and parts to be incorporated into export products. They may vary their product designs to cater to the demand of local consumers or industrial users, taking advantage of their technological know-how about the products. To embark on new product frontiers, local Taiwanese subsidiaries rely on strategic assets that they have accumulated in local production, in addition to their technological know-how. With the Chinese connections, accumulation of location-specific assets in Southeast Asia is not difficult.

Small Taiwanese firms are keen on local markets from the very beginning of their overseas production, although they are primarily export-oriented. This is probably because they foresee the dissipation over time of their labor-based competitiveness and the potentiality of the local market provides an insurance against the event of losing export markets.

Increased local sales implies that local subsidiaries gain more autonomy in marketing. Independent marketing units and marketing channels need to be established at the subsidiaries when the proportion of local sales is large. Establishment of marketing channels usually entails linkages to local sales networks with which parent firms are totally out of touch. To develop products for the local markets also calls for independent R&D units to engage in product innovation, or at least in product adaptation to suit the local tastes and standards. Local sales are also an important driving force in other areas of localization, such as material sourcing and technological adaptation.

In addition to local sales, Taiwanese affiliates also use their overseas base to serve regional markets, namely, the Southeast Asian market. Since the whole of Southeast Asia is undergoing an unprecedented period of rapid growth, the regional market offers a good prospect for Taiwanese firms that maintain a manufacturing base in the area. If not for the existing trade barriers that impede intra-regional trade, a regional small-firm network with Taiwan's small firms serving as connecting points could easily be formed.

In sum, when we follow the history of FDI by Taiwanese small- and medium-sized firms, we see little evidence of an evolutionary process of internationalization: from export, to sales subsidiary, and then to production subsidiary. Taiwanese small firms skip the first two steps and embark directly on production subsidiaries. In doing so, they take advantage of the local overseas Chinese network to overcome the foreignness of operating abroad without previous contacts to accumulate 'strategic' asset (Dunning and Narula 1996).

In fact, FDI by Taiwanese small affiliates can hardly be called an 'internationalization' process. At most, they run a two-plant operation in two different countries. They spend more resources in localizing their overseas subsidiaries than in establishing a truly international production network centrally controlled by headquarters in Taiwan. There are indeed resource interflows between parent companies in Taiwan and overseas affiliates, but only a small fraction of these can be called genuine intra-firm trade involving proprietary asset. More often, the parent firm serves only as an outpost to tap into the resources available in its Taiwanese network, upon which Taiwan's small- and medium-sized firms depend for competitiveness. The proprietary assets of small firms are normally embodied in the owners, who reside with the overseas subsidiaries, or at least spend substantial time abroad. Without the presence of these owners, the strength of the proprietary assets cannot be exploited and the subsidiaries are not viable.

Because small firms are short of managerial resources, cross-border operations often prove to be too costly for them to sustain on a long-term basis. Localization is thus a survival strategy. Overseas affiliates which are successful in localization grow and may surpass the size of the parent. Parent firms that do not find a way to restructure themselves, or lack managerial resources to run a viable transnational operation, degenerate into a liaison office taking orders from the overseas subsidiaries. Even if the parent firms succeed in restructuring, and survive the 'hollowing-out' risk, their dominance of the overseas subsidiaries decreases over time and the two eventually become parallel operations interacting like business allies rather than parent–subsidiary.

11.2 Small-Firm FDI and Industrial Restructuring in Taiwan

Whether FDI leads to a hollowing-out of the domestic industry (deindustrialization) is an issue that has been debated but remains unsettled. Some argue that FDI creates jobs at the headquarters which provide technical and managerial services to overseas subsidiaries (Lipsey 1994). FDI enables investing companies to preserve export market share which otherwise would have been lost to competitors from local origins or from low-wage countries. Preservation of market share also saves jobs and some domestic production. Others argue that FDI is tantamount to industry dislocation and export of jobs from home. Outflow of capital crowds out domestic investment, eventually leading to a hollowing-out of domestic industry (Aaronovitch et al. 1981).

Theoretically speaking, if FDI results in a relocation of domestic industries without replacement at home, it will contribute to deindustrialization; if FDI is only a part of an industrial restructuring process, deindustrialization may be avoided. Industrial restructuring at home following FDI may take place through three channels: within one firm, within an industry, or between industrial sectors.

First, some firms, particularly large ones, may introduce new product lines to replace the old ones which have been transplanted overseas. This is an effort to exploit the power of their firm-specific asset, which is often embodied in their employees, especially the skilled workers. Laying off employees runs the risk of leaking special know-how to competitors. Therefore, arrangements will be made to reemploy these workers in new production units. Usually such a placement plan is well thought out before a foreign investment project is undertaken. This is the case of intra-firm restructuring.

Such intra-firm restructuring is particularly noticeable among Japanese enterprises (Hara 1989), which until recently practiced the lifetime employment system. Their ability to introduce new product lines suggests the accessibility of new technologies and the existence of firm-specific know-how that can be deployed to new frontiers. All this is made possible by exploiting the economies of scope within business conglomerates (*keiretsu*). For example, when the production of TV sets is relocated abroad, domestic production may shift to computer monitors, which benefit from technological externalities of TV production. This type of restructuring often results in a horizontal integration between home and overseas production whereby economies of scale in marketing can be exploited. Since product diversity is the key to intra-firm restructuring, large firms are more capable of restructuring than small firms.

Second, relocated overseas production may be linked forward or backward to domestic industries. Through this linkage, overseas production may nourish downstream or upstream industries at home. This is part of the network linkage that we alluded to at the beginning of the book. This results in an intra-industry or inter-industry restructuring, depending on how broadly an industry is defined. The key to this type of restructuring is vertical integration and network linkage. The more vertically integrated are the industries at home and the more lasting are the network linkages across borders, the more likely this type of restructuring will take place. Most multinational firms prefer to source from their home market, particularly the headquarters, to avoid adjustment costs in overseas production. In that case, linkages to domestic networks are durable. Again, Japanese multinational firms are famous for insisting on this link-up to keep their competitive edge abroad (Kotabe and Omura 1989). Since linkages to Taiwan's networks from Taiwanese affiliates are vulnerable, we may expect FDI-induced restructuring of this type to be unreliable.

Third, resources that are released domestically by transplantation of existing production can be transferred to new sectors in the home economy. This follows the classical argument that resources find their own way to full employment as long as the market mechanism is unimpeded. This is intersectoral restructuring.

Based on the above arguments, whether FDI leads to deindustrialization seems to be an empirical issue. In the following subsection, we will briefly examine the Taiwanese case to see the interrelationship between FDI and industrial restructuring, in light of the nature of network linkage that we have discussed in the previous chapters.

11.2.1 FDI and Restructuring

With massive FDI since 1986, the weight of manufacturing activity in Taiwan's economy has decreased rapidly. In 1986, manufacturing accounted for 39.4 percent of GNP. In 1996, the manufacturing share in GNP fell to only 28.1 percent. In a short span of ten years, the share of manufacturing output fell by 11.3 percent. If deindustrialization is defined as 'the dismantling of a country's manufacturing base' (Caslin 1987, p. 240) and dismantling is taken to mean rapid decline of output share, Taiwan seems to exemplify a classical case of deindustrialization. In the same time span, employment in the manufacturing sector in Taiwan decreased by 265 118 jobs, almost 10 percent of the initial employment level in 1986.

However, with a few exceptional industries, the absolute value of manufacturing output did not decrease in 1986–96. The decline of manufacturing share in GNP was attributable to a rapid increase in service output whose share rose from 47.3 percent in 1986 to 61.1 percent in 1996. Despite the decline in manufacturing employment, the unemployment rate in Taiwan remained consistently below 3 percent except for a few abnormal months in 1996. The phenomenon seems to indicate a restructuring of the economy more than a 'hollowing-out' of industry.

If we look at some major industries in which Taiwanese FDI in Southeast Asia was active, we can find that the association of FDI with deindustrialization is unwarranted. For example, the shares of the three leading FDI industries, namely electrical and electronic products, chemicals, and basic metal and metal products, in manufacturing output all increased substantially between 1986 and 1996. Some major FDI industries, for example, the textile and plastic products industries, saw their shares in manufacturing output decline, however.

In fact, the greatest increase in output share in the manufacturing sector between 1986 and 1996 occurred in the chemicals and electrical and electronic products industry. Introduction of new product lines was prevalent in these two industries and new product innovations replaced outgoing ones. This was in sharp contrast to the textile and plastics industries where technological change was the norm of restructuring, but product innovation was not pervasive.

11.2.2 Intra-Firm Restructuring

As in Western countries, intra-firm restructuring took place mainly within large enterprises. For example, large Taiwanese textile firms embarked on the production of textile fibers after relocating their garment operations abroad. Staying within the perimeters of the industry in which they had ample experience was the basic principle of intra-firm restructuring. Examples are manufacturers of consumer electronics moving into computer assembly, and computer assembly firms moving to semiconductors. In the restructuring process, the investors take advantage of the know-how that they have accumulated in the original business and apply it in related fields. The firm may also exploit the business relationship it has developed in previous business undertakings to establish a relationship with new business partners. The more knowledge externalities can be exploited and the more easily a business relationship can be carried over to a new horizon, the more possibilities exist for intra-firm restructuring. Therefore, firms operating in a more dynamic industry or firms possessing more generic knowledge with widespread applications stand a better chance of succeeding in intra-firm restructuring. For example, firms in the garment and footwear, leather products, wood products, and plastic products industries face a smaller scope for restructuring compared to those in the chemicals and electronics because the latter industries are more dynamic.

Small- and medium-sized firms are intrinsically disadvantaged in intra-firm restructuring. Many Taiwanese SMEs closed their domestic operations after making overseas investment. Some SMEs, however, took advantage of their network resources to make intra-firm restructuring and switched to a new industry. The key to success in this kind of transition depends on the technology gap between the old and the new industry and whether someone within the business network can offer assistance. Help may come from a major client, a major supplier, or other related firms. However, since the technology needed for transition is likely to be proprietary rather than standardized, small firms generally have to make some commitment to the network before a technology transfer is possible. As a result, the loosely knit small-firm networks in Taiwan are giving way to more integrated networks in which some dominant firms control the proprietary assets. The dominant firms are usually large firms which possess superior R&D capabilities. This is why large firms have played an increasing role in Taiwan's manufacturing output and exports. Small firms, which have become increasingly reliant on large firms for technological support and increasingly locked in to network relations, assume the relatively labor-intensive segments of the production process. This explains why the contribution of SMEs to manufacturing employment has increased along with the decline in SMEs' shares in output and exports.

The decline of loosely knit small-firm networks has been evident in conventional light manufacturing industries in Taiwan, such as garments, wood products, footwear, plastic products, sporting goods, and so on. On the rise have been more integrated networks dominated by product innovators or brand-name producers. Membership of these networks is fixed or semi-fixed with members making long-term commitments to designated roles. Examples are computer industry networks.

11.2.3 Intra-Industry Restructuring

Intra-industry restructuring may take two forms: one is a vertical shift, the other is a horizontal shift. Vertical shift refers to movement from downstream production to upstream production, or vice versa. For example, when the garment industry moves abroad, domestic production may shift to fabrics, yarn, or textile fibers. Whether this happens depends on the linkage between overseas production and domestic industries. The linkage may also go the other way from upstream to downstream products. For example, overseas production of gray fabric may encourage the expansion of domestic production of finished fabric, resulting in a boost to the printing and finishing industry. Production of electronics parts and components abroad may likewise promote the domestic assembly of electronic products.

Another form of intra-industry restructuring is the horizontal shift of products. Horizontal shift may also take place within one firm whereby an overseas investor differentiates its overseas production from domestic production by product quality. But extra-firm restructuring is also common whereby old firms relocate abroad and new firms emerge to take their place. Inevitably the switch is facilitated by the knowledge which has been accumulated and stored in the home society. For example, when small-sized computer monitors were shifted to Southeast Asia for production, Taiwan's production moved to large-sized monitors. When the production of cotton textiles was relocated to Southeast Asia, Taiwan turned to the production of polyester textiles.

The extent to which horizontal shift can occur depends on the degree of horizontal differentiation that can be made out of the industry. As an example, take the garment industry which relocated to Southeast Asia *en masse* in the late 1980s. To differentiate domestic products from overseas ones, Taiwan needed to develop design capability and brand-name garments. Since both design capability and brand name were nonexistent and could not be established easily with the existing knowledge pertinent to manufacturing, intra-industry restructuring was largely absent in Taiwan's garment industry.

In contrast, the electronics industry is a typical industry exemplifying extensive intra-industry restructuring following FDI. Taiwan was also a major producer and exporter of consumer electronics (such as TV sets and cassette recorders) and electronics components. Rising labor costs in the 1980s drove this industry to Southeast Asia and other areas. Domestic production shifted to computers, and components and peripherals. The computer industry attracted entry of new as well as well-established electronics firms. The foundation for this smooth transition was the production knowledge that had been accumulated in the 1970s and 1980s.

11.2.4 Network Linkage and Restructuring

Despite a vulnerable network linkage with the domestic industry, Taiwanese subsidiaries in Southeast Asia nonetheless generated linkage effects to facilitate intra-industry restructuring in Taiwan since 1986. The garment industry is a good example. Garment firms were the front runners of Taiwanese FDI in Southeast Asia. After relocating production lines overseas, most garment firms reduced or removed major production capacity at home. In general, large firms and those possessing brand names in the domestic market were more capable than small firms in retaining domestic production after FDI. Taiwan continued to export some apparel products despite massive FDI, partly because export quotas in the US, Canada, and Europe acted to protect Taiwan's market share, partly because of Taiwan's unique production environment. A flexible production network cultivated over long years' experience of serving export markets gave Taiwan a unique capability to switch product lines swiftly and to deliver products promptly. Even small garment firms strove to maintain a small-scale production capacity in Taiwan to produce for short orders after they invested in Southeast Asia. Preparation for production and actual production times were shorter in Taiwan because of a well-knit network comprising suppliers and subcontractors who could divide the job in a very efficient and flexible manner.

If a garment firm was too small to maintain even small-scale production at home, it at least kept an office in Taiwan to provide logistical support to overseas production. The logistical support included mainly marketing and procurement functions, such as accepting orders, sample preparation and demonstration, procurement and collections of materials in preparation for production. Sample preparation is a very important process in soliciting orders. Normally, when a potential client indicates an intention to purchase a certain type of product, multiple samples need to be prepared in a short span of time for the client to inspect and to choose from. For the small-volume market, the capacity to make samples fast and precise is essential to the competition for orders. Taiwan is known for its superior capacity in supplying small-volume, large-variety orders. Making samples also entails the design capability of transforming the vague ideas of clients into real visualization of products and this capability needs to be maintained at the headquarters to ensure nimbleness.

Logistical support in procurement of parts and materials in preparation for production is also essential to the flexibility of overseas production. When an order is accepted and planned to be carried out in an overseas subsidiary, parts and materials which are not available at the overseas location need to be procured and shipped overseas in the shortest time possible. Note that even in overseas production, quick delivery constitutes the competitive edge of Taiwanese subsidiaries over local firms as both groups face the same wages. Any disruption in the supply of parts and materials will delay the production schedule and undermine the core competitiveness of Taiwanese subsidiaries. Although over time Taiwanese subsidiaries cut the proportion of materials sourced from Taiwan, they still procured from Taiwan some specialty products.

Initial production of Taiwanese subsidiaries is normally furnished by orders transferred from parent firms. Gradually, overseas subsidiaries accumulate new assets and explore new sources of clients. To beat off local competition, logistical support from the parent firm and the resources available from Taiwan's production networks are their weapons. New clients typically came from new export markets and, like their parent firms, OEM contracts were the typical form of engagement. Low labor costs in overseas locations, combined with network resources in Taiwan, underscore the comparative advantage of Taiwanese subsidiaries in Southeast Asia. In the case of garments, most Southeast Asian subsidiaries of Taiwanese garment firms purchase fabrics from Taiwan and procurement is conducted by parent firms. In fact, it is advantageous to import fabrics from Taiwan because Taiwan provides more variety, accepts smaller orders, and promises a shorter delivery time. It is in these areas that network linkages to Taiwan were maintained in spite of mounting pressure to localize.

FDI, together with network linkages, reshaped Taiwan's textile industry dramatically. In 1986, garments accounted for 36.6 percent of the textile industry output, fabrics and yarns accounted for 50.7 percent, and man-made fibers accounted for the remaining 12.7 percent. In 1996, the share of garments in textiles output sharply decreased to only 19.2 percent while that of fabrics and yarns increased to 59.0 percent and man-made fibers to 21.8 percent. In fact, the absolute value of the garment production declined in 1986–96 while the other two subsectors of textiles both gained.

Since network linkages to Taiwan generally have weakened over time and those remaining strong are product-specific, Taiwan's manufacturing industry has become much more concentrated after restructuring in 1986–96. Three major industries, namely electrical and electronic products, chemicals, basic metal and metal products, combined to account for 57.0 percent of the manufacturing output in 1996, a big jump from 39.5 percent in 1986. These three sectors also contributed to 56.0 percent of domestic capital formation and the creation of 161 736 new manufacturing jobs in 1986–96.

11.3 Implications for East Asian Dynamism

The surge of Taiwanese FDI in recent years is reminiscent of the 'flying-geese' pattern of economic development advocated by Akamatsu (1961) and other Japanese scholars. 'The flying-geese paradigm of economic development describes a phenomenon in which a group of economies, closely interacting with one another, advance together as a whole, led by a predominant economy as the growth center, followed by progressively less developed economies in a hierarchical pattern homologous to that formed by a flock of flying geese' (Ozawa 1993, p. 102).

The predominant economy in East Asian dynamism is Japan. Japan led the flock of East Asian 'flying geese'. Behind it followed the Asian NICs. In the third ranks are members of ASEAN (excluding Singapore, which is a member of NICs) and the coastal provinces of China. In the fourth ranks may be Vietnam and other Indochinese countries.

Japan embarked on a course of FDI in the late 1960s, with Asian NICs as its primary target. Labor-intensive, export-oriented industries relocated from Japan to NICs *en masse*, adding fuel to the industrial development locomotives of the latter countries. Taiwan, Korea, Singapore, and Hong Kong have since taken over these labor-intensive industries and become the world's major exporters of textiles, electronic products, and other light manufactures. Meanwhile, Japan has since undergone a process of internal restructuring whereby a series of capital- and technology-intensive industries has been developed to replace the labor-intensive ones. The decade of 1970s was the prime time when this sequential restructuring took place in Japan and the NICs. Underlying this restructuring process were the changing factor endowments and technological capabilities of both parties.

The second wave of major FDI in East Asia came after the 1985 Plaza Accord, following which the Japanese yen, the new taipi, and the Korean won all entered the fast track of appreciation. This time, Japan's FDI, comprising mainly capital-intensive industries, headed toward the US and Europe, with members of ASEAN taking the secondary position as host countries, and NICs being virtually ignored. In terms of technological sophistication, those headed toward the US and Europe were more technologically advanced than those headed toward ASEAN member-countries. The relocation of labor-intensive light manufacturing was mainly performed by NICs, with ASEAN members and China targeted as major destinations (World Bank 1989).

Although the second wave of FDI is just over ten years old, the observable consequences have been reminiscent of those of the first wave of FDI. ASEAN countries, together with China, have overtaken NICs as the world's major exporters of textiles, electronic products, and other light manufactures. Meanwhile, NICs have launched a campaign to host the second sequence of capital- and technology-intensive industries, with varying degrees of success. The flock of geese has obviously moved forward, and along the way, the interactions within the group, in terms of investment, trade, technology diffusion, and labor migration, have been heightened to an unprecedented level. The leading role of Japan is unscathed, but now NICs are also capable of discharging excess production capacity and financial resources to help propel the growth engines of the third-tier economies along East Asia's dynamic path.

A systematic study of multinational firms based in NICs is yet to be done. Our study on the Taiwanese case has uncovered important differences between Taiwanese FDI in Southeast Asia today and Japanese FDI in NICs approximately 15 years ago. Although both FDI phenomena share the same characteristics of labor intensiveness and export orientation, and in both cases, small- and medium-sized firms played a significant role, the two cases differed, evidently, in terms of group behavior.

Japanese FDI is a concerted action by the firms within a business group, known as *keiretsu*. When the group ventures abroad, each member of the group adjusts their functions to accommodate the move, with *sogo shosha* (a general trading firm) playing the leading role (Panglaykim 1983, p. 85). The action is backed by the whole group, which often includes banks, contractors, factories, trading firms, consultants, research laboratories, and so on. The actions of Japanese multinational firms are therefore integrated and centrally coordinated. The operations of overseas affiliates are centrally controlled by headquarters in Japan and are positioned to serve the global (or regional) interests of the group. Japanese multinationals may also localize, but localization often takes the form of increasing the presence of *keiretsu* members in the host country. That is, they replicate the *keiretsu* networks in the local economies.

In contrast, Taiwanese FDI is normally an individual action with little coordination between firms. Only on a few occasions have we observed large assemblers investing in conjunction with their subcontractors. Taiwanese transnationals usually lack a master plan for globalization. Their FDI endeavor is, in essence, a survival strategy. Internationalization of Taiwanese firms is a piecewise process with a short planning horizon. They will plan for the second step only after succeeding in the first step and the second-step actions are conditional on the first-step experience. They respond to market pressures and opportunities by engaging in overseas production. When Taiwanese firms invest in a particular country in flocks, it is mainly because there are market forces driving them; it is a common action of unrelated firms. When supporting industries follow the pioneer investors by locating abroad, it is the market demand that attracted the attention of followers. In a sense, Taiwanese FDI is coordinated by market forces, with industrial networks in Taiwan transmitting relevant information.

The unorchestrated FDI makes Taiwanese investors isolated in local economies. Unlike the Japanese FDI, in which banks often precede the establishment of production subsidiaries, banks are conspicuously missing in Taiwanese FDI. Isolation makes Taiwanese affiliates desperate for local association, and they often rely on personal connections to make associations. Local networks formed in host countries are usually a hybrid of local,

Taiwanese, and other transnational firms. In essence, Taiwanese small transnational firms do not reproduce Taiwan's networks overseas; instead they integrate with, or, more precisely, get absorbed into, local networks.

Although Japan is the undisputed leader in East Asian dynamism, its contribution to host countries via FDI is often questioned. Many scholars believe that it was mainly domestic capital formation that contributed to the economic development of NICs (see, for instance, Koo 1993). Technology transfer and local linkages of Japanese multinationals are considered sketchy and inconsequential (see, for instance, Hill 1988). Furthermore, Japanese parent firms' unyielding control of key components and parts often compels host countries to continue to depend on Japanese technology. Even NICs today still resent their continuing trade deficits with Japan resulting from this irrevocable dependency.

In contrast, Taiwanese transnationals have little control over key components and parts, which are either imported from third-party countries or produced by independent suppliers in Taiwan. Parent firms in Taiwan have little incentive or capacity to keep crucial technologies out of the reach of overseas affiliates as a means of maintaining technological superiority. Small firms, in particular, are only concerned with the viability of subsidiaries, making sure that the proprietary assets embodied in the owners continue to generate economic rents from these subsidiaries, because their business lives at home may have been severed. Large firms usually engage in horizontal division of labor, with limited vertical integration between parents and subsidiaries. The parent firms may furnish overseas subsidiaries with some semi-finished products to which key components and parts are out-sourced rather than internally produced.

Therefore, the inter-economy restructuring within East Asia as induced by Japanese FDI is a sequential and orderly process (Ozawa 1993), in which technology is partitioned and transferred piece by piece to ensure a hierarchical structure dominated by Japan. Normally, old technology will not be transferred unless new technology has been adopted at home. Inter-economy restructuring induced by Taiwanese FDI is more or less an industrial migration, through which the entirety of Taiwan-owned technology crosses borders as long as the local economies have the absorption capacity. We can identify at least the following industries as having emigrated from Taiwan since 1986: shoes, garments, luggage, toys, sporting goods, and kitchenware.

Industrial migration has a greater impact on source and host economies than does Japanese-style, or for that matter, American-style, FDI. Industrial migration involves a transfer from one country to the other of a complete set of industrial resources, including technology, market access, production facilities, and human resources. Like human migration, industrial migration is driven by the conviction that the destination economy provides higher returns on the relevant assets. In fact, industrial migration is often accompanied by migration of key personnel in the migrating firms. Although emigrated industries maintain some linkages with Taiwan's networks, the transactions between Taiwan's networks and overseas subsidiaries involve more and more intangibles, such as market and technological information, and fewer and fewer tangibles such as components and parts.

In traditional American and Japanese FDI, investing firms seek to exploit the value of proprietary assets which have the nature of a public good, meaning return can be obtained at relatively low marginal costs (Caves 1971). In Taiwan's FDI, particularly that of small- and medium-sized firms, when the proprietary asset is transferred abroad, its applicability at home is substantially diminished. Because Taiwanese firms operate in competitive industries and competitors in these industries face the same external environment, when one firm feels it is advantageous to migrate, the rest feel the same way. Therefore, they often migrate in flocks, and their supporting industries follow in their footsteps. The unorchestrated FDI often turns out to be a concerted industrial migration.

The wave of industrial migration starts on a small scale with few firms, but both the scale and number of firms grow over time. It is common to observe that overseas Taiwanese subsidiaries operate on a scale larger than their original size in Taiwan. Since migrant firms compete with one another on the new soil, they have to employ their best technology and mobilize all available resources to combat the competition. There is little room for managerial slack or withholing certain technology to keep the parent firm in a superior position. The result is an unimpeded transfusion of resources from Taiwan to the host countries, contributing to the industrial development of the latter. Since migration incurs sunk costs, and adaptation to local conditions creates location-specific assets, Taiwanese overseas subsidiaries do not easily exit the host country once they settle down there. They adjust to changing macroeconomic conditions to stay competitive, just like other local firms.

The result of this type of FDI is a fast but perhaps disorderly restructuring of the economies involved. While the recipient countries are given an impetus to move the ranks in a flying-geese formation, the investing country is under the risk of dropping out of the formation. The key is that feedback from the recipient countries to the investing country is limited and diminishing over time. The investing country has to create new industries, probably unrelated to outgoing ones, to retain its rank in the league of Asian flying geese rather than to prosper from the growth of overseas investment. This implies that a very fast pace of economic restructuring has to take place at home if an industrial hollowing-out is to be avoided. This requires new technologies, and, today, the leading goose (Japan) seems to be unprepared to provide them either through FDI or other forms of technology trade. Since Japan itself has slowed down in moving up the technological ladder, its technological distance from the second-tier NICs seems to have been shortened so much that technology trade is less advantageous than it used to be. Today, interactions between Japan and the second-tier NICs are limited to commodity trade. Japan seems to consider its moral responsibility in East Asia to be providing a market to supplant the US market as an outlet for the export drives of the other regional economies (Ozawa 1993). Whether Taiwan, together with other NICs, is able to obtain needed technology to keep the second-rank position in the East Asian flying-geese formation and to keep the formation moving forward remains to be seen.

Appendix: Questionnaire

1. Company information
   Name ____________________
   Date of establishment ___________
   Major products _______________
   Sales ____________ US dollars (1993)
   Capital (1993)
   ☐ below US$1 million
   ☐ US$1–3 million
   ☐ US$3–5 million
   ☐ US$5–10 million
   ☐ above US$10 million
   Country origin of investors:
   Taiwan capital share _____ %
   Local capital share _____ %
   Third-party country capital share ____ %
   (e.g., Japan, Hong Kong, etc.)
   Other capital share _____ %
   Is there a parent company in Taiwan: Yes ☐ No ☐
   Are there any restrictions on export ratio imposed by the host government? Yes ☐ No ☐
   Are there any restrictions on local content imposed by the host government? Yes ☐ No ☐

2. How much time elapsed between when you first applied for investment and when you actually started operating?
   ____ years ____ months

3. Nature of the company:
   ☐ started new
   ☐ acquired, merged, or joined existing company
   ☐ other (specify ________________)

4. Reasons to invest overseas (please rank, marking 1 for the most important reason, 2 for the second most important, etc.)
   - ☐ The appreciation of NT in the home country has eroded the competitiveness of products
   - ☐ To take advantage of low-cost labor
   - ☐ To secure a supply of raw materials
   - ☐ To take advantage of low-cost energy and water resources
   - ☐ To take advantage of low-cost land
   - ☐ To expand sales in the local market or markets in other countries
   - ☐ To avoid trade restrictions
   - ☐ To collect market information
   - ☐ To avoid environmental regulations in Taiwan
   - ☐ Joint actions with other firms
   - ☐ Other (Please specify ______________)

5. What are the reasons you chose the current location over other Southeast Asian countries to invest? (multiple choice)
   - ☐ also invest in other Southeast Asian countries
   - ☐ cheap labor
   - ☐ political stability
   - ☐ good infrastructure
   - ☐ sound legal framework and commercial practices
   - ☐ racial homogeneity
   - ☐ good supporting industries
   - ☐ good potential for local market
   - ☐ good personal connections
   - ☐ high level of education
   - ☐ attractive fiscal incentives
   - ☐ favorable status for exporting to third-party countries
   - ☐ lack of government regulations and controls
   - ☐ other (specify ___________)

6. Sources of components and parts
   Procure from local suppliers _____ %
   Import from third-party countries _____ %
   (e.g., Japan, Singapore, etc.)
   Import from other suppliers in Taiwan _____ %
   Import from the parent company _____ %

7. Sources of machinery and equipment
   Procure from local suppliers ____ %
   Import from third-party countries ____ %
   Import from suppliers in Taiwan ____ %
   Old machinery relocated from the parent company ____ %

8. Sources of financing
   Provided by local investors in the host country __ %
   Provided by local financial institutions ____ %
   Provided by financial institutions in Taiwan ____ %
   Provided by financial institutions in third-party countries ____ %
   Provided by the parent company _____ %
   Provided by curb market or other informal financial sources _____ %

9. Market for the products (by sales value)
   Sold in local market ___ %
   Export to third-party countries __ %
   Export to the parent company in Taiwan ____ %
   Export to other companies in Taiwan ____ %

10. Marketing channels for the products
    Marketed by yourself _____ %
    Marketed by local trading companies _____ %
    Marketed by trading companies in other countries
    (including Taiwan) _____ %
    Marketed by the parent company _____ %

11. Employment of your company
    Total number of employees ________ (1993)
    Where staff ____
    R&D personnel ____
    Skilled labor ____
    Unskilled labor ____
    * skilled labor is defined as the labor whose work requires extensive experience or 3 months' pre-occupational training.

12. Number of employees from Taiwan _____ (skip if no parent firm)
    Expatriates are in charge of (multiple choice)
    ☐ All operations (as president or vice president)
    ☐ Finance
    ☐ Marketing
    ☐ Production
    ☐ Planning or R&D
    ☐ Personnel
    ☐ Other (specify____________)

13. How do you improve your products and production process?
    (multiple choice)

☐ through own R&D
☐ imitating other local companies
☐ acquiring technology from other advanced countries
☐ technology transfer from the parent company
☐ other (specify___________)

14. Sales in past three years
    1991 _______ US dollars (growth rate ____ %)
    1992 _______ US dollars (growth rate ____ %)
    1993 _______ US dollars (growth rate ____ %)

15. In how many years do you expect to recover the capital invested?
    _______ years

16. Disposition of your profits
    retained in the company for operation or for expansion ____ %
    reinvested in other projects locally ____ %
    remitted to Taiwan ____ %

17. Please assess the degree of technology transfer in the following fields from the parent company and mark in the corresponding block (0 means no technology transfer has been made in this field and the related function is fully controlled by the parent company; 100% means technology transfer in this field is complete and the subsidiary assumes the full responsibility of the related function):

Fields of Technology	Degree of Technology Transfer										
	0	10%	20%	30%	40%	50%	60%	70%	80%	90%	100%
operation technology											
maintenance and inspection											
quality control											
process control											
technological improvement											
introduction of new technology											
product design											

	0	10%	20%	30%	40%	50%	60%	70%	80%	90%	100%
product innovation											
development of metal molds and machine tools											
development of manufacturing equipment and facilities											

18. Please indicate who makes the decision in the following fields at the present time by marking in the appropriate blocks:

Decision maker	Fields of Decision				
	Finance	Marketing	Production	Personnel	R&D
The parent company makes the decision					
Expatriate managers make the decision with regular influence from the parent company					
Expatriates managers make independent decisions					
Local management make independent decisions					

Who is expected to make the same decision five years from now?

Decision maker	Fields of Decision				
	Finance	Marketing	Production	Personnel	R&D
The parent company makes the decision					
Expatriate managers make the decision with regular influence from the parent company					
Expatriates managers make independent decisions					
Local management make independent decisions					

19. The following questions regard the comparison of business operations between your company and indigenous firms producing similar products in the closest locality. Please mark on the appropriate blank with respect to their business activity. The extent of comparison is scaled in four scores as follows: higher than local firms, the same as local firms, lower than local firms, and cannot compare.

	Compare with local firms			
	higher	same	lower	can't compare
(1) average production value per employee per year	☐	☐	☐	☐
(2) unit price of product	☐	☐	☐	☐
(3) scale of production	☐	☐	☐	☐
(4) degree of automation	☐	☐	☐	☐
(5) capacity of quality control	☐	☐	☐	☐
(6) level of production technology	☐	☐	☐	☐
(7) marketing capacity	☐	☐	☐	☐
(8) quality of after-sales services	☐	☐	☐	☐
(9) capacity for new product development	☐	☐	☐	☐
(10) capacity for technology innovation and process improvement	☐	☐	☐	☐
(11) soundness of internal management.	☐	☐	☐	☐
(12) product flexibility	☐	☐	☐	☐
(13) ratio of local procurement	☐	☐	☐	☐
(14) training and education of local employees	☐	☐	☐	☐
(15) export ratio	☐	☐	☐	☐
(16) average returns to investment	☐	☐	☐	☐
(17) company image	☐	☐	☐	☐

20. The following questions regard the comparison of business operations between your company and subsidiaries based in advanced countries (e.g., the US, Japan, Europe, etc.). Please mark on the appropriate blank with respect to their business activity. The extent of comparison is scaled in four scores as follows: higher than advanced countries' subsidiaries, the same as advanced countries' subsidiaries, lower than advanced countries' subsidiaries and cannot compare.

	Compare with subsidiaries of advanced countries			
	higher	same	lower	can't compare
(1) technology spillover	☐	☐	☐	☐
(2) ratio of local procurement	☐	☐	☐	☐
(3) degree of joint research and development with local firms	☐	☐	☐	☐
(4) proportion of unskilled labor in total employment	☐	☐	☐	☐
(5) job training and education of local employees	☐	☐	☐	☐
(6) ratio of export to total sales	☐	☐	☐	☐
(7) capital intensity	☐	☐	☐	☐
(8) willingness to build plants in remote areas	☐	☐	☐	☐

21. The following questions regard the description of your business operations in the host country. Please mark on the appropriate blank expressing the extent to which you agree with the statement. The extent of agreement is scaled in six levels as follows:
[1] Strongly agree, [2] Agree, [3] Somewhat agree,
[4] Somewhat disagree, [5] Disagree, [6] Strongly disagree

	[1]	[2]	[3]	[4]	[5]	[6]
(1) Taiwanese firms regularly introduce new products and stimulate local investment in the related industries . .	☐	☐	☐	☐	☐	☐
(2) Taiwanese firms regularly transfer appropriate technology through joint venture or technical assistance to local firms	☐	☐	☐	☐	☐	☐
(3) Taiwanese firms regularly offer technical services to local suppliers . .	☐	☐	☐	☐	☐	☐
(4) Taiwanese firms successfully build a supplier network in the host country	☐	☐	☐	☐	☐	☐

(5) Taiwanese firms use local materials adequately ☐ ☐ ☐ ☐ ☐ ☐

(6) Taiwanese firms provide sufficient training to local employees ☐ ☐ ☐ ☐ ☐ ☐

(7) Taiwanese firms make great contributions to job creation ☐ ☐ ☐ ☐ ☐ ☐

(8) The management systems of Taiwanese firms are often adopted by local firms ☐ ☐ ☐ ☐ ☐ ☐

(9) Most capital of Taiwanese firms is provided by the parent company or foreign financial institutions ☐ ☐ ☐ ☐ ☐ ☐

(10) The turnover rate of skilled employees in Taiwanese firms is high, leading to spillover of technology ☐ ☐ ☐ ☐ ☐ ☐

(11) Taiwanese firms hire more unskilled employees than other subsidiaries and create more job opportunities for unskilled labor ☐ ☐ ☐ ☐ ☐ ☐

(12) Taiwanese firms contribute to export significantly ☐ ☐ ☐ ☐ ☐ ☐

(13) Local enterprises have a good image of Taiwanese enterprises ☐ ☐ ☐ ☐ ☐ ☐

(14) Taiwanese firms maintain a good relationship with local governments ☐ ☐ ☐ ☐ ☐ ☐

(15) Taiwanese firms get along with local people well ☐ ☐ ☐ ☐ ☐ ☐

(16) Taiwanese firms make a large contribution to host country's economic growth ☐ ☐ ☐ ☐ ☐ ☐

22. The following questions regard the image of Taiwanese overseas firms in the host country. Please mark on the appropriate blank expressing the extent to which you agree with the statement. The extent of agreement is scaled in six levels as follows:
[1] Strongly agree, [2] Agree, [3] Somewhat agree,
[4] Somewhat disagree, [5] Disagree, [6] Strongly disagree

[1] [2] [3] [4] [5] [6]

(1) Taiwanese firms care about the welfare of workers ☐ ☐ ☐ ☐ ☐ ☐

(2)	Taiwanese firms care about the comfort and safety of the work environment	☐	☐	☐	☐	☐	☐
(3)	Taiwanese firms are ardent in public affairs	☐	☐	☐	☐	☐	☐
(4)	Customers are confident about the product quality of Taiwanese firms . .	☐	☐	☐	☐	☐	☐
(5)	Managers of Taiwanese firms have good personalities	☐	☐	☐	☐	☐	☐
(6)	Taiwanese firms care about product design and often introduce new products to the market	☐	☐	☐	☐	☐	☐
(7)	Taiwanese firms have an international view of operation	☐	☐	☐	☐	☐	☐
(8)	Taiwanese firms have an efficient management system	☐	☐	☐	☐	☐	☐
(9)	Taiwanese firms are active in R&D . .	☐	☐	☐	☐	☐	☐
(10)	Customers are satisfied with the sales and after-sales service provided by Taiwanese firms	☐	☐	☐	☐	☐	☐
(11)	Taiwanese firms maintain a harmonious relationship with their workers and labor disputes are rare . .	☐	☐	☐	☐	☐	☐

Bibliography

Aaronovitch, S., R. Smith, J. Gardiner and R. Moore (1981), *The Political Economy of British Capitalism, a Marxist Analysis,* London: McGraw-Hill.

Adachi, Fumihiko (1991), 'Small and Medium Sized Firms in Japan's Foreign Direct Investment', in Tran Van Tho (ed.), *Japan's Direct Investment in Thailand: Patterns and Issues*, Tokyo: Japan Center for Economic Research, pp. 48–65.

Akamatsu, Kaname (1961), 'A Theory of Unbalanced Growth in the World Economy', *Weltwirtschaftliches Archiv*, **86**, 196–215.

Akamatsu, Kaname (1962), 'A Historical Pattern of Economic Growth in Developing Countries', *The Developing Economies*, **1** (1), 3–25.

Allen, T. (1973), *Direct Investment of Japanese Enterprises in Southeast Asia: A Study of Motivations, Characteristics and Attitudes*, Study No. 1, The Economic Cooperation Center for the Asian and Pacific Region, Bangkok.

Amin, Ash and Nigel Thrift (eds) (1994), *Globalization, Institutions and Regional Development in Europe,* London: Oxford University Press.

Aoki, T. (1992), 'Japanese FDI and the Forming of Networks in the Asia–Pacific Region: Experience in Malaysia and Its Implications', in Shojiro Tokunaga (ed.), *Japan's Foreign Investment and Asian Economic Interdependence*, Tokyo: University of Tokyo Press, pp. 73–110.

APEC (1998), *The Impacts of Investment Rule-Making and Liberalization*, Singapore: APEC Economic Committee.

Aquino, Thomas G. and Antoinette B. Bolaños (1995), 'Foreign Investment Inflows and Political Stability in the Phillippines', in Nomura Research Institute and Institute of Southeast Asian Studies (eds), *The New Wave of Foreign Direct Investment in Asia*, Singapore: Institute of Southeast Asian Studies, pp. 174–96.

Ariff, M. (1991), 'The Changing Role of Foreign Direct Investment', in H. Yokoyama and T. Mokhtar (eds), *Malaysian Economy in Transition*, Tokyo: Institute of Developing Economies, pp. 67–90.

Ariff, M. (1992), 'Foreign Direct Investment in Malaysia: Trends, Determinants and Implications', in M. Ariff and H. Yokoyama (eds), *Foreign Direct Investment in Malaysia*, Tokyo: Institute of Developing

Economies, pp. 1–24.

Arrow, Kenneth (1969), 'Classificatory Notes on the Production and Transmission of Technological Knowledge', *American Economic Review: Papers and Proceedings*, **52**, 29–35.

Athukorala, P. and J. Menon (1994), 'Foreign Direct Investment and Export-led Industrialisation: The Malaysian Experience', mimeo, Melbourne: Monash University.

Attakorn, V. (1975), *Role of Japanese Investment in Thailand*, Bangkok, Thailand: Odiun Store Publishing.

Audretsch, David B. and Maryann P. Feldman (1994), 'External Economies and Spatial Clustering', in P.R. Krugman and A. Venables (eds), *The Location of Economic Activity: New Theories and Evidence*, London: Centre for Economic Policy Research (CEPR).

Bandaralage, J.S. and D. T. Nguyen (1994), 'The Role of Foreign Direct Investment in a Transitional Economy: The Case of Viet Nam', mimeo, Griffith University, December.

Barnet, Richard J. and Ronald E. Muller (1974), *Global Reach: The Power of the Multinational Corporations*, New York: Simon and Schuster.

Bergsten, C.F., T. Horst and T. Moran (1978), *American Multinationals and American Interests*, Washington, DC: Brookings Institution.

Bhattacharya, Amar and Mari Pangestu (1993), *Indonesia: Development Transformation and Public Policy*, Lessons of East Asia Series, Washington, DC: World Bank.

Buckley, Peter (1979), 'Foreign Investment Success for Smaller Firms', *Multinational Business*, **3**, 12–9.

Buckley, Peter and Mark Casson (1976), *The Future of the Multinational Enterprise*, London: Macmillan Press.

Buckley, Peter, Gerald Newbould and Jane Thurwell (1988), *Foreign Direct Investment by Smaller UK Firms*, London: Macmillan Press.

Caslin, Terry (1987), 'De-industrialization in the UK', in Howard Vane and Terry Caslin (eds), *Current Controversies in Economics*, Oxford: Basil Blackwell, pp. 256–92.

Caves, Richard (1971), 'International Corporations: The Industrial Economics of Foreign Investment', *Economica*, **38**, 1–27.

Caves, Richard (1974), 'Causes of Direct Investment: Foreign Firms' Shares in Canadian and United Kingdom Manufacturing Industries', *Review of Economics and Statistics*, **56**, 279–93.

Chen, Homin and Tain-Jy Chen (1998), 'Foreign Direct Investment as a Strategic Linkage', *Thunderbird International Business Review*, **40** (1), 13–30.

Chen, Tain-Jy (1992a), 'Determinants of Taiwan's Direct Foreign Investment: The Case of a Newly Industrializing Country', *Journal of Development*

Economics, **39**, 397–407.

Chen, Tain-Jy (1992b), 'Technical Change and Technical Adaptation of Multinational Firms: The Case of Taiwan's Electronics Industry', *Economic Development and Cultural Change*, **40**, 867–81.

Chen, Tain-Jy, Ying-Hua Ku and Meng-chun Liu (1995), 'Direct Foreign Investment in High-wage vs. Low-wage Countries: the Case of Taiwan', in P. Drysdale and E. Chen (eds), *Corporate Links and Foreign Direct Investment in Asia and the Pacific,* Pymble, NSW, Australia: Harper Educational, pp. 262–74.

Chen, Tain-Jy and Hsien-Yang Su (1987), *Tui Wai Tou Tzu Te Cheng Ts'e Chien T'ao (Assessment of Foreign Investment Policies)*, project report, Taipei: Chung-Hua Institution for Economic Research.

Chen, Tain-Jy and De-Piao Tang (1987), 'Offshore Assembly and Short-Run Labor–Labor Substitution', *Weltwirtschaftliches Archiv*, **123** (1), 140–48.

Chen, Tain-Jy and Wen-Thuen Wang (1995), 'Globalization of Taiwan's Electronics Industry', in Chien-nan Wang (ed.), *Globalization, Regionalization, and Taiwan's Economy*, Taipei: Chung-Hua Institution for Economic Research, pp. 215–36.

Chou, Tein-Chen (1988), 'Concentration and Profitability in a Dichotomous Economy: The Case of Taiwan', *International Journal of Industrial Organization*, **6**(4), 409–28.

Council for Economic Planning and Development (CEPD) (1992), *Tai-wan Tou Tzu Cheng Che Ping Ku Pao Kao* (*A Study of Taiwan's Direct Foreign Investment*), project report, Taipei: CEPD.

Dahlman, Carl J. (1993), Comment on 'Accumulating Technological Capability in Developing Countries' by Bell and Pavitt and 'Technology Gaps between Industrial and Developing Countries' by Pack in Lawrence Summers and Shekhar Shah (eds), *Proceedings of the World Bank Annual Conference on Development Economics, 1992,* Washington, DC: World Bank, pp. 313–15.

Dahlman, Carl J., et al. (1991), 'Technology Strategy for Industrial Competitiveness: A Case Study of Thailand', in World Bank, Plan, Part II, Washington, DC and in *Energy Department Working Paper,* Industrial Paper No. 24, World Bank, April.

Dietz, James (1985), 'Export–Enclave Economics, International Corporations, and Development', *Journal of Economic Issues*, **19** (2), 512–22.

Dunning, John H. (1995), 'Reappraising the Eclectic Paradigm in an Age of Alliance Capitalism', *Journal of International Business Studies*, **26** (3), 461–91.

Dunning, John H. and R. Narula (1996), 'The Investment Development Path Revisited: Some Emerging Issues', in John H. Dunning and R. Narula (eds), *Foreign Direct Investment and Government: Catalysts for Economic*

Restructuring, London: Routledge, pp. 1–41.

Enos, John, Sanjaya Lall and Mikyung Yun (1996), 'Transfer of Technology - An Update', mimeo, Oxford University.

Fei, John (1989), 'Chinese Cultural Values and Industrial Capitalism', Conference on Confucianism and Economic Development in East Asia (proceedings), Taipei: Chung-Hua Institution for Economic Research.

Fong, C.O. (1990), 'Direct Foreign Investment in Malaysia', in K.Y. Chen (ed.), *Foreign Investment in Asia*, Tokyo: Asian Productivity Organization, pp. 191–229.

Geringer, J.M. (1986), *Criteria for Selecting Partners for Joint Ventures in Industrialized Market Economies*, PhD dissertation, University of Washington, Seattle.

Giddy, Ian and Stephen Young (1982), 'Conventional Theory and Unconventional Multinationals: Do New Forms of Multinational Enterprises Require New Theories?' in Alan Rugman (ed.), *New Theories of the Multinational Enterprise*, London: Croom Helm, pp.55–78.

Gilroy, Bernard M. (1993), *Networking in Multinational Enterprises: The Importance of Strategic Alliances*, Columbia, SC: University of South Carolina Press.

Gomes-Casseres, Benjamin (1989), 'Ownership Structures of Foreign Subsidiaries', *Journal of Economic Behavior and Organization*, **11**, 1–25.

Grubel, Herbert and Peter Lloyd (1975), *Intra-industry Trade: The Theory and Measurement of International Trade in Differentiated Products*, London: Macmillan Press.

Hallen, Lars, Jan Johanson and Nazeem Seyed-Mohamed (1991), 'Interfirm Adaptation in Business Relationships', *Journal of Marketing*, **55** (2), 29–37.

Hamilton, Gary (1996), 'The Organizational Foundations of Western and Chinese Commerce: A Historical and Comparative Analysis', in Gary Hamilton (ed.), *Asian Business Network*, New York: Walter de Gruyter, pp. 43–57.

Hamilton, Gary and Tony Waters (1995), 'Chinese Capitalism in Thailand: Embedded Networks and Industrial Structure', in P. Drysdale and E. Chen (eds), *Corporate Links and Foreign Direct Investment in Asia and the Pacific*, Pymble, NSW, Australia: Harper Educational, pp. 87–111.

Hara, Masayuki (1989), 'Kigyo Nai Sangyo Chosei: Takaku-ka to Choku-setsu Toshi' (Industrial Restructuring within the Firm: Diversification and Foreign Direct Investment), *Sekai Keizai Hyoron,*, **33** (8), 1–21.

Harrison, Bennett (1994), *Lean and Mean: The Changing Landscape of Power in the Age of Flexibility*, New York: Basic Books.

Hasan, I. (1981), *Direct Foreign Investment in Indonesian Manufacturing: A Bargaining Approach*, PhD dissertation, University of California, Berkeley.

Hayashida, Masato (1993), 'Entrepreneurship in Taiwan and Korea: A

Comparison', Policy Paper no. 109E, Tokyo: International Institute for Global Peace.

Hill, Hal (1985), 'Subcontracting, Technological Diffusion and the Development of Small Enterprise in Philippine Manufacturing', *Journal of Developing Areas*, **19** (2), 245–61.

Hill, Hal (1988), *Foreign Investment and Industrialization in Indonesia*, Oxford University Press.

Horst, Thomas (1972), 'Firms and Industry Determinants of the Decision to Invest Abroad: an Empirical Study', *Review of Economics and Statistics*, **54**, 258–66.

Hsing, You-tien (1997), 'The Work of Networks in Taiwan's Export Fashion Shoe Industry', working paper, Center for Human Settlements, University of British Columbia.

Hymer, Stephen (1960), *The International Operations of National Firms: A Study of Direct Foreign Investment*, PhD thesis, MIT (Cambridge: MIT Press, 1976).

Japanese Ministry of International Trade and Industry (1994), *Survey of Overseas Investments by Small and Medium Enterprises*, Tokyo: MITI.

Jedel, M.J. and D. Kujawa (1976), 'Management and Employment Practices of Foreign Direct Investors in the United States', in *Foreign Direct Investment in the United States*, **5**, Appendix I, Report to Congress, US Department of Commerce.

Johanson, Jan and L. Mattsson (1987), 'Internationalization in Industry System - A Network Approach', in N. Hood and J. Vahlne (eds), *Strategies in Global Competition*, London: Routledge, pp. 287–315.

Johanson, Jan and Jan-Eric Vahlne (1977), 'The Internationalization Process of the Firm: A Model of Knowledge Development and Increasing Foreign Market Commitments', *Journal of International Business Studies*, **8** (1), 23–32.

Johanson, Jan and Jan-Eric Vahlne (1990), 'The Mechanism of Internationalization', *International Marketing Review*, **7** (4), 11–24.

Kanthachai, N. et al. (1987), *Technology and Skills in Thailand*, Singapore: Institute of Southeast Asian Studies.

Kaosa-ard, M. (1992), 'Manufacturing Growth: A Blessing for All!', in *TDRI Synthesis Report Volume I*, TDRI 1992 The Year-End Conference, Bangkok: TDRI.

Karnjanapunka, P. (1978), *Joint-Venture Business in Thailand: A Case Study of Thai–Japanese Joint-Venture*, MS thesis, Thammasat University.

Kojima, Kiyoshi (1973), 'A Macroeconomic Approach to Foreign Direct Investment', *Hitotsubashi Journal of Economics*, **14**, 1–21.

Kojima, Kiyoshi (1978), *Direct Foreign Investment: A Japanese Model of Multinational Business Operation*, New York: Praeger.

Koo, Bohn-Young (1993), 'Foreign Investment and Economic Performance in Korea', in Sanjaya Lall (ed.), *Transnational Corporations and Economic Development*, United Nations Library on Transnational Corporations, volume 3, New York: United Nations, pp. 288–313.

Kotabe, Masaaki and Glenn Omura (1989), 'Sourcing Strategies of European and Japanese Multinationals: A Comparison', *Journal of International Business Studies*, **20** (1), 113–30.

Ku, Ying-Hua (1994), 'The Impact of Taiwanese Investment in Malaysia', mimeo, Taipei: Chung-Hua Institution for Economic Research.

Lall, Sanjaya (1979), 'The Indirect Employment Effects of Multinational Enterprises in Developing Countries', Employment Effects of Multinational Enterprises Working Paper No. 3, Geneva: International Labor Office.

Lall, Sarjaya (1980), 'Monopolistic Advantages and Foreign Involvement by US Manufacturing Industry', *Oxford Economic Papers*, **32**, 102–22.

Lall, Sanjaya (1993), 'Introduction: Transnational Corporations and Economic Development', in S. Lall (ed.), *Transnational Corporations and Economic Development*, United Nations Library on Transnational Corporations, volume 3, New York: United Nations, pp. 1–30.

Lall, Sanjaya (1996), 'The Investment Development Path: Some Conclusions', in John H. Dunning and R. Narula (eds), *Foreign Direct Investment and Governments: Catalysts for Economic Restructuring*, London: Routledge, pp. 423–41.

Lall, S. and P. Streeten (1977), *Foreign Investment, Transnationals and Developing Countries*, London: Macmillan Press.

Lall, S. and P. Streeten (1993), 'TNCs and Welfare of Host Countries: Analytical Considerations', in Sanjaya Lall (ed.), *Transnational Corporations and Economic Development*, United Nations Library on Transnational Corporations, volume 3, New York: United Nations, pp. 43–75.

Le, Van Be and Nguyen Van Vien (1994), 'Direct Investment of Taiwan's Small- and Medium-Sized Firms in Vietnam', paper presented at Workshop on Taiwan's Small and Medium-Sized Firms' Investment in Southeast Asia, Taipei: Chung-Hua Institution for Economic Research, November 18–19.

Lecraw, Donald (1977), 'Direct Investment by Firms from Less Developed Countries', *Oxford Economic Papers*, **29**, 442–57.

Lecraw, Donald (1979), 'Choice of Technology in Low Wage Countries: A Non-Neoclassical Approach', *Quarterly Journal of Economics*, **53**, 631–54.

Lee, Chung (1980), 'United States and Japanese Direct Investment in Korea: A Comparative Study', *Hitotsubashi Journal of Economics*, **20**, 26–41.

Lee, Chung (1984), 'On Japanese Macroeconomic Theories of Direct Foreign Investment', *Economic Development and Cultural Change*, **32**, 713–23.

Liebau, E. and P. Wahnschaffe (1992), 'Management Strategies of

Multinationals in Developing Countries', *Intereconomics*, **27**, pp. 190–98.

Lin, An-Loh (1995), 'Trade Effects of Foreign Direct Investment: Evidence for Taiwan with Four ASEAN Countries', *Weltwirtschaftliches Archiv*, **131**(4), 737–47.

Lin, Ts'ung-Ming (1994), 'Wo Kuo Chi Chih Chiao Yu Fa Chan Yu Chung Hsiao Chi Yeh Jen Li Yun Yung Chih Chien T'ao Yu Chan Wang' (Vocational Education and Small- and Medium-Sized Firms in Taiwan: Reviews and Prospects), paper presented at the Conference on Development of Small- and Medium- Sized Enterprises. Taipei: Chung-Hua Institution for Economic Research, March 3–4.

Lindblom, C.E. (1977), *Politics and Markets*, New York: Basic Books.

Lipsey, R. (1991), 'Direct Foreign Investment and Structural Change in Developing Asia, Japan, and the United States' in E.D. Ramstetter (ed.), *Direct Foreign Investment in Asia's Developing Economies and Structural Change in the Asia Pacific Region*, Boulder, CO: Westview Press.

Lipsey, R. (1994), 'Outward Direct Investment and the US Economy', *National Bureau of Economic Research Working Paper No. 4691*, Cambridge, MA: NBER.

Lucas, Robert (1989), 'On the Mechanics of Economic Development', *Journal of Monetary Economics*, **22**, 3–42.

Markusen, J.R. (1983), 'Factor Movement and Commodity Trade as Complements', *Journal of International Economics*, **14**, 341–56.

Mason, Hal (1980), 'A Comment on Professor Kojima's Japanese Type versus American Type of Technology Transfer', *Hitotsubashi Journal of Economics*, **20**, 42–52.

Morley, Samuel and Gordon Smith (1977), 'Limited Search and the Technology Choices of Multinational Firms in Brazil', *Quarterly Journal of Economics*, **91**, 263–87.

Mukai, Juichi (1990), *Gendai Nihon Kigyo to Takokuseki Sogo Kinyu Kikan* (Modern Japanese Enterprises and Multinational Financial Institutions), Tokyo: Dobunkan.

Mundell, Robert (1957), 'International Trade and Factor Mobility', *American Economic Review*, **47**, 321–35.

National Science Council, ROC (1994), *Indicators of Sciences and Technology*, Taipei: National Science Council.

Naya, S. and P. Imada (1988), *Trade and Investment Linkage in ASEAN Countries*, Honolulu: East–West Center.

Nohria, Nitin and Carlos Garcia-Pont (1991), 'Global Strategic Linkages and Industry Structure', *Strategic Management Journal*, **12** (special issue), 102–24.

Ozawa, Terutomo (1979), 'International Investment and Industrial Structure: New Theoretical Implications from the Japanese Experience', *Oxford*

Economic Papers, **31**, 72–92.

Ozawa, Terutomo (1985), *International Transfer of Technology by Japan's Small and Medium Enterprises in Developing Countries*, New York: UNCTAD.

Ozawa, Terutomo (1993), 'The Dynamics of Pacific Rim Industrialization: How Mexico Can Join the Asian Flock of Flying Geese', in Daniel Chudnovsky (ed.), *Transnational Corporations and Industrialization*, United Nations Library on Transnational Corporations, volume 11, New York: United Nations, pp. 100–114.

Panglaykim, P. (1983), *Japanese Direct Investment in ASEAN: The Indonesian Experience*, Singapore: Maruzen Asia.

Pearce, R.D. (1989), *The Internationalization of Research and Development by Multinational Enterprises*, London: Macmillan Press.

Perrow, Charles (1992), 'Small-Firm Networks', in Nitin Nohria and Robert Eccles (eds), *Networks and Organizations: Structure, Form, and Action*, Boston, MA: Harvard Business School Press, pp. 445-70.

Petri, Peter (1992), 'Platforms in the Pacific: The Trade Effects of Direct Investment in Thailand', *Journal of Asian Economics*, **3** (2), 173–96.

Pongpisanupichit, J. (1985), *Private Direct Foreign Investment and Thai Economy*, PhD dissertation, Cornell University.

Pongpisanupichit, J. and B. Pussarungsri (1992), *Flow of Capital in Asia–Pacific: Thai Prospective,* project report, Asia–Pacific Project, Bangkok: TDRI.

Poorpongskorn, N. (1992), 'The Change of Labor Market toward the Labor Shortage' (in Thai), mimeo, Bangkok: TDRI.

Pugel, T.A. (1981), 'The Determinants of Foreign Direct Investment: an Analysis of US Manufacturing Industries', *Managerial and Decision Economics*, **2** (December), 220–28.

Pupphavesa, W. and N. Grewe (1994), 'Matching Investment Opportunities and Relocation of Industries: Thailand's Prospective', mimeo, Bangkok: TDRI.

Pupphavesa, W. and B. Pussarungsri (1995), 'Foreign Direct Investment and Industrial Restructuring in Thailand', in Nomura Research Institute and Institute of Southeast Asian Studies (eds), *The New Wave of Foreign Direct Investment in Asia*, Singapore: Institute of Southeast Asian Studies, pp. 160–73.

Pussarungsri, B. and N. Thongpakdee (1992), 'How to Strengthen Cooperation Among Thai Affliates of Taiwanese Companies and Local Thai Companies', mimeo, Bangkok: TDRI.

Redding, Gordon (1991), 'Weak Organizations and Strong Linkages: Managerial Ideology and Chinese Family Business Network', in Gary Hamilton (ed.), *Business Networks and Economic Development in East and*

Southeast Asia, Hong Kong: Centre of Asian Studies, University of Hong Kong, pp. 30–47.

Riedel, James (1975), 'The Nature and Determinants of Export-Oriented Direct Foreign Investment in a Developing Country: A Case Study of Taiwan', *Weltwirtschaftliches Archiv*, **111** (3), 58–87.

Riedel, James (1993), 'Viet Nam: On the Trail of the Tigers', *World Economy*, **16** (4), 401–22.

Sabolo, Yves (1975), 'Employment and Unemployment, 1960–1990', *International Labor Review*, **112** (6), 401–17.

Sato, Yukihito (1994), 'Taiwan No Semento Kojo Ni Okeru Ginon Keisei' (Skill Formation in Taiwan's Cement Factories), *Ajia Keizai*, **35** (9), 33–48.

Schann, J. L. (1983), *Parent Control and Joint Venture Success: The Case of Mexico,* unpublished doctoral dissertation, University of Western Ontario.

Schmitz, A. and P. Helmberger (1970), 'Factor Mobility and International Trade: The Case of Complementarity', *American Economic Review*, **60**, 761–7.

Seetoo, Dah-Hsian (1994), 'Tai-wan Chung Hsiao Chi Yeh Te Chin Yin Che Rei' (Business Strategies of Taiwan's Small- and Medium-Sized Enterprises), paper presented at Conference on Development of Small- and Medium-Sized Enterprises, Taipei: Chung-Hua Institution for Economic Research, March 3–4.

Sibunruang, A. (1984), *Foreign Direct Investment and Manufactured Exports in Thailand*, PhD dissertation, University of Sussex.

Sibunruang, A. (1986), *Foreign Direct Investment and Manufactured Exports from Thailand,* Bangkok: Chulalongkorn University Social Research Institute.

Sibunruang, A. and P. Brimble (1988), 'The Employment Effects of Manufacturing Multinational Enterprises in Thailand', Multinational Enterprises Programme, Working Paper No. 54, Geneva: International Office.

Sibunruang-Brimble, A. (1992), 'Changing Pattern of Foreign Direct Investment', paper presented at Pacific Economic Outlook Specialists Meeting, March 1992, Osaka.

Small and Medium Enterprise Agency, Japan (1992), 'Actual Situation of Internationalization of Small and Medium Enterprises', December 1992, Tokyo: Small and Medium Enterprise Agency.

Steinmann, H., B. Kumar and A. Wasner (1980), 'Conceptualizing the Internationalization Process of Medium-Sized Firms: Some Preliminary Considerations for a Research Design', *Management International Review*, **20**, 52–66.

Stopford, John and Louis Wells (1972), *Managing the Multinational Enterprise*, New York: Basic Books.

Suehiro, Akira (1991), *Tai No Zaibatsu* (Conglomerates in Thailand), Tokyo: Dobunkan.
Tambunleartchai, S. (1980), 'Attitude and Experience in Japanese–Thai Joint Venture Investment', in Medhi Krongkaew (ed.), *Current Development in Thai–Japanese Economic Relations: Trade and Investment,* Bangkok: Thammasat University Press.
TDRI (1989), 'Direct Foreign Investment and Capital Flow', paper prepared for TDRI's Year-End Conference 1989, Bangkok: TDRI.
TDRI (1994), *AFTA, and Trade and FDI in Thailand*, Final Draft, Bangkok: TDRI.
Teece, David (1977), 'Technology Transfer by Multinational Firms: The Resources of Transfering Technological Know-How', *Economic Journal*, **87**, 242–61.
Thee, Kian Wie (ed.) (1985), *Kaitan-Kaitan Vertikal Antar Perusahaan dan Pengembangan Sistem Subkontraktor di Indonesia: Beberapa Studi Kasus* (Vertical Interfirm Linkages and the Development of the Subcontracting System in Indonesia: Several Case Studies), *Masyarakat Indonesia*, **12** (3), special issue, pp. 219–88.
Thee, Kian Wie (1991), 'The Surge of Asian NIC Investment into Indonesia', *Bulletin of Indonesian Economic Studies*, **27** (3), 55–88.
Thee, Kian Wie and Mari Pangestu (1998), Technological Capability and Indonesian Manufactured Exports, in Dieter Ernst, Tom Ganiatsos and Lynn Mytelka (eds) *Technological Capabilities and Export Success in Asia*, London: Routledge (forthcoming).
UNCTAD (1984), 'International Transfer of Technology to Developing Countries by Small and Medium-Sized Enterprises', Geneva: Report by UNCTAD Secretariat, TD/B/C6/119.
UNCTAD (1993), *Small and Medium-Sized Transnational Corporations: Role, Impact and Policy Implications*, New York: United Nations.
UNCTAD (1994), *Small- and Medium-Sized Transnational Corporations, Executive Summary and Report on the Osaka Conference*, New York: United Nations.
UNCTC (1991), *World Investment Report 1991*, New York: United Nations.
Urata, Shujiro (1993), 'Japan's Foreign Direct Investment and Technology Transfer in the Asia–Pacific Region', paper presented at the Conference on Internationalization of Taiwan Industry, Taipei: Chung-Hua Institution for Economic Research, June 7.
van Hoesel, Roger (1996), 'Taiwan Foreign Direct Investment and the Transformation of the Economy', in J.H. Dunning and R. Narula (eds), *Foreign Direct Investment and Government: Catalysts for Economic Restructuring*, London: Routledge, pp. 280–315.
van Hoorn, Th. P. (1979), 'Strategic Planning in Small and Medium-Sized

Companies', *Long Range Planning*, **2**, 84–91.

Vernon, R. (1966), 'International Investment and International Trade in The Product Cycle', *Quarterly Journal of Economics*, **80**, 190–207.

Vernon, Raymond (1971), *Sovereignty at Bay: The Multinational Spread of US Enterprises,* New York: Basic Books.

Vernon, Raymond (1979), 'The Product Cycle Hypothesis in a New International Environment', *Oxford Bulletin of Economics and Statistics*, **41**, 255–67.

Weisskoff, Richard and Edward Wolff (1977), 'Linkages and Leakages: Industrial Tracking in an Enclave Economy', *Economic Development and Cultural Change*, **25**, 607–28.

Wells, Louis (1973), 'Economic Man and Engineering Man: Choice of Technology in a Low-Wage Country', *Public Policy*, **21** (3), 319–42.

Wells, Louis (1983), *Third World Multinationals*, Cambridge: MIT Press.

Wells, L. and V. Warren (1979), 'Developing Country Investors in Indonesia', *Bulletin of Indonesian Economic Studies*, **15** (1), 69–84.

Wheeler, David and Ashoka Mody (1992), 'International Investment Location Decisions: the Case of US Firms', *Journal of International Economics*, **33**, 57–76.

White, E. (1983), 'The Role of Third World Multinationals and Small and Medium-Sized Companies in the Industrialization Strategies of Developing Countries', in *Industrial Development Strategies and Policies for Developing Countries*, Vienna: United Nations Industrial Development Organization.

Wolf, Bernard (1977), 'Industrial Diversification and Internationalization: Some Empirical Evidence', *Journal of Industrial Economics*, **26**, 177–91.

Wong, Poh Kam (1991), *Technology Development through Subcontracting Linkages*, Tokyo: Asian Productivity Organization.

World Bank (1989), 'Foreign Direct Investment from the Newly Industrialized Economies', Industry and Energy Department, Industry Series Paper, No. 22, World Bank, Washington, DC.

Yeoman, Wayne (1968), *Selection of Production Processes for the Manufacturing Subsidiaries of US Based Multinational Corporations*, DBA thesis, Harvard Business School.

Yonekura, Minoru (1988), 'Chukan, Chusho Denki Kigyo No Kaigai Shinshutsu' (Overseas Operations of Medium and Medium-Small Electronics Firms), *Sekai Keizai Hyoron*, **32** (4), 52–9.

Yoshihara, Kunio (1994), *The Nation and Economic Growth: The Philippines and Thailand*, New York: Oxford University Press.

Index